IMAGES
of America

African Americans of Pine Bluff and Jefferson County

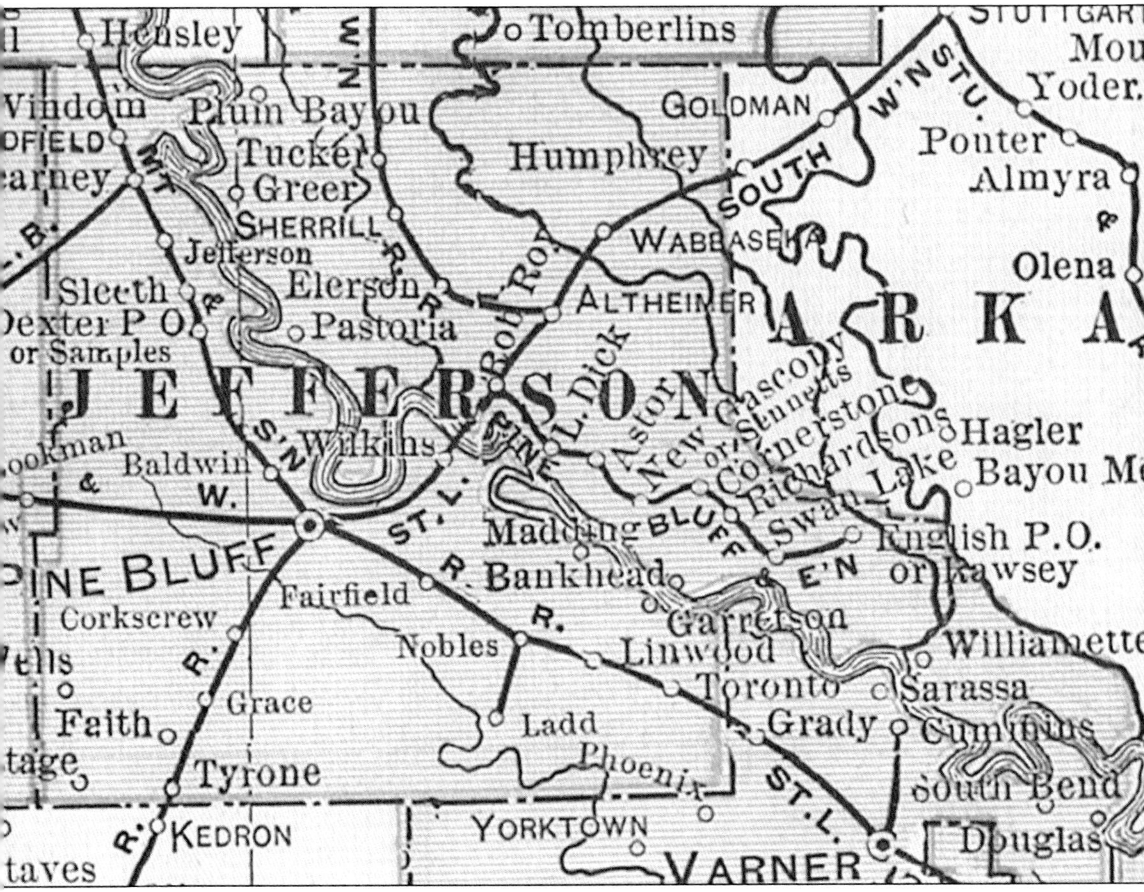

This 1898 map shows the boundaries and towns of Jefferson County, Arkansas. (Courtesy of Hearthstone Legacy Publications.

On the Cover: Winston Alexander, owner of the College Grocery, waves merrily from a float during a 1950s Arkansas Agricultural, Mechanical & Normal (AM&N) College homecoming parade in downtown Pine Bluff. (Courtesy of Karen Dancy Dickson.)

IMAGES
of America

AFRICAN AMERICANS OF PINE BLUFF AND JEFFERSON COUNTY

Jimmy Cunningham Jr.
and Donna Cunningham

ARCADIA
PUBLISHING

ISBN 978-0-7385-9884-0

Published by Arcadia Publishing
Charleston, South Carolina

Printed in the United States of America

Library of Congress Control Number: 2012949905

For all general information, please contact Arcadia Publishing:
Telephone 843-853-2070
Fax 843-853-0044
E-mail sales@arcadiapublishing.com
For customer service and orders:
Toll-Free 1-888-313-2665

Visit us on the Internet at www.arcadiapublishing.com

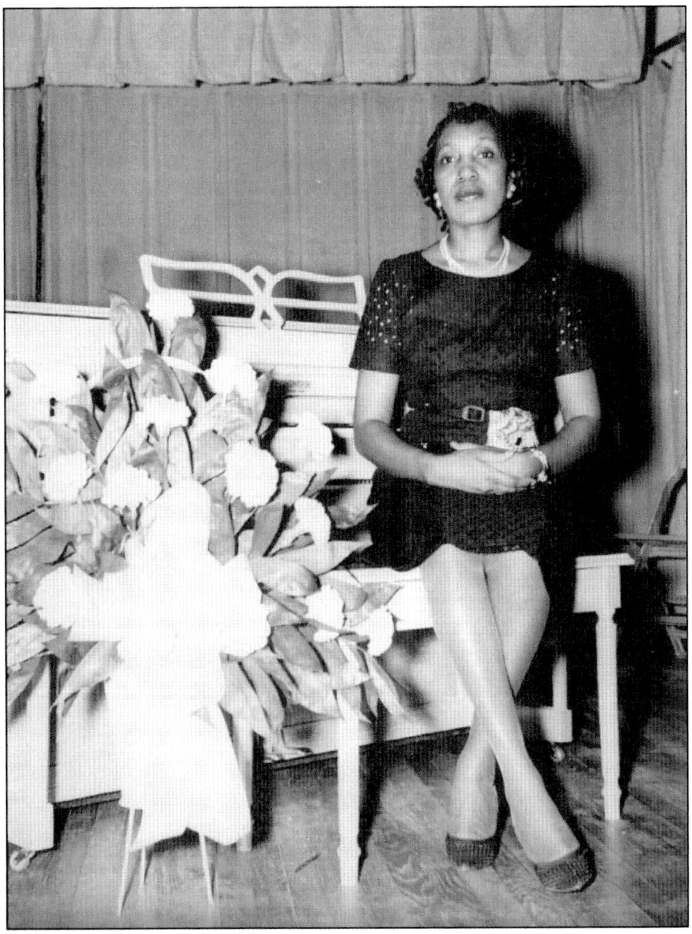

This book is dedicated to Bernice Cunningham-Terry whose passionate commitment to young people and family, profound devotion to God, and prodigious love of turnip greens bespoke the very best of the African American spirit in Jefferson County, Pine Bluff, Arkansas, the Delta, and the South. (Courtesy of Donna Cunningham.)

Contents

Acknowledgments

If the African proverb, "It takes a village to raise a child," is correct, then it also takes a village to write a local history. Many thanks to those organizations and individuals that provided images, information, or other forms of critical assistance for this book, including the Arkansas History Commission, the Special Collections Department of the University of Arkansas Libraries, the Pine Bluff/Jefferson County Historical Museum, the University of Arkansas at Pine Bluff (UAPB), the University of Arkansas–Division of Agriculture, US Naval Academy–Nimitz Library, National Museum of the Air Force, the *Arkansas Times*, African American Images Publishing Company, Mosaic Templars Cultural Center, A'Lelia Bundles, Juanita Currie, Dr. Granville Coggs, Raye Montague, Paul Purdue, Carol Williams Rankins, Laura Parker Castoro, Kevin Cole, Karen Dancy Dickson, George Wylie, Ralph Fitzgerald, Myrtus Henry, Johnathan Henry, Paolo Harrell, Lewis Delavan, Naomi LaVeux Summerville, Dr. Loyd Lasker Jr., Richard Redus, Julius Lester, Phoebe Roaf, Queen Yancy, Dr. Mars Hill, Jerry Sims, Delores Broughton, John Flowers, Ben Berry, Ruth Rice, Dr. Mildred Henry, Ena Hartman, Eva Burks, Alvin Starks, George Cooks, Rev. Walter May, Margie Bell, Rev. and Mrs. Clifton O'Neal, Louise Dalton, Dr. Bob Cochran, Lola Gordon, Rosalyn Burks, Jymmeka Moore, Dr. John Haddock Jr., Camuriel Cunningham, Renee Peterson, and Jeffrey McMurray.

Further, Alicia Cunningham deserves big kudos for her loving support. It pays to marry the right woman! We also thank the blues, which we played incessantly, inspiring us throughout this book's writing. We knew that between Howlin' Wolf songs, Kibb's Barbeque sandwiches, and Friday night catfish dinners, we would eventually finish this project. More importantly, we thank God for sparking this idea in us and wondrously blessing it to fruition. Only a God of love and humor could orchestrate the planting of seeds in us from years ago to blossom in the writing of this work today.

Unfortunately, we could not include all of the stellar accomplishments of African Americans in Jefferson County because of the size constraints of this book. Any future histories should surely include a sports section with people like Coach Andrew Butler, Basil Shabazz, Torri Hunter, Willie Roaf, Joe Barry Carrell, Monte Coleman, Eric Mitchell, and many others. Families like the Kearneys, the Moreheads, the Barons, the McKissics, and others too numerous to name offer key examples of black excellence in the area and should also be explored in future works.

We will be placing a copy of a complete bibliography in the Pine Bluff /Jefferson County Library for those who wish to pursue further research. If you would like to contact us, please feel free to do so at jmmyjam@mac.com or at msre39@gmail.com.

INTRODUCTION

Jefferson County, with Pine Buff as its county seat, stands as a cultural and historical mecca of the Delta and the original center of African American influence in the state of Arkansas. In these twin roles serving a state and a region, African Americans of Jefferson County, and particularly those of Pine Bluff, have innovated, endured, and achieved in breathtaking fashion. The scope of these achievements in the face of profound adversity illustrates a rare combination of genius and resilience.

From the county's beginnings in 1829 and Pine Bluff's selection as its seat in 1832, the area has been a place of expanding borders. The county largely sits inside the western edge of the Mississippi Alluvial Plain (the Mississippi Delta) with a small portion, about 25 percent, extending into the adjacent Arkansas Timberlands region. Pine Bluff, the largest city in the county, was originally completely inside the Delta, sandwiched between the Arkansas River and Bayou Bartholomew until its borders later grew partially into the Timberlands. Other Jefferson County towns with predominately black populations, such as Altheimer, Humphrey, Moscow, Sherrill, and Wabbaseka, are all completely inside the Delta.

Since the flood of blacks into the county following the defeat of rebel forces during the Civil War, the cultural landscape has been dynamic. While other Delta locales such as Clarksdale, Mississippi; Helena, Arkansas; and Vicksburg, Mississippi are generally known for legendary contributions in specific fields such as music, the military, or agriculture, Pine Bluff/Jefferson County's history shows a much broader reach. The area has been a virtual mecca attracting or producing African Americans who have achieved milestones in every imaginable field, including music, military, agriculture, science, art, business, civil rights, education, medicine, literature, and a host of other areas. No major political, social, cultural, or religious movements in black America have escaped Pine Bluff/Jefferson County's significant involvement or contributions.

Notwithstanding its Delta regional roots, Pine Bluff/Jefferson County has also been vital to the state of Arkansas. While cities like Little Rock and Helena played immensely important roles in early Arkansas black history, no city was more vital to African Americans during the period of 1865 to 1915 than Pine Bluff. Indicators underscoring the area's significance as the state's original center of black influence include the 1873 establishment of Branch Normal College, later known as the University of Arkansas at Pine Bluff (UAPB), which produced critical black leadership throughout Arkansas; the 1898 formation of a vital statewide education association for blacks organized in Pine Bluff, serving the needs of black youth and teachers throughout Arkansas; the 1880s founding of the "Colored" State Fair in Pine Bluff, which brought an estimated 20,000 blacks together from across the state annually to network, socialize, and share; and the sheer dominance by black Jefferson County legislators in state government (the county led all others in the state from 1868 to 1893 in the total number of terms held by blacks).

Additionally, the presence of the black business community was inordinately large in proportion to the city's size. At the turn of the 20th century, blacks in Pine Bluff owned four barbershops, nineteen grocery stores, four butcher shops, three boot and shoe shops, four blacksmith shops, five saloons, twelve restaurants, the state's and the Delta's first black-owned bank, and two hotels, according to *The Arkansas Delta: Land of Paradox*. Indeed, Carl Moneyhon points out in *Arkansas and the New South: 1874-1929* that the Pine Bluff business directory of 1900 listed over 250 African American businessmen and women with trades largely serving the black community. The concentration of black wealth in Jefferson County during this time was unparalleled. After updating data presented in *Black Property Owners of the South: 1790-1915* with that of all six black Pine Bluff magnates whose estates exceeded $20,000 in value by 1900, the adjusted record shows Pine Bluff had the largest per capita concentration of wealthy blacks in Arkansas and the Mississippi Delta, and one of the largest in the entire South during this era. Prominent estates included that of Wiley Jones (estimated worth in 1900: $250,000; 2010 value: $6.5 million), Ferdinand Havis (estimated worth in 1900: $100,000; 2010 value: $2.6 million), J.C. Jones (estimated worth in 1900: $100,000; 2010 value: $2.6 million), and J.C. Corbin (estimated worth in 1900: $75,000; 2010 value: $1.9 million), according to Norman Wood in *The White Side of a Black Subject*. Additionally, Pine Bluff planter Pleasant Tate had an estimated worth of $40,000 in 1889 (2010 value: $958,000), as noted *in Jefferson County, Arkansas 1889 History*, while E.E. Fluker, a local merchant, had an estimated worth of $25,000 (2010 value: $646,350). Though power later shifted to Little Rock as demographics changed approaching World War I, Pine Bluff/Jefferson County laid the original foundation for black influence in the state and has continued to contribute significantly for decades.

When considering the pivotal role that Pine Bluff/Jefferson County's black community has played in the development of the Mississippi Delta and the state of Arkansas, it is humbling to consider the antebellum beginnings of this journey. The following condensed passage, taken from Jun and Louise DeHorney's *Just the Typical American Negro*, offers an actual account of the arrival of a slave on a Pine Bluff/Jefferson County area plantation in the early to mid 1800s:

> The master was driving the wagon bringing a new addition to the plantation, an African slave. The new arrival had a chain around his neck with his hands chained to the back of the wagon while trotting. He wore no shirt nor shoes and his feet were bleeding very badly. All the slaves gathered round and the master told us to get back because this one was buck wild. The master said he had shoes on his feet when he bought him, but he must have pulled them off somewhere in Louisiana.
>
> So they took the African and put him in a shed, no bed, only some straw to lay on. The master put a bucket of water in the shed and gave him some corn mush. They shut the door and you could hear that African raising cane. Every day he raised cane and was hostile to everybody. The master didn't believe in whipping his slaves, but he would have other slaves to do it for him. Yet, for some reason he chose not to have this African whipped. He decided to sell him as he had no success in all his efforts to break him in.
>
> The day he left was like the day he came. He was shackled with no shoes and trotting behind the wagon. All the slaves came to see him off. As he was leaving, a small grin appeared on his face as if in relief, the only time he had ever displayed his common humanity.

While African Americans of Pine Bluff/Jefferson County have had a journey that has been indisputably brutal at times and wonderfully exhilarating at others, most residents would agree with the words of the old gospel song, "You Brought Me From a Mighty Long Way." Herein, a small window into this journey is presented.

One

Early Years

In October '63, I runned away and went to Pine Bluff to get to the Yankees . . . Heerd the hounds a howling chasing for to get after us. Then we hide in dark woods. It was cold frosty weather. Two days and two nights we travelled . . . When we gets to the Yankee camp all our troubles was over . . . Was there more runaways? Oh Lord, yes, hundreds I reckon.

—Boston Blackwell, former North Little Rock slave
Works Progress Administration (WPA) Slave Narratives

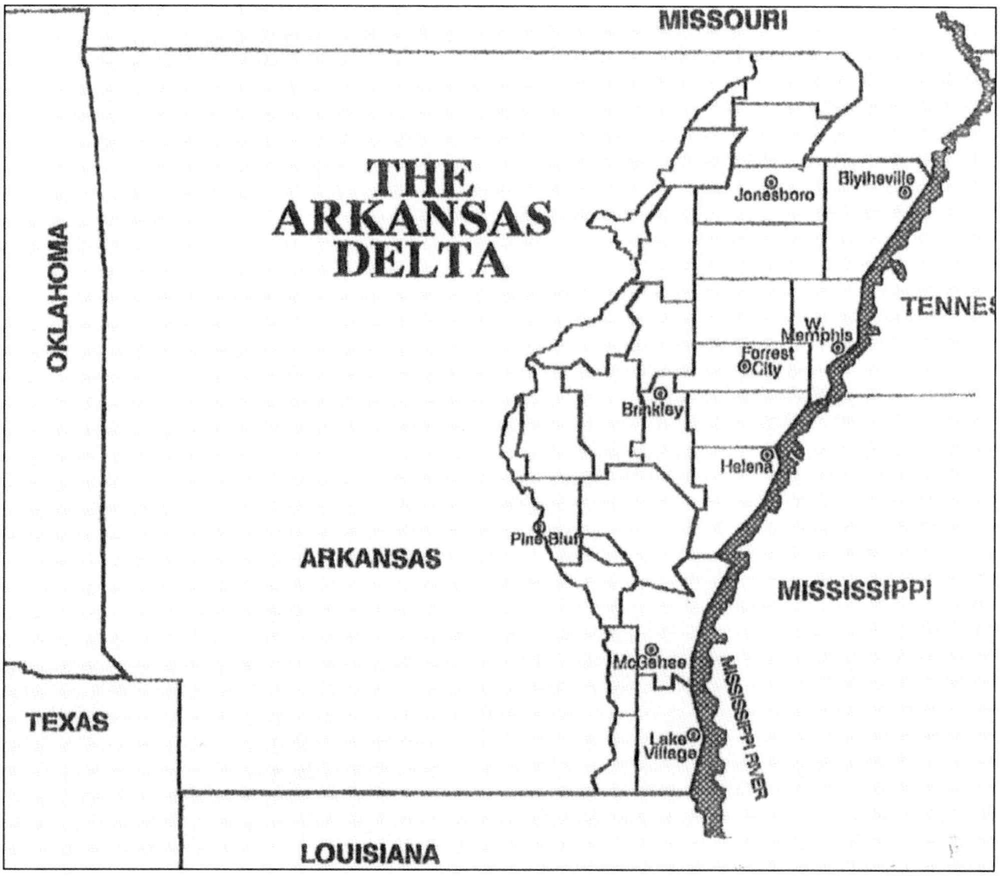

The history of African Americans in Jefferson County is inextricably bound to the Arkansas Delta, where 75 percent of the county's land is situated. This region, formerly a swath of dense forests and swamps, became known for its fertile soil when early 1800s settlers discovered its superior yields for cotton and other products. This discovery inevitably made the Delta, and by extension, Jefferson County, a stronghold of slavery in the years to come. (Courtesy of the Delta Cultural Center.)

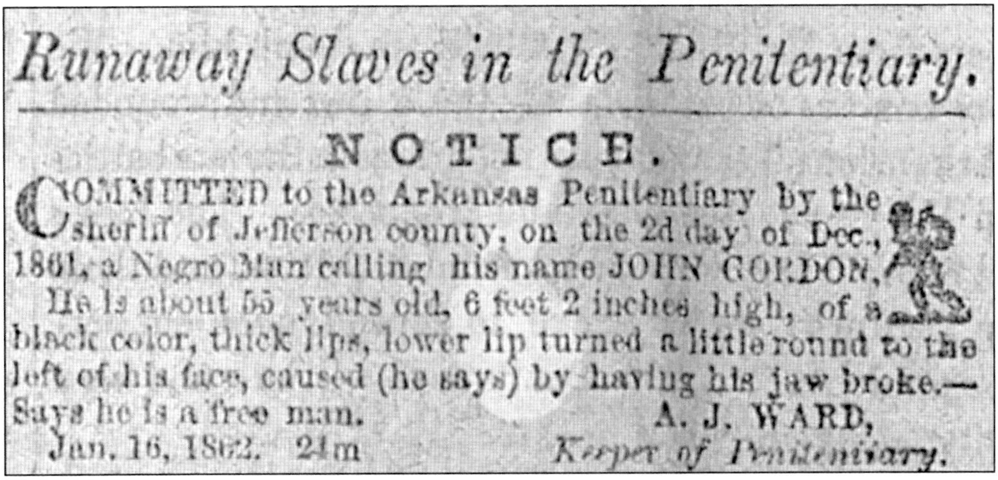

Runaway Slaves in the Penitentiary.

NOTICE.

COMMITTED to the Arkansas Penitentiary by the sheriff of Jefferson county, on the 2d day of Dec., 1861, a Negro Man calling his name JOHN GORDON. He is about 55 years old, 6 feet 2 inches high, of a black color, thick lips, lower lip turned a little round to the left of his face, caused (he says) by having his jaw broke.—Says he is a free man.

A. J. WARD,
Keeper of Penitentiary.

Jan. 16, 1862. 24m

Between 1840 and the time of this unknown newspaper's notice in 1862, the slave population had grown almost 700 percent in Jefferson County. This was due primarily to the increased demand for cotton, which was bolstered by the area's strategic position as a hub on both the Arkansas River and Bayou Bartholomew. According to the 1860 census, Jefferson County had the fourth highest number of 1,000-acre plantations in the state and the third highest number of slaves. (Courtesy of the National Archives.)

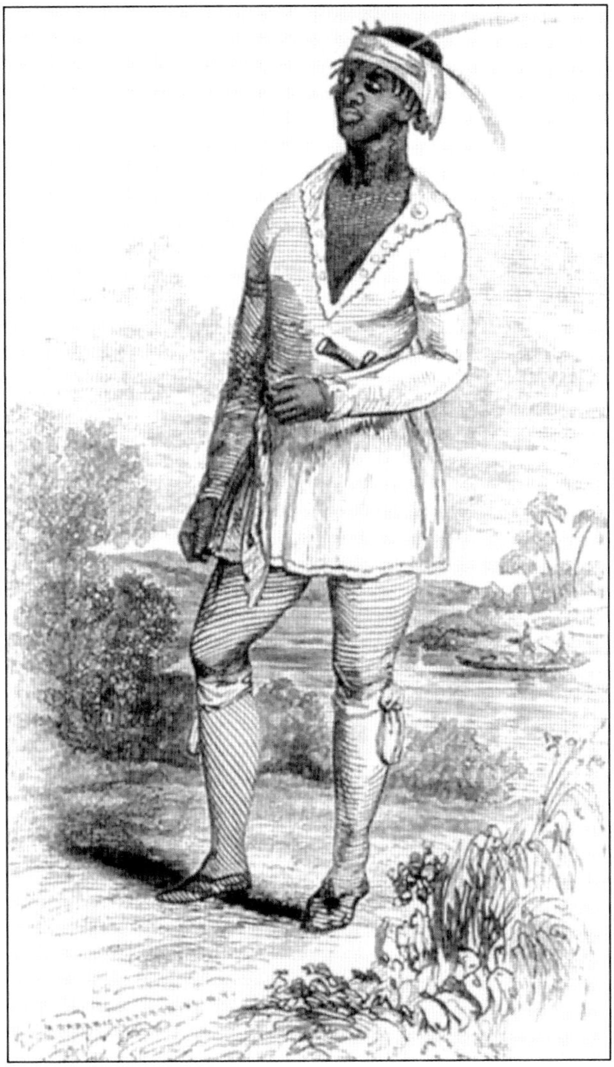

John Horse, a Black Seminole warrior, slave rebellion organizer, and leader of the largest mass exodus of slaves in US history, landed in Pine Bluff in 1842 on the steamboat *Swan*. Horse, along with hundreds of Native and Black Seminole Indians, was relocated from Florida to Oklahoma following the Second Seminole War. Jefferson County was the site for several steamboat stops relocating Black Seminoles and others. (Courtesy of Florida State University Archives.)

In this c. 1855 image, the female slave on a Delta estate, likely from Pine Bluff or another neighboring town, according to the Library of Congress notes, served as a nanny for a child. At the peak of slavery, Jefferson County had about 7,000 slaves out of a total population of more than 14,000. (Courtesy of the Library of Congress.)

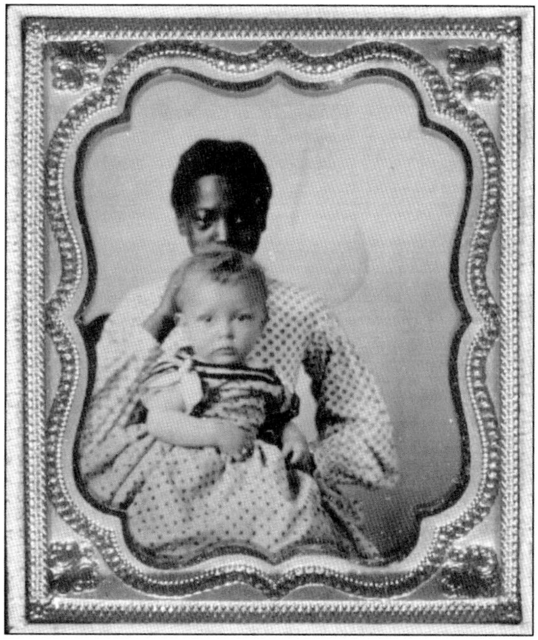

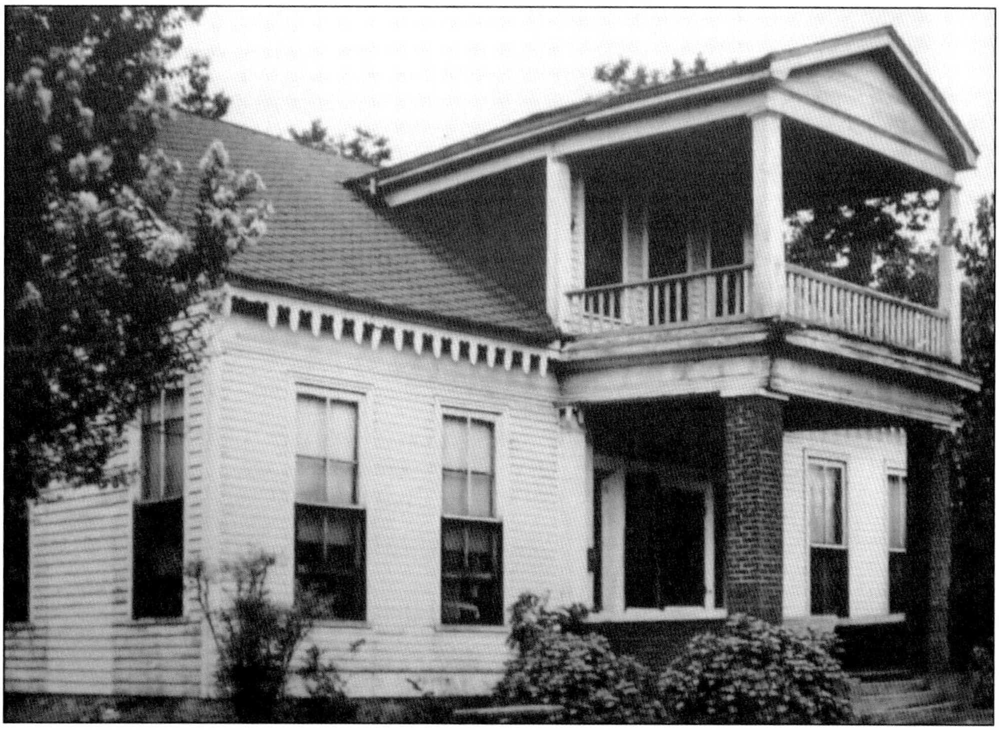

The Taylor-Portis House was built by slaves in 1844. The Taylor and Portis families were among Pine Bluff's early slave-owning plantation aristocracy that reaped profits from the surrounding rich Delta farmland. The Barraques, Sheppards, and Blackwells were just a few of the many other slave-owning families from plantations that dotted the county landscape. The Taylor-Portis House sat on the lot where P.K. Miller Mortuary is currently located (Second Avenue and State Street). (Courtesy of Lites-Wallis Collection.)

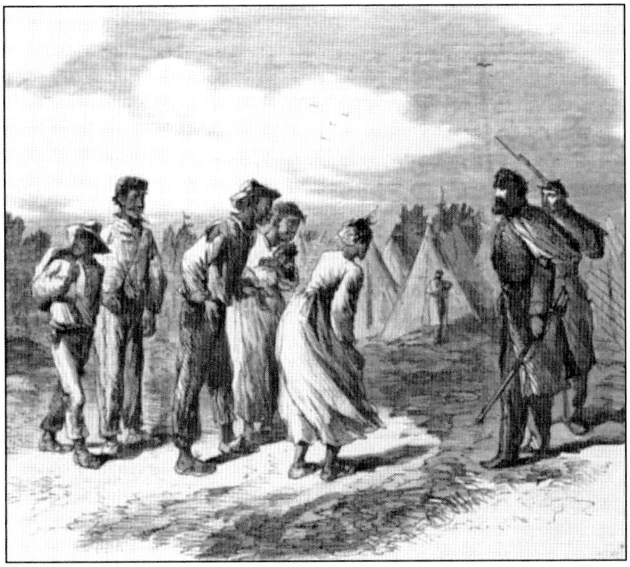

An estimated two to four contraband camps were set up in Jefferson County by Union soldiers for thousands of runaway slaves. As a haven throughout the Delta and southern Arkansas, these camps provided food, shelter, and medical attention to runaway slaves and helped fuel an overwhelming influx of African Americans following the defeat of rebel forces. Also of note, 300 black men from the contraband camps fought with Union soldiers to quell an 1863 Confederate attack on Pine Bluff. (Courtesy of the American Antiquarian Society.)

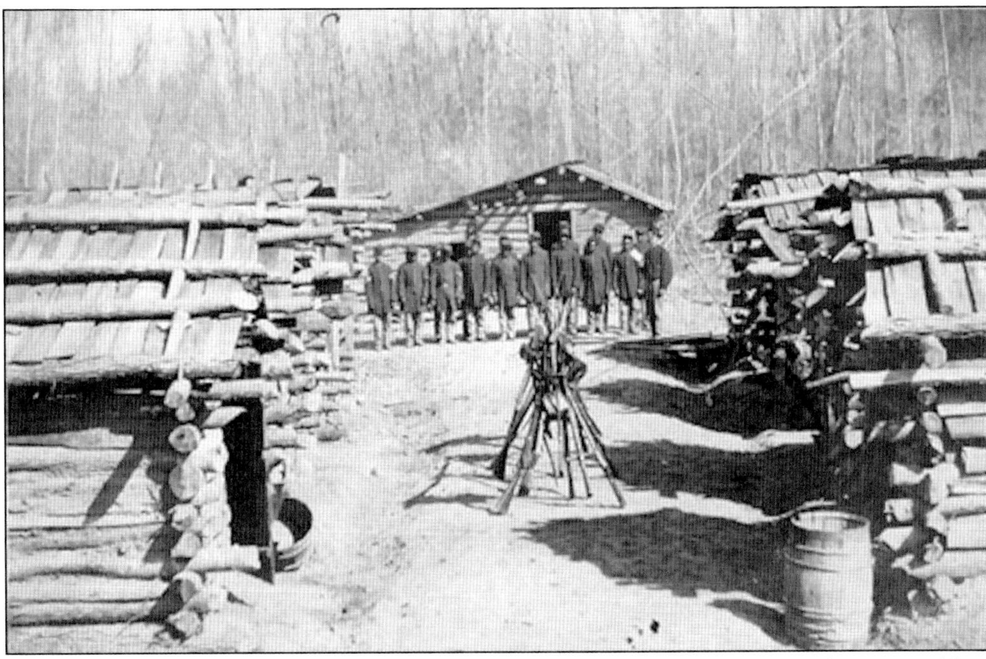

These soldiers of the 64th Colored Infantry in Palmyra Bend, Mississippi, were the same soldiers who were stationed in Pine Bluff and fought in a skirmish with hostile forces on July 2, 1864, during the Civil War. At least three other African American regiments served in Pine Bluff during the war. The most famous was the 1st Kansas Colored Infantry (stationed in Pine Bluff in 1865), which was the very first black unit to fight during the conflict when it engaged troops in the Battle of Island Mound (Missouri) in 1862. (Courtesy of Library of Congress.)

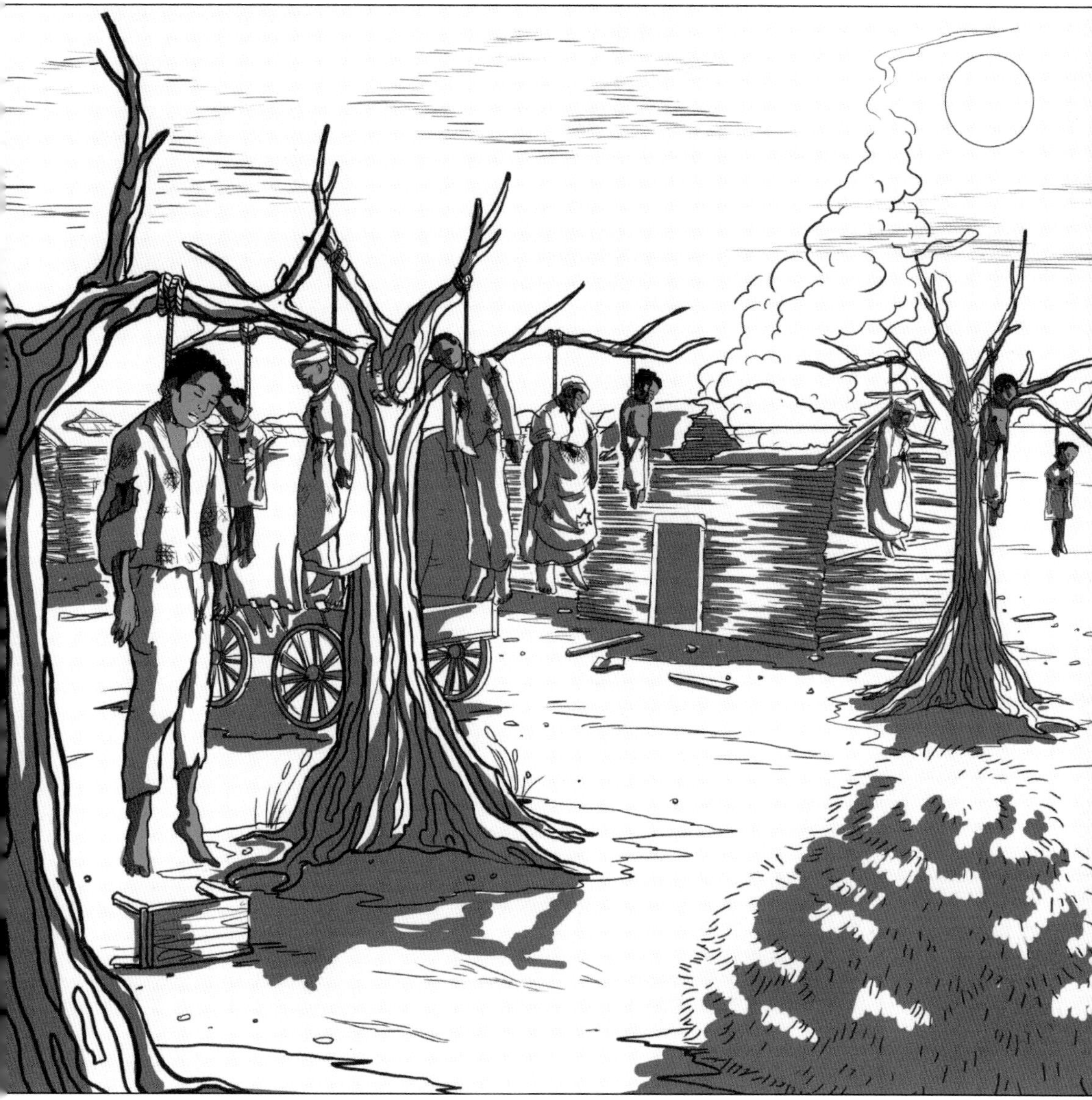

In March 1866, approximately 24 African Americans were lynched just outside of Pine Bluff, according to a letter from William Mallet to US senator Thaddeus Stevens. The letter reads in part, "the rebs had some Kind of dispute with some Freedmen, but it was no more thaut about until that night the Negroes Cabbens were seen to be on fire, the next Morning . . . I Saw a sight that apald Me. 24 Negro Men Woman and Children weare hanging to trees all around the Cabbins." If this sole account is accurate, this was the largest mass lynching in the United States, exceeding the previous 1891 record set in New Orleans. Lynching was an insidious tool of intimidation used throughout the South. According to the *New York Times* on February 15, 1892, two black men—Gulbert Harris and John Kelly—were lynched directly in front of the Jefferson County Courthouse as 5,000 to 10,000 spectators watched. With nine lynchings from 1889 to 1909, along with the 1866 mass lynching, the area also has the dubious title of the most lynchings of any county in Arkansas. (Courtesy of Jimmy Cunningham Jr.)

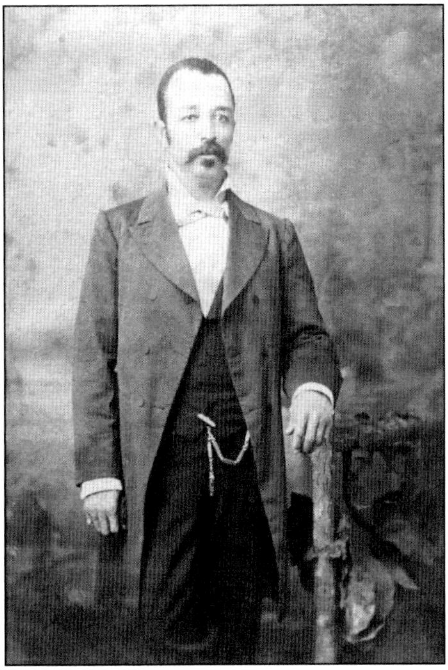

Wiley Jones, pictured here around 1885, was a former slave who came from Georgia to Pine Bluff at the age of five. He became a barber while saving his money and investing in real estate. Eventually, Jones became the richest black man in Arkansas and the entire Mississippi Delta. He owned a Pine Bluff trolley car company, a horseracing track, and real estate holdings, including a resort in Sulphur Springs, as well as several other business ventures. His net value at his death was estimated to be around $250,000. (Courtesy of A'Lelia Bundles.)

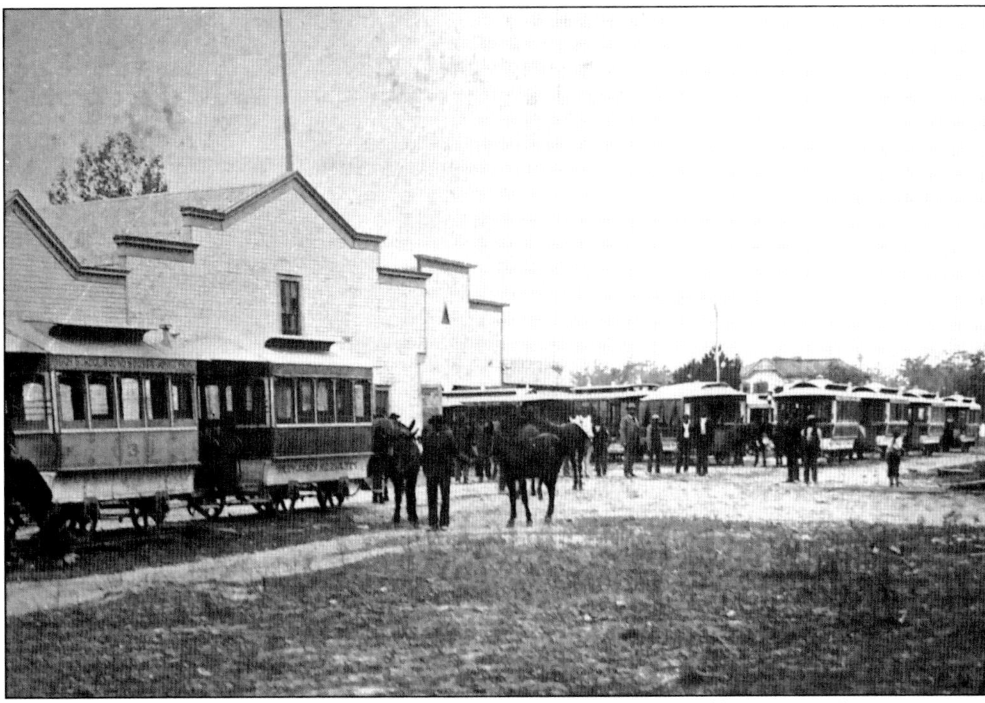

Wiley Jones's horse-drawn trolley car company in Pine Bluff, pictured here around 1890, was one of the first such black-owned companies in the nation. These grounds, located near 17th Avenue and Main Street, were part of his 55-acre park, which was home to bicycle races, fairs, and other assorted celebrations. Adjacent to the park was Jones' Colored State Fairgrounds, which, according to the *Encyclopedia of African American Business History*, drew 20,000 people per year. The grounds boasted horse stables and an amphitheater. (Courtesy of A'Lelia Bundles.)

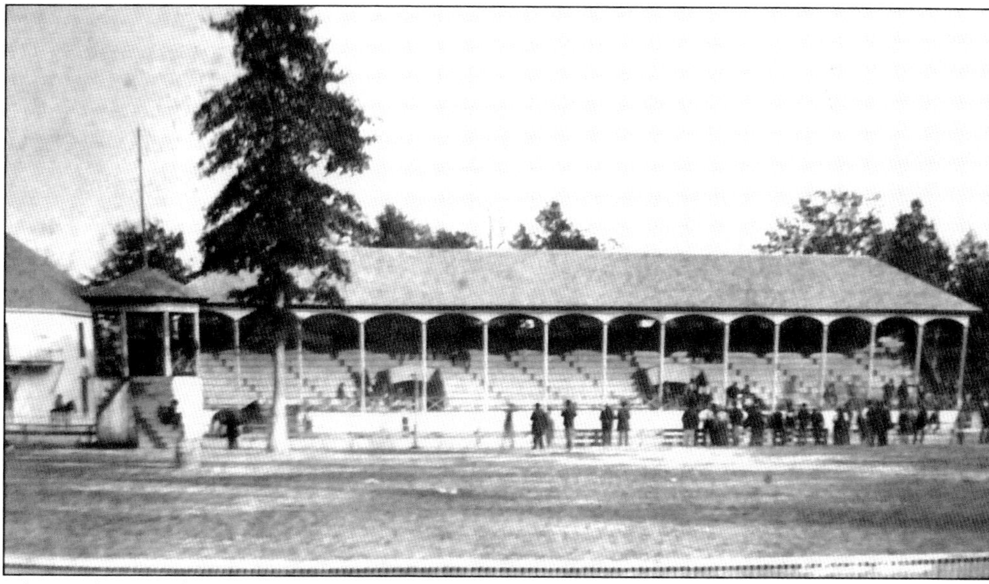

This is the grandstand of Wiley Jones's horseracing track. Jones had up to 24 stallions in his stable, including his favorite racing horse, Excalibur. One horse was valued at $25,000, according to Booker T. Washington in *The Negro In Business*. (Courtesy of A'Lelia Bundles.)

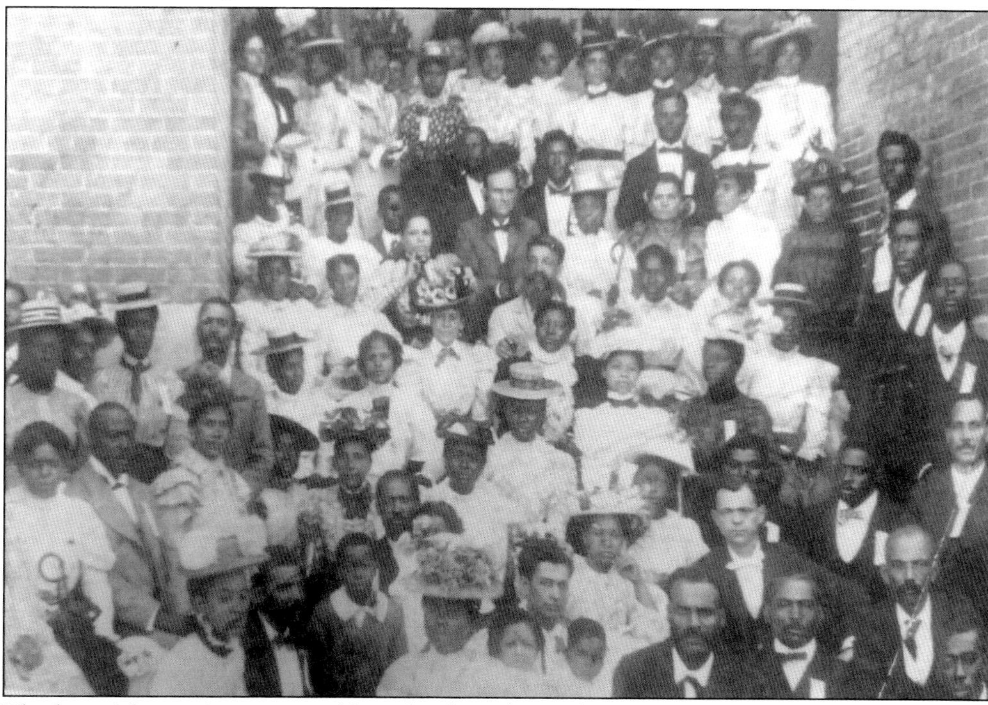

The best African American public school teachers selected from around the state attend an annual summer institute in Pine Bluff supervised by the president of Branch Normal College (later UAPB), Joseph C. Corbin, in 1895. Corbin and fellow educator Rufus Childress went on to form the Teachers Association of Arkansas in 1898, which enrolled more than 50 percent of black teachers in the state and was the forerunner of the current Arkansas Teachers Association. (Courtesy of the Henri Linton Collection.)

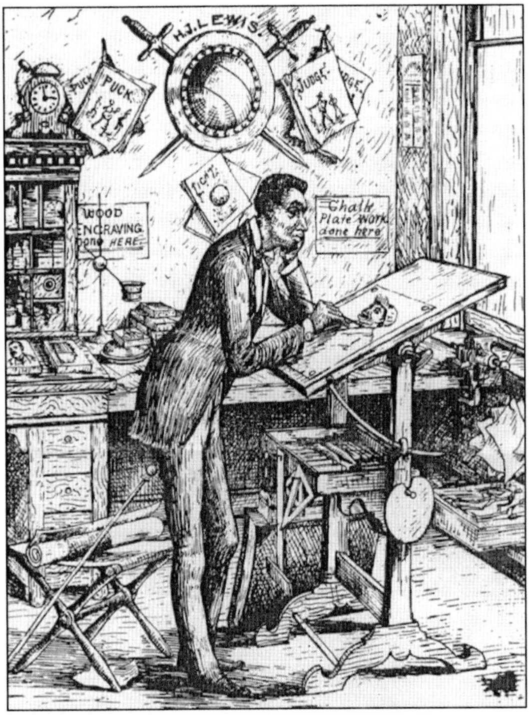

This c. 1890 self-portrait of the nation's first African American political cartoonist, Henry Lewis Jackson, shows the Mississippi-born, 20-year Pine Bluff resident laboriously sketching. His artistic talent blossomed during his time in Pine Bluff with his first non-political drawings published nationally while there. Eventually, Jackson took a position with the Indiana-based weekly black newspaper the *Freeman*. (Courtesy of the Dusable Museum of African American History.)

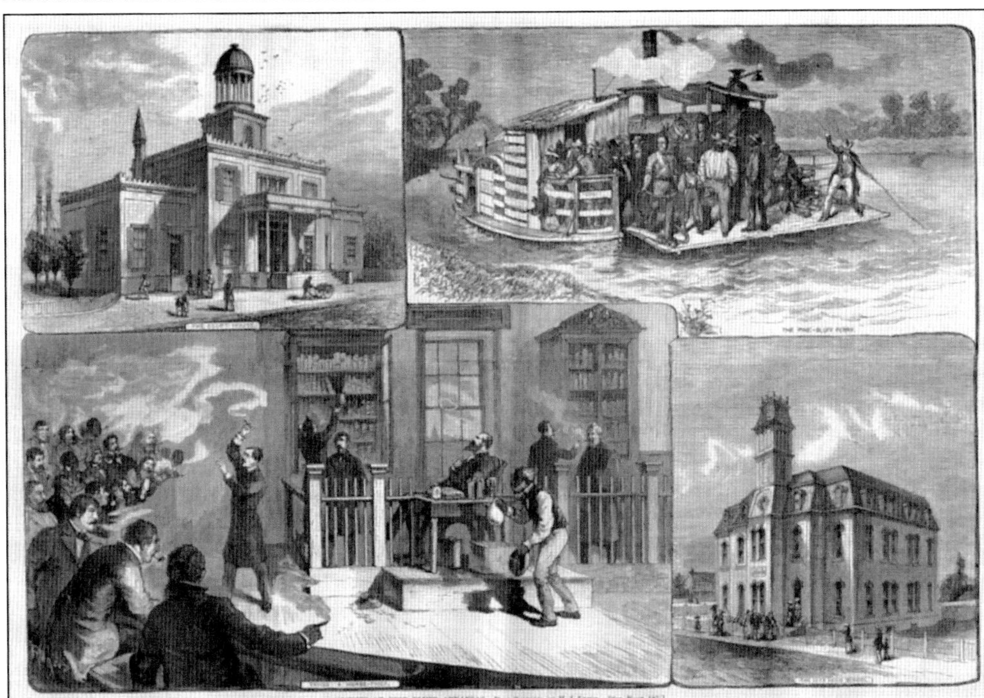

Henry Jackson Lewis's artwork appeared in *Harper's Weekly* magazine in 1879 before his switch to political cartoons. Here, he illustrates Jefferson County scenes from the courthouse, the Arkansas River, the trial of an accused horse thief, and a local high school. (Courtesy of New York Public Library.)

Two unidentified Pine Bluff women pose in stylish attire indicative of a middle class background in this c. 1895 photograph. By the turn of the 20th century, the county had developed a small but vibrant black middle class. African American women of status were engaged in benevolent societies such as the Mother's League, organized in 1893, and social/literary groups such as the Ne Plus Ultra Club. (Courtesy of Paul Perdue.)

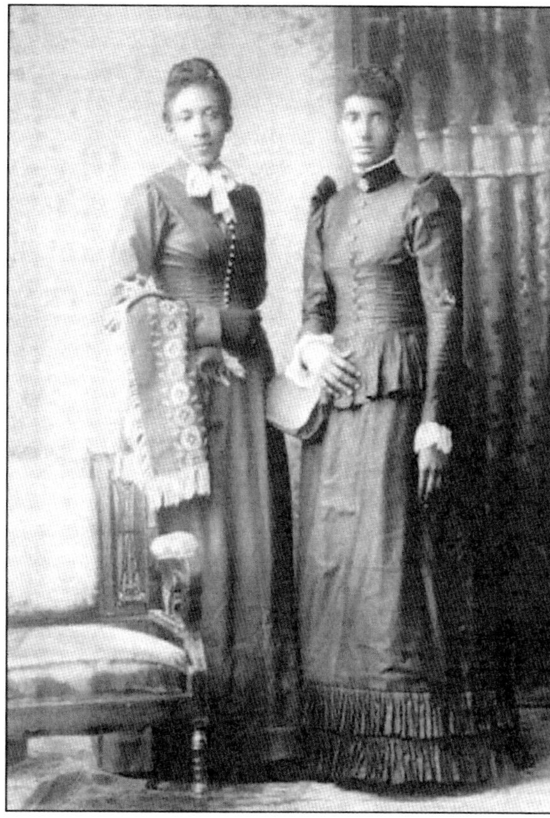

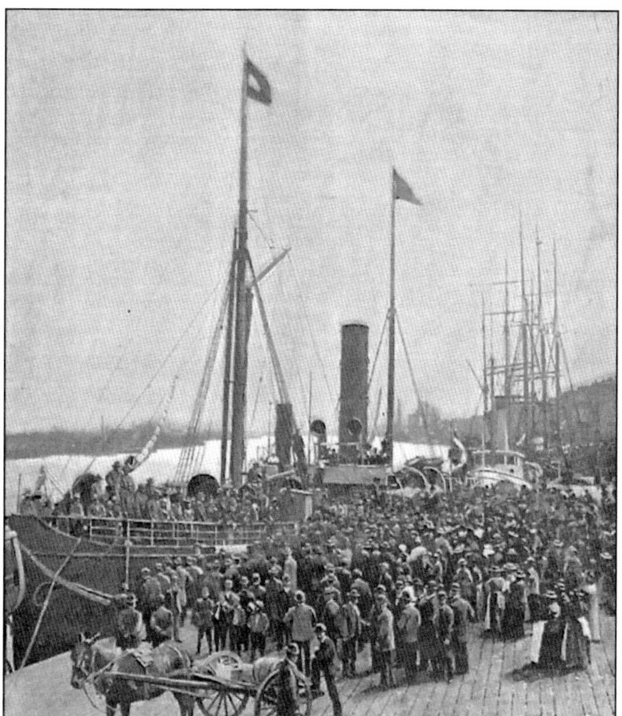

The steamship *Horsa*, pictured here in March 1895, departs from Savannah, Georgia, carrying over 100 Jefferson County passengers headed to the African nation of Liberia. Frustrated with the virulent racism of the post-Reconstruction era, a Jefferson County resident wrote that 900 additional area blacks were ready to go to Liberia, according to Kenneth Barnes in *Journey of Hope: The Back to Africa Movement in Arkansas in the Late 1800s*. (Courtesy of New York Public Library.)

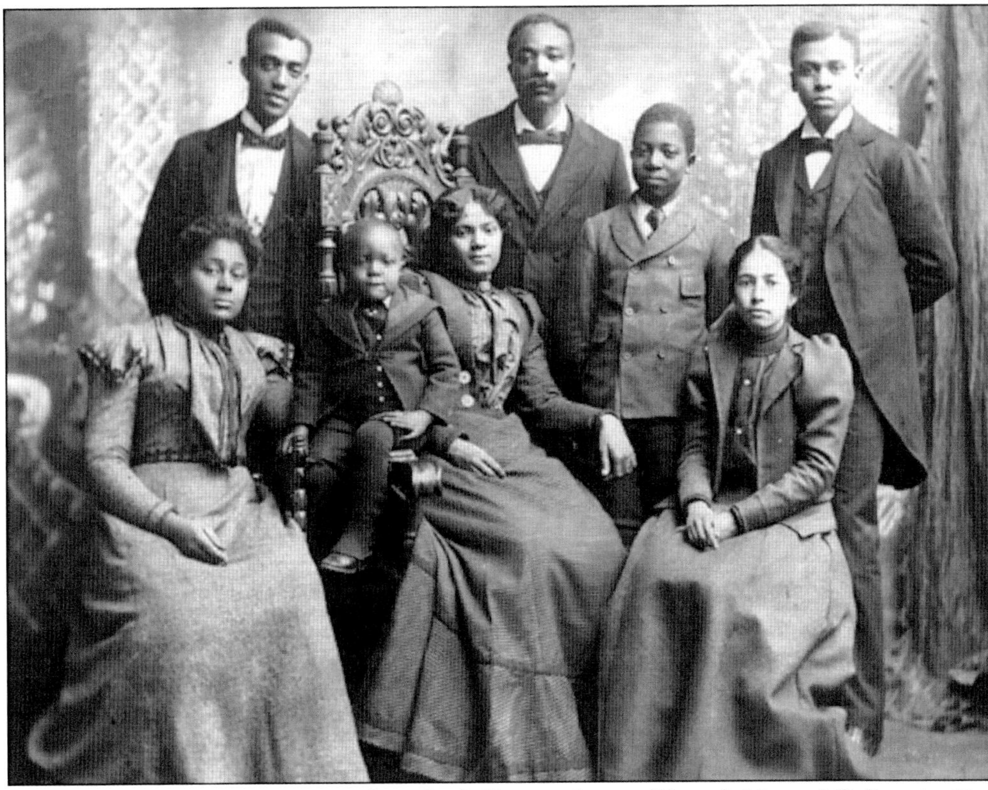

Amanda Davis (first woman seated on the left), a graduate of Branch Normal College in Pine Bluff, awaits departure in 1898 from New York to Liberia so she may begin her teaching assignment there along with other Methodist Arkansas missionaries. (Courtesy of Library of Congress.)

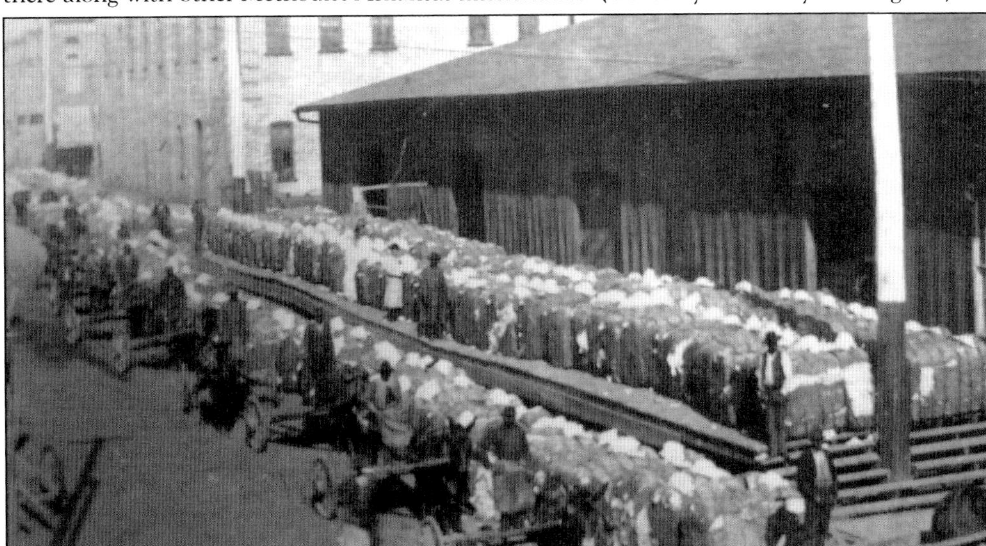

African American drivers transport cotton from around the county to downtown Pine Bluff. This 1893 picture, taken for an exhibit at the Chicago World's Fair, illustrates how integral the cotton market was to the area. According to a report in 1888, Jefferson County was second in the entire South in the total number of cotton bales produced. (Courtesy of Dr. George Talbot.)

Ferdinand "Ferd" Havis, former slave of mixed parentage, was one of Jefferson County's most powerful black politicians and one of the richest in the late 1800s. Havis served as an alderman, state representative, county assessor, and in other assorted positions. He was part of the new black Republican majority in Jefferson County, which agreed to share power with whites by guaranteeing political offices to both races during Reconstruction. (Courtesy of Arkansas History Commission.)

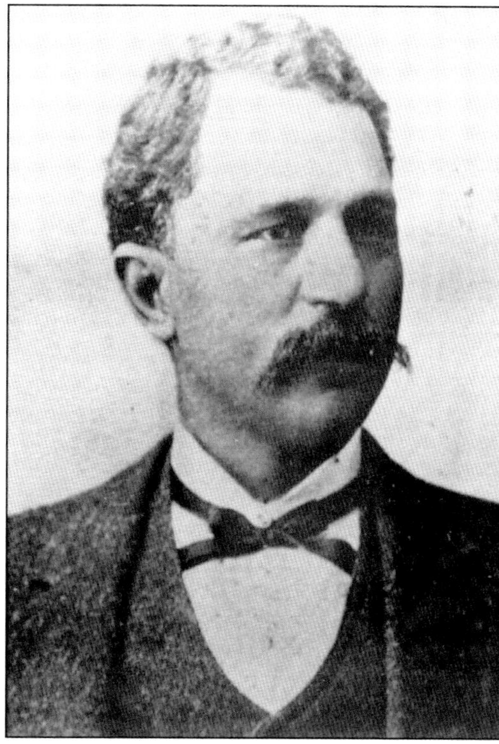

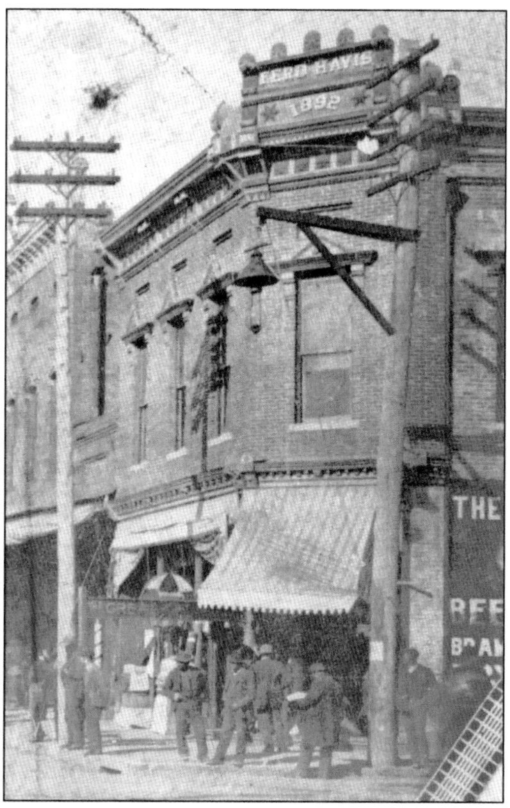

In 1893, Ferd Havis's building on Third and Main Street was a tavern and a popular meeting place among Pine Bluff's black society. In addition to his tavern, Havis also owned 2,000 acres of land, several tenement houses, and a barbershop. His actual estimated worth was around $100,000. He was called "the Colored Millionaire." (Courtesy of the Butler Center for Arkansas Studies.)

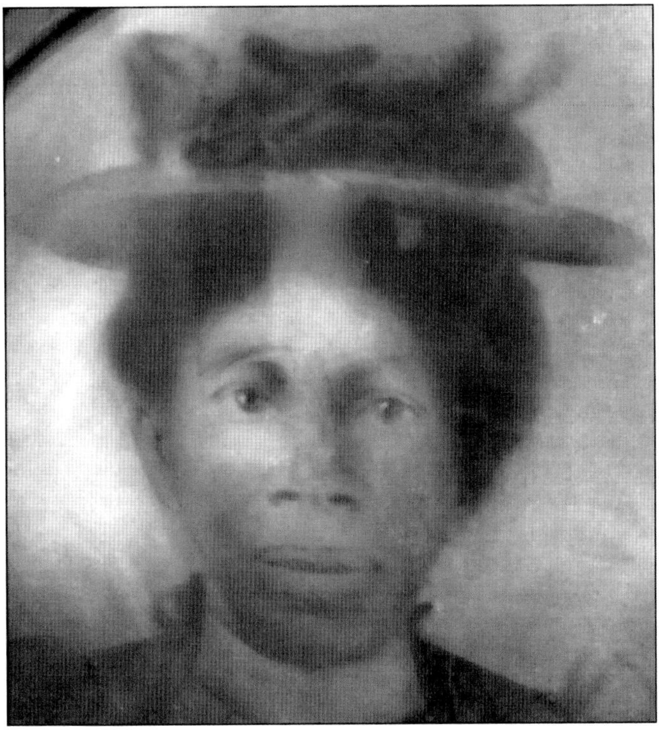

Jane Oliver, born a slave in 1862, was one of Jefferson County's early African American female landowners. After borrowing $100 from banker R.M. Knox, she purchased 202 acres of land for farming and selling timber. She managed her business affairs and paid off her loans all without ever learning how to write, according to her 1938 interview with Bernice Bowden. Jane Oliver Apartments, a Pine Bluff housing project, bore her name for years. (Courtesy of Pine Bluff/Jefferson County Historical Museum.)

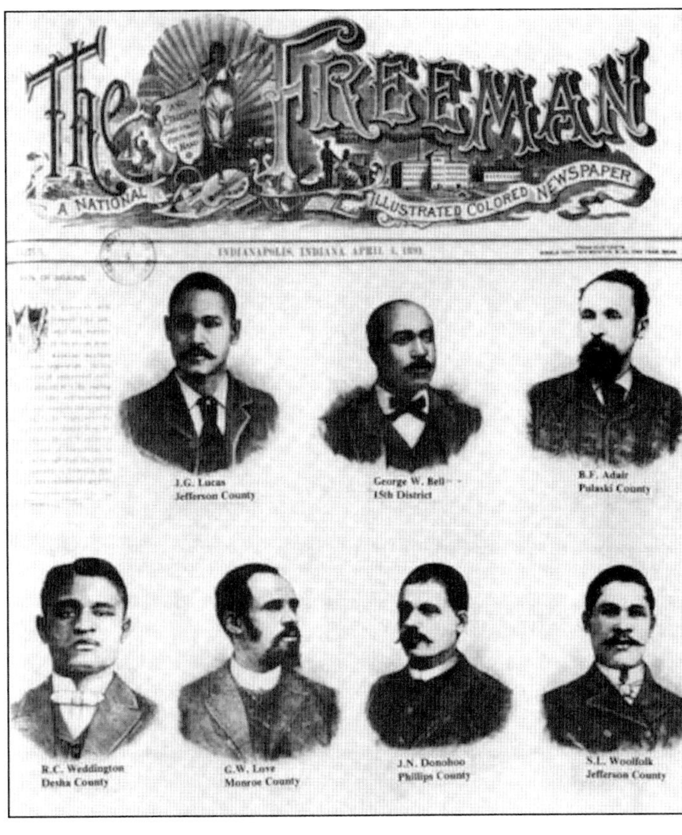

The Freeman
A National Illustrated Colored Newspaper

J.G. Lucas
Jefferson County

George W. Bell
15th District

B.F. Adair
Pulaski County

R.C. Weddington
Desha County

G.W. Love
Monroe County

J.N. Donohoo
Phillips County

S.L. Woolfolk
Jefferson County

This 1891 edition of the Indiana-based African American newspaper *The Freeman* shows only two black legislators from Jefferson County: J.G. Lucas (top row, left) and S.L. Woolfolk (bottom row, right). However, Jefferson County legislators dominated Arkansas state politics in representation from 1868 to 1893 with 33 total terms held by black legislators compared with Phillips County (23 terms held by blacks) and Pulaski County (9 terms held by blacks). (Courtesy of Special Collections Department, University of Arkansas Libraries.)

Two

Music, Art, and Entertainment

My hair is arising, my flesh begin to crawl, I had a dream last night baby, another mule in my doggone stall!

—Big Bill Broonzy, "Big Bill Blues"

Grammy nominee and Blues Hall of Famer "Big Bill" Broonzy, born Lee Conley Bradley, was one of the nation's biggest blues stars of the 1930s and 1940s. According to blues historian Robert Reisman, Broonzy was born in Jefferson County near Lake Dick and moved to Pine Bluff. He learned to play the fiddle there and was paid to perform at picnics and country dances. He eventually settled in Chicago and learned to play the guitar. With numerous hit songs in the United States and appearances ranging from Carnegie Hall to juke joints and clubs across the country, he is also credited with introducing European audiences to the blues in the 1950s. His work influenced Muddy Waters, Howlin' Wolf, Eric Clapton, and the Rolling Stones. Lyrics from his song, "Black, White and Brown," were quoted during the 2009 US presidential inauguration by Rev. Joseph Lowrey. (Courtesy of Associated Press [AP] Images/Bettman Corbis.)

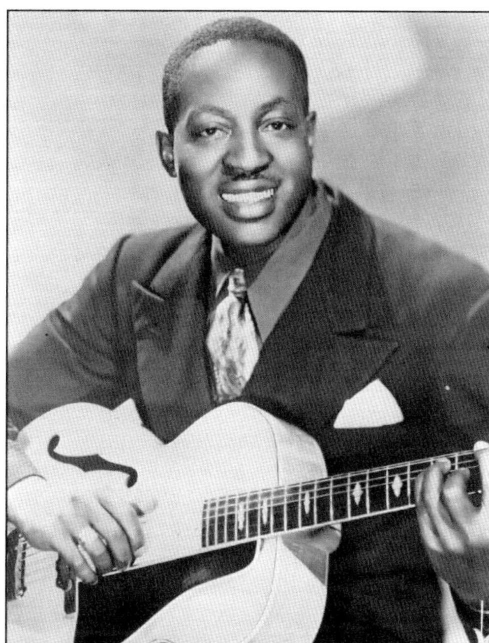

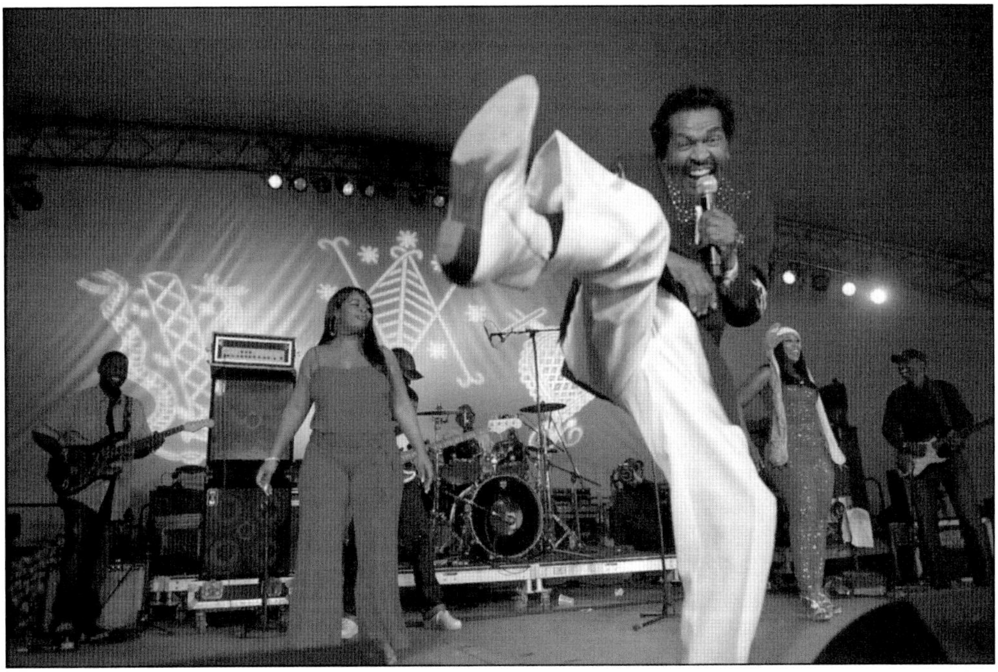

Another Grammy nominee and Blues Hall of Famer, Bobby Rush moved to Pine Bluff with his family when he was 11 years old. It was in Pine Bluff that Rush formed his first band playing at a juke joint called Nappy's, situated behind a sawmill. It was also in Pine Bluff where he formed key associations with blues artists Boyd Gilmore, Elmore James, Howlin' Wolf, Driftin' Slim, "Moose" Walker, and others. Rush was recently named the International Ambassador of the Blues by the Tennessee legislature. (Courtesy of AP Images/Adrienne Battistella/Picture Group.)

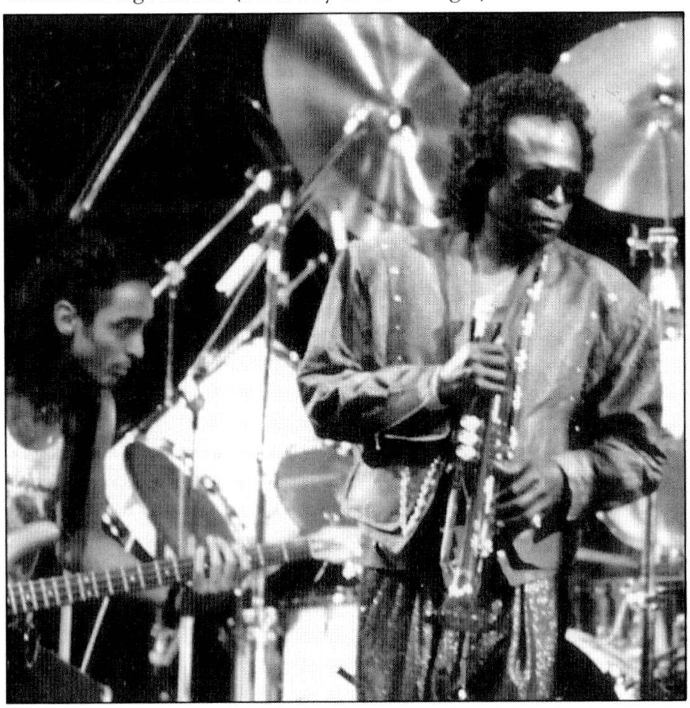

Grammy Award–winning jazz artist Miles Davis spent his summers growing up on his grandfather's farm in Noble Lake (in Jefferson County). His father was a native of Jefferson County, whose family fought rural white residents to keep their prosperous farm. In *Miles: The Autobiography*, Davis discusses his many Jefferson County childhood experiences and attributes the blues-influenced gospel sounds he heard at the area's country churches with giving him his earliest music influences. (Courtesy of Oliver Nurock.)

William "Smokie" Norful Jr., a Grammy-winning gospel artist, performs at the White House for a celebration of Black Music Month in 2005. Norful grew up largely in Pine Bluff, attended college there, and taught history in the local public school district before launching a successful singing career. Norful's father, Rev. Dr. W.M. Norful Sr., retired in 2012 as pastor at his Pine Bluff childhood church home of St. John African Methodist Episcopal (AME) Church. (Courtesy of Krisanne Johnson.)

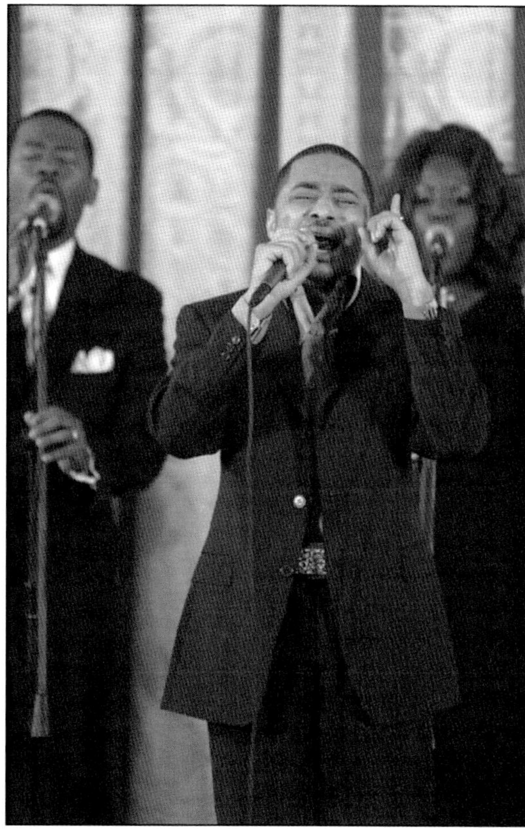

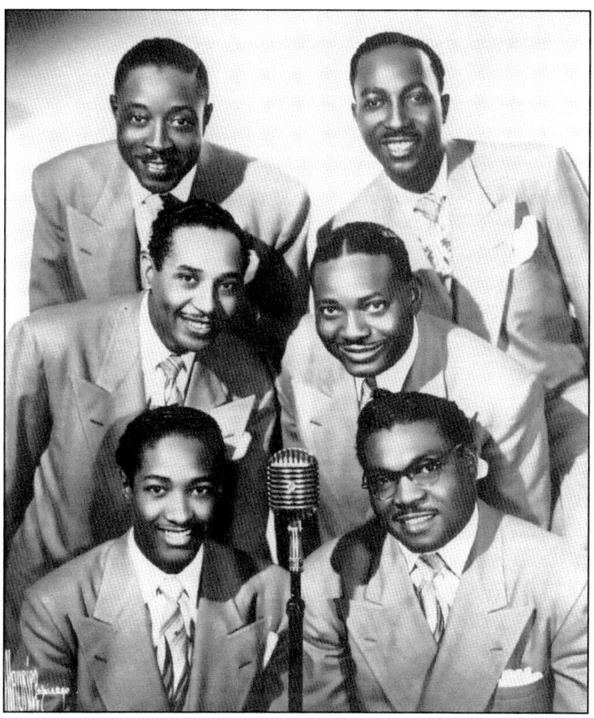

Sometime around 1950, Sam Cooke (first row, left), then an unknown performer, joined the gospel group the Soul Stirrers and made his professional debut in Pine Bluff, according to Arthur Kempton in *Boogaloo: The Quintessence of American Popular Music*. Reportedly, he only knew two songs but made it through the performance. Cooke later started a solo career as an R&B artist, making a string of legendary hits. He received a posthumous Grammy for Lifetime Achievement in 1999. (Courtesy of Michael Ochs Archives/Getty Images.)

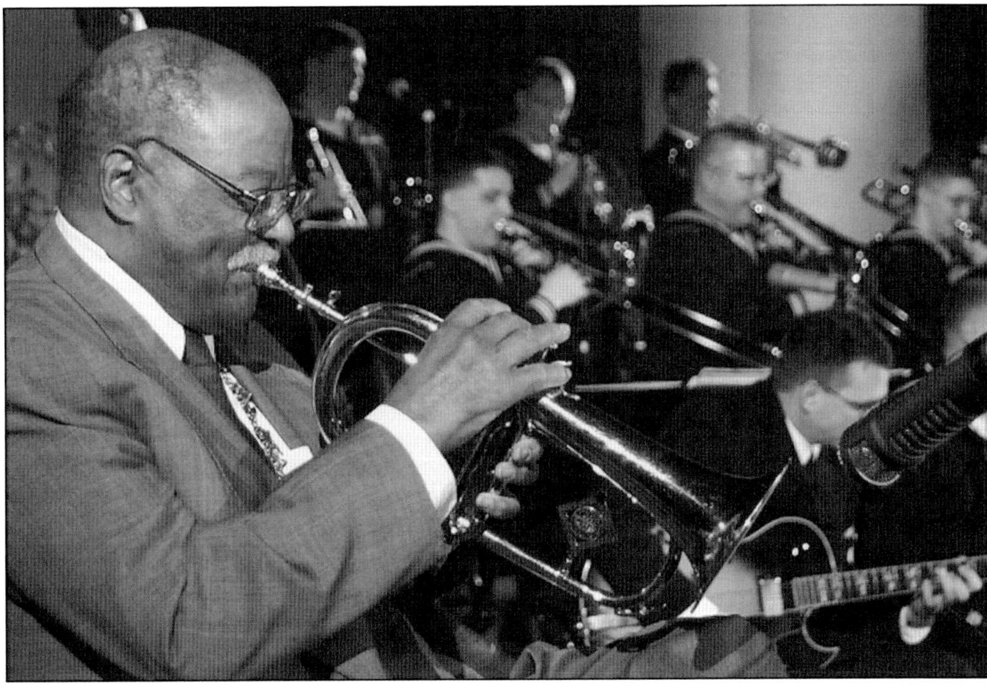

St. Louis–born and Grammy Lifetime Achievement Award–winner Clark Terry moved to Pine Bluff in his senior years and has never stopped influencing music. He has mentored local musicians, played for eager Pine Bluff crowds, and inspired area jazz festivals. Terry's career spans 70 years as a trumpeter and flugelhornist having performed for eight US presidents. One of the most recorded musicians in the history of jazz, with more than 900 recordings, he has played with Quincy Jones, Duke Ellington, Count Basie, Billie Holiday, Ray Charles, Aretha Franklin, Sara Vaughn, and many others. (Courtesy of Micheal Worner.)

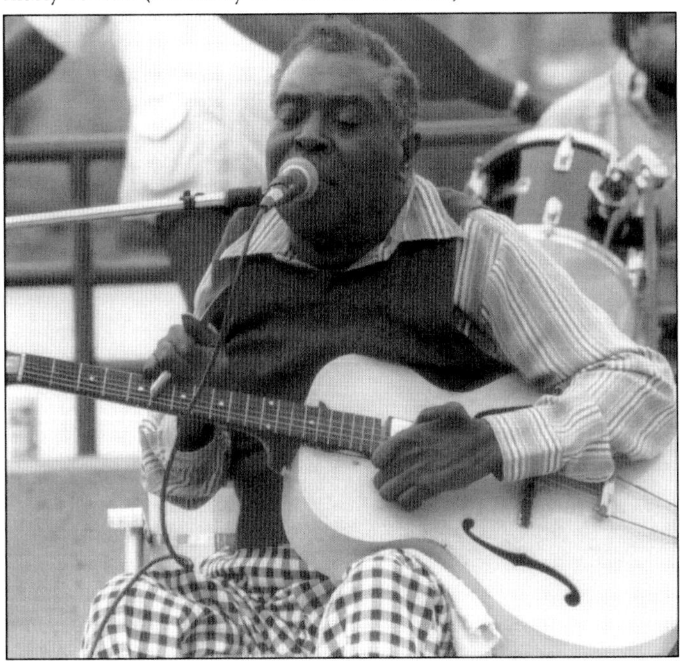

Cedell Davis, a 45-year resident of Pine Bluff, blues guitarist/vocalist, and National Endowment for the Arts National Heritage Fellow nominee, employs a butter knife to create chords. During the late 1950s, Davis moved to Pine Bluff and began playing at the Jack Rabbit juke joint, where he performed regularly with other legendary blues musicians such as Robert Knighthawk, Elmore James, and Houston Stackhouse. His Fat Possum Records recordings have garnered international acclaim among blues fans. (Courtesy of Paul Barrows.)

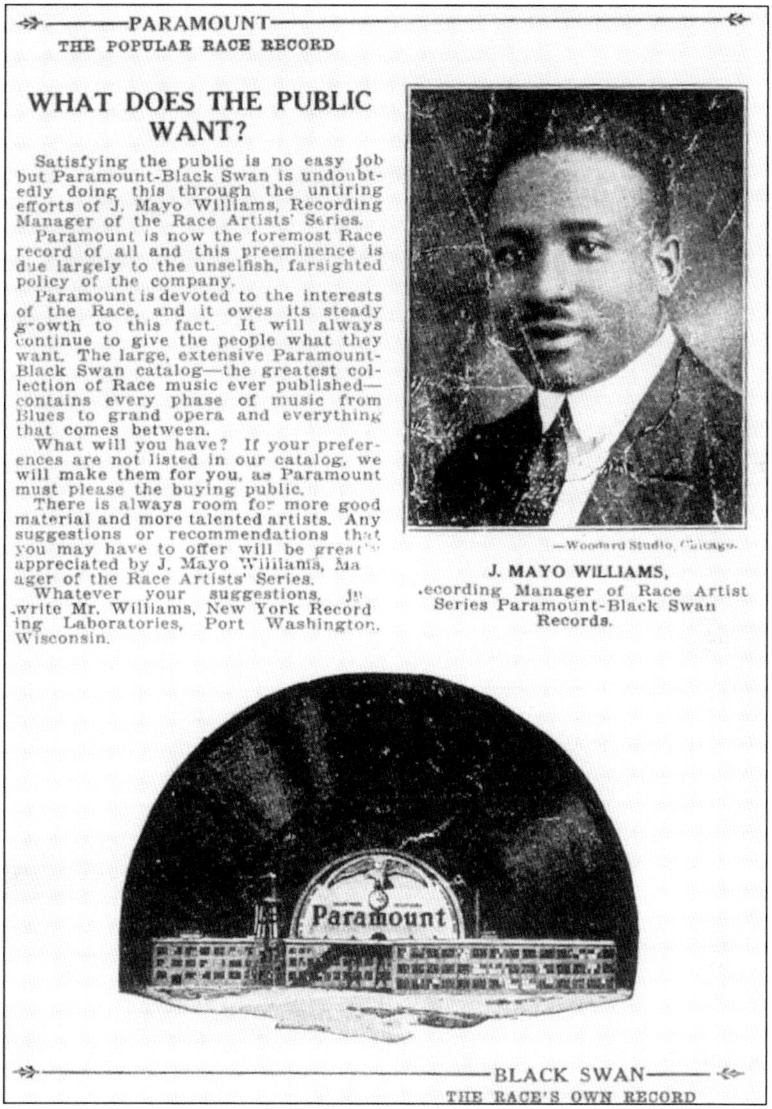

PARAMOUNT

THE POPULAR RACE RECORD

WHAT DOES THE PUBLIC WANT?

Satisfying the public is no easy job but Paramount-Black Swan is undoubtedly doing this through the untiring efforts of J. Mayo Williams, Recording Manager of the Race Artists' Series.

Paramount is now the foremost Race record of all and this preeminence is due largely to the unselfish, farsighted policy of the company.

Paramount is devoted to the interests of the Race, and it owes its steady growth to this fact. It will always continue to give the people what they want. The large, extensive Paramount-Black Swan catalog—the greatest collection of Race music ever published—contains every phase of music from Blues to grand opera and everything that comes between.

What will you have? If your preferences are not listed in our catalog, we will make them for you, as Paramount must please the buying public.

There is always room for more good material and more talented artists. Any suggestions or recommendations that you may have to offer will be greatly appreciated by J. Mayo Williams, Manager of the Race Artists' Series.

Whatever your suggestions, just write Mr. Williams, New York Recording Laboratories, Port Washington, Wisconsin.

—Woodard Studio, Chicago.

J. MAYO WILLIAMS,
Recording Manager of Race Artist Series Paramount-Black Swan Records.

BLACK SWAN

THE RACE'S OWN RECORD

Pine Bluff native and Blues Hall of Famer J. Mayo "Ink" Williams was a trailblazing legend as the first African American record producer at a major record company. William Kenney states in *Recorded Music in American Life* that Williams "built the longest running and most productive career of any African American in the phonograph business before World War II." Williams worked for Paramount and Decca Records from the 1920s to 1930s, later forming his own labels in the 1940s largely based in blues music. The list of artists he discovered, produced, wrote for, and/or recorded reads as a virtual who's who of early black popular music, including such artists as Ma Rainey, Papa Charlie Jackson, Blind Lemon Jefferson, Tampa Red, Jelly Roll Morton, King Oliver, Mahalia Jackson, Alberta Hunter, Sister Rosetta Tharpe, Marie Knight, Louis Jordan, Roosevelt Sykes, Sleepy John Estes, Ida Cox, Muddy Waters, Peetie Wheatstraw, Joe Williams, Thomas Dorsey, Clarence "Pinetop" Smith, Leroy Carr, Georgia White, "Bumble Bee Slim," Trixie Smith, and many others. Few black producers have ever worked with such an enormous slice of the leading talent of their era. Also, Williams, along with activist Paul Robeson, was one of the first three African Americans to play in the National Football League in the early 1920s. (Courtesy of Alex van der Tuuk.)

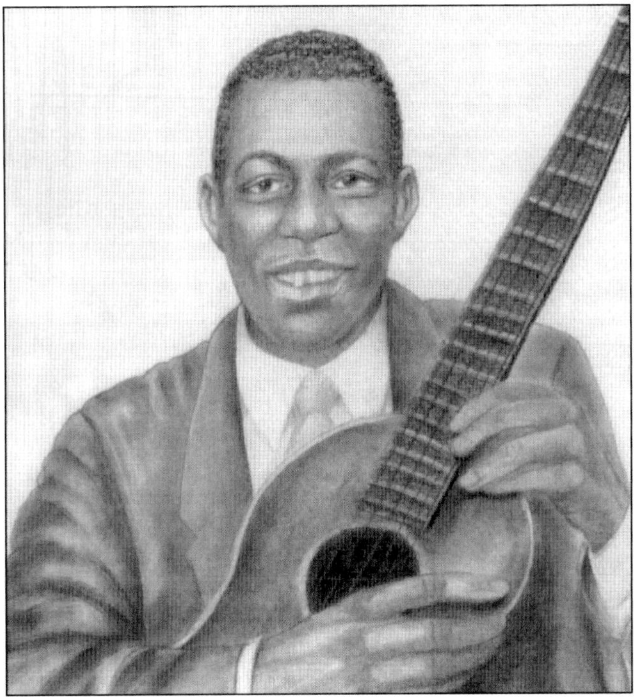

Casey Bill Weldon, born in Pine Bluff, was one of the great pioneer slide guitar blues artists of the 1920s and 1930s. He was known largely as a solo artist who produced hits like "Somebody Changed the Lock on My Door" and "WPA Blues." He recorded over 200 songs as a solo artist, as a member of the Memphis Jug Band, and with his wife, legendary Blues Hall of Famer Memphis Minnie. Weldon played a National steel guitar on his lap and was known as the "Hawaiian Guitar Wizard." (Courtesy of M. Allegro.)

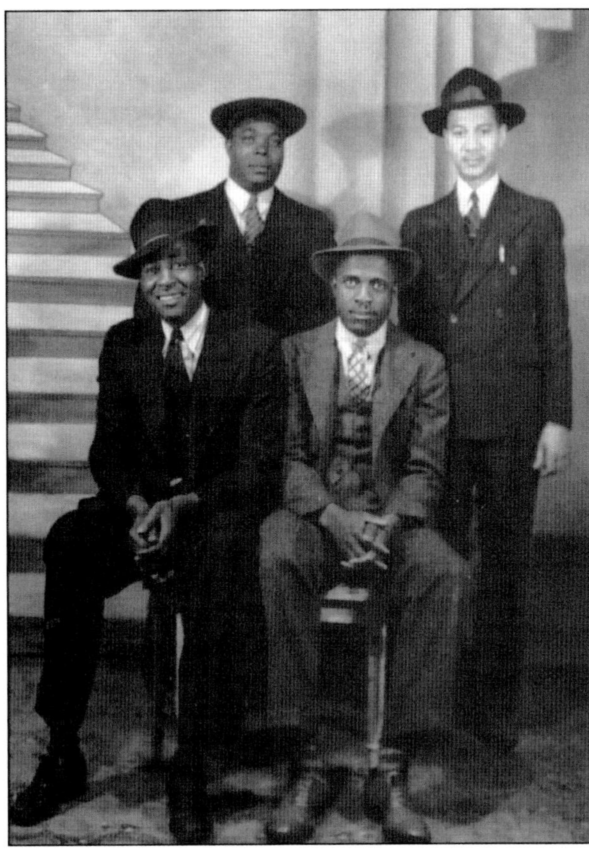

Joshua Altheimer (standing, right), described as "the greatest blues pianist on records" by French music historians Hugues Pannasie and Madeleine Gautier in their *1956 Guide to Jazz,* was born in Altheimer. During the 1930s, he was the primary pianist for Big Bill Broonzy (seated, left), but also played for other greats such as "Sonny Boy" Williamson I, Washboard Sam, Jazz Gillum, Lonnie Johnson, and others. His talents were cut short when he died in 1940 from pneumonia at the age of 30. This is the only known image of Altheimer. (Courtesy of Michael Ochs Archives/Getty Images.)

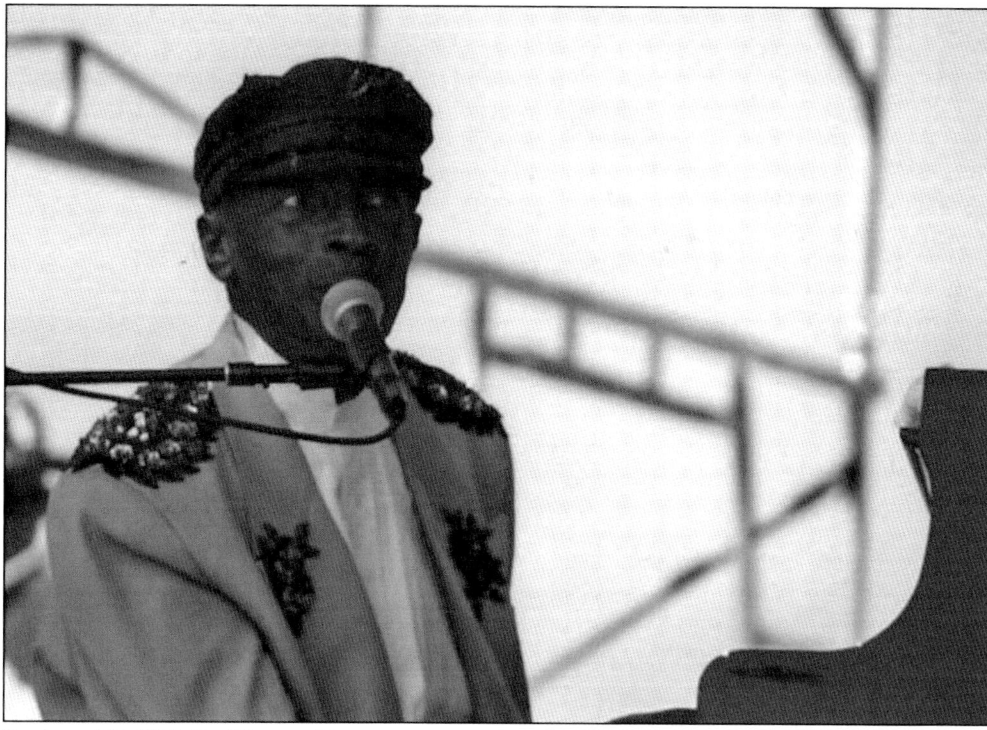

Rock and Roll Hall of Famer, Grammy nominee, and blues/R&B legend Charles Brown, a Texas City, Texas, native, moved to Pine Bluff in the early 1940s to start a career in chemistry at the Pine Bluff Arsenal and hone his musical skills on the side. However, frustrated with discrimination at the arsenal, he later moved to California where he went into the music industry full-fledged and recorded blues standards like "Merry Christmas Baby" and a series of chart topping hits from the mid-1940s to the early 1960s. (Courtesy of Sumori.)

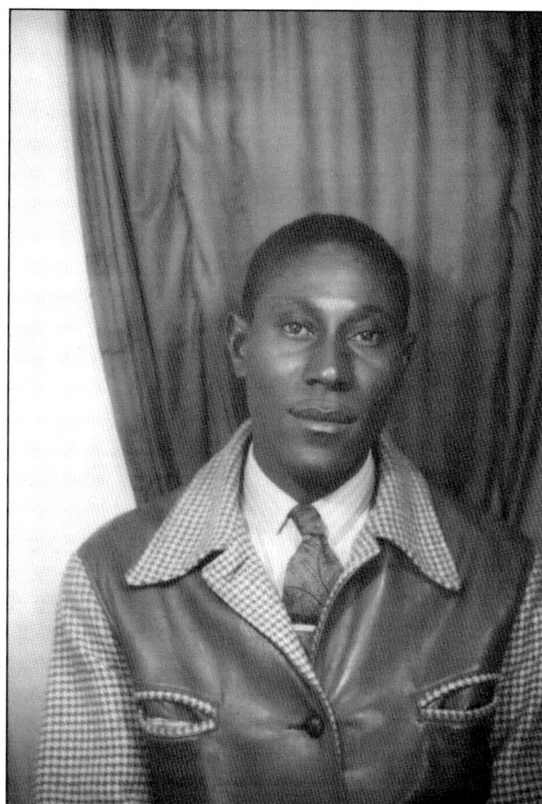

Curtis Rice, shown here in 1940, was an Arkansas gospel music sensation. Born in Sherrill, he later moved to Pine Bluff and joined the highly acclaimed gospel quartet the Spiritual Five until 1972. That same year, he formed the Rice Spiritual Singers for which he became best known. Rice was in constant demand at every church program imaginable throughout south Arkansas and the Delta. (Courtesy of Arkansas History Commission.)

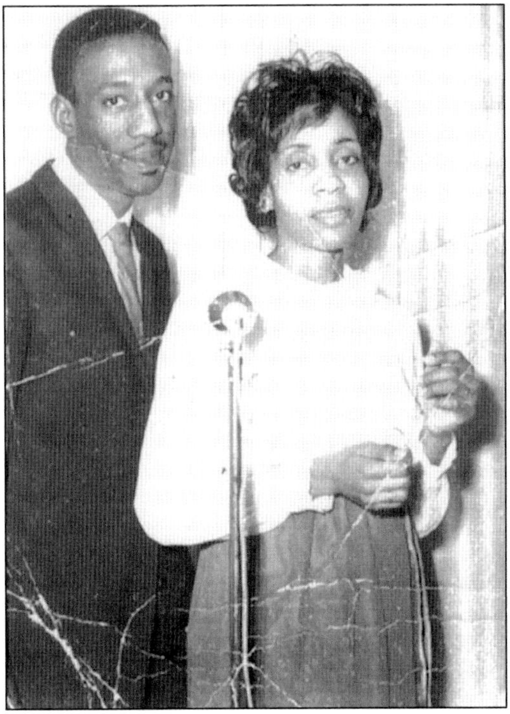

The Williams Singers of Pine Bluff, composed of husband and wife U.Z. and Jessie B. Williams, enthralled gospel audiences for years beginning in 1960. They traveled throughout the South with gospel greats such as Sister Rosetta Tharpe, Brother Joe Mays, the Angelic Gospel Singers, the Pearl Gospel Singers, and many others. It is no wonder that their grandchild Ashely Williams won the $10,000 first-place prize at the Steve Harvey Hoodie Awards national singing competition in 2012. (Courtesy of Carol Williams Rankin.)

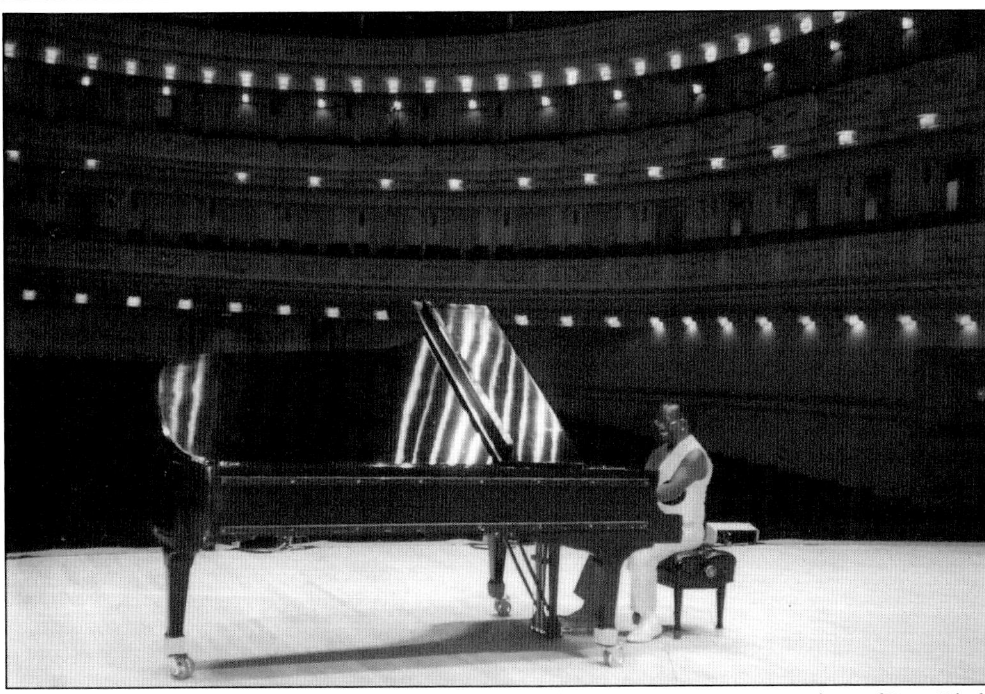

James "Jimmy" McKissic, an internationally acclaimed concert pianist, is a product of Pine Bluff. He began playing the piano at the age of three and has since played for three US presidents, multiple heads of state, and at venues of all kinds. His annual concerts at Carnegie Hall have received critical praise, and his performances in countries across the globe have entertained tens of thousands. (Courtesy of Pine Bluff Commercial.)

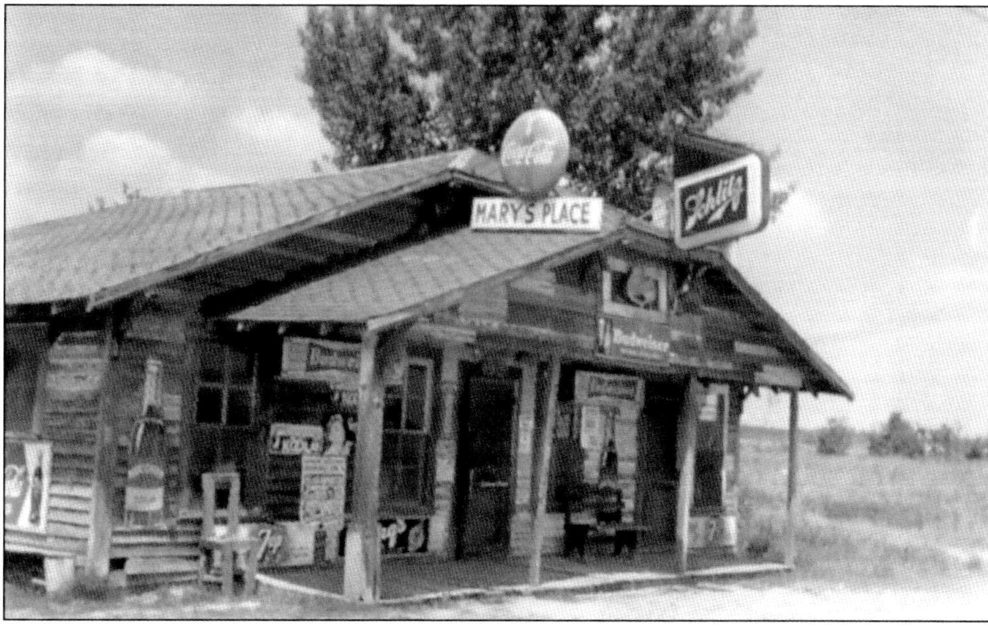

Mary's Place, located near Humphrey, offered locals a chance to hear good blues and catch up on the daily area happenings. (Courtesy of Special Collections Department, University of Arkansas Libraries.)

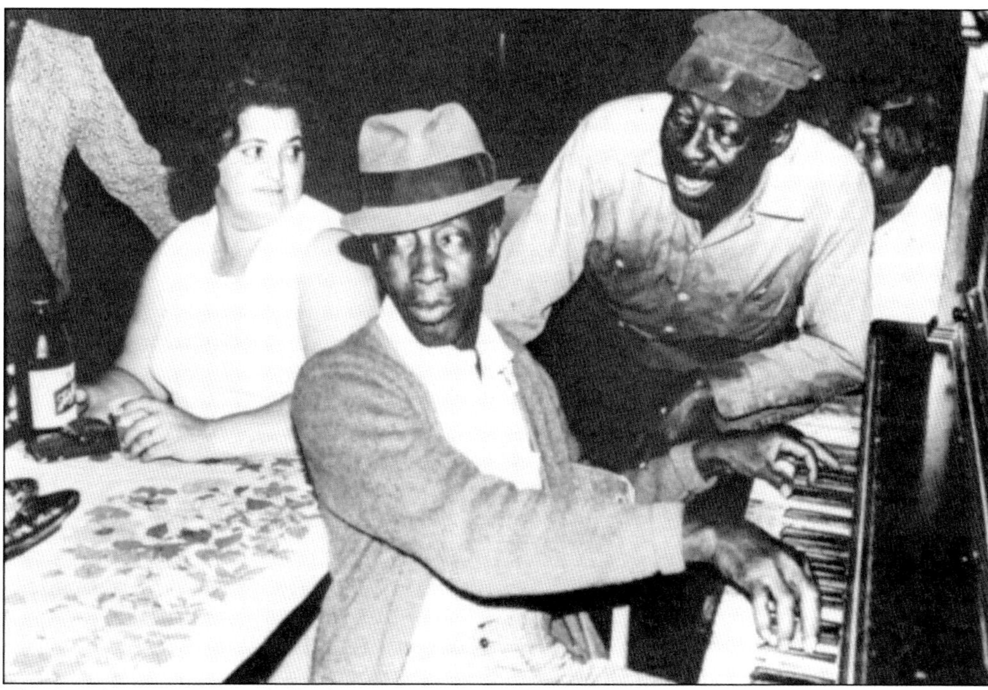

The Jungle Hut, a Pine Bluff juke joint, was typical of the local blues scene featuring live music, liquor, and social camaraderie in 1976. However, because of shifts in musical tastes and formats, traditional juke joints with live blues artists had begun to give way to larger clubs with deejays, like PJ's Disco, Fat Daddy's/Monroe's, the Elk's Lodge, and other venues by the late 1970s. (Courtesy of Arkansas History Commission.)

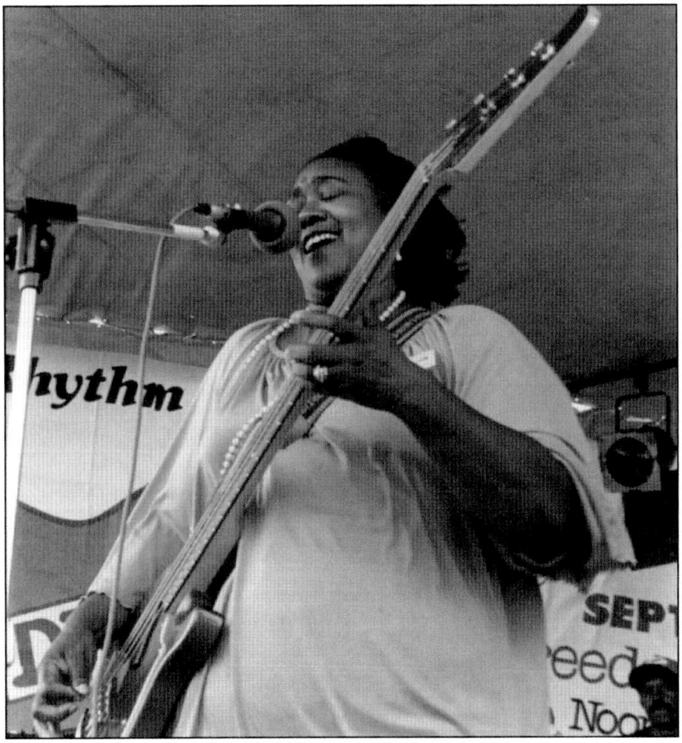

"Queen" Sylvia Embry, born and raised in Wabbaseka, belts out blues with feeling. As a female blues bass guitarist and vocalist with her own group, the Chicago-based Embry was an absolute rarity. The *Encyclopedia of Blues* described her work as powerful and creative and called her "one of the most interesting blues women in the post–World War II era." (Courtesy of University of Mississippi.)

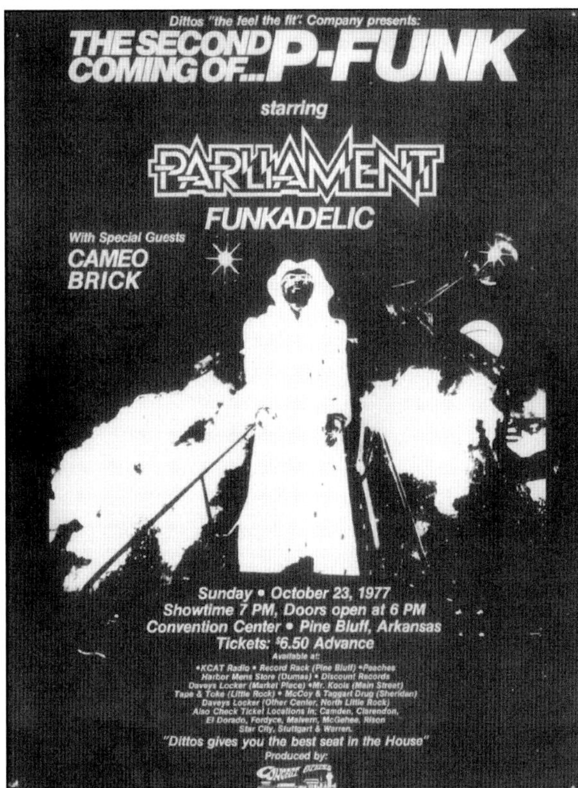

A 1977 concert poster of the popular group Parliament shows the caliber of stars that came to Pine Bluff in the Convention Center's early years. For the black community, this meant seeing the best R&B acts, including the likes of Marvin Gaye, Teddy Pendergrass, Prince, Evelyn Champagne King, Luther Vandross, Rick James, Tina Marie, the Barkays, the Time, Frankie Beverly/Maze, Natalie Cole, the O'Jays, the Isley Brothers, Dionne Warwick, the Commodores, the Emotions, and many others. (Courtesy of Jimmy Cunningham Jr.)

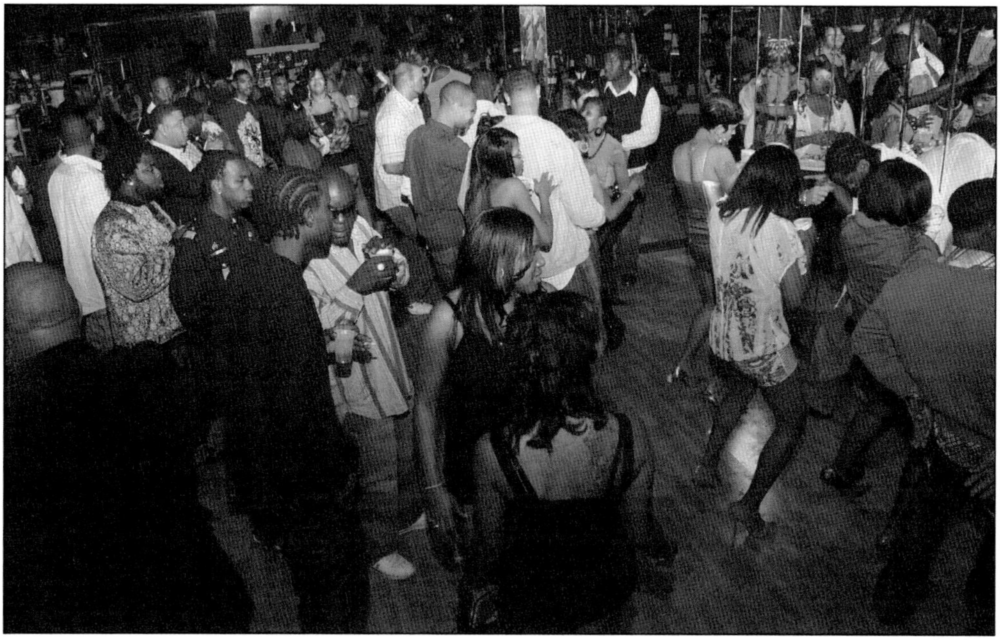

Patrons of PJ's Disco crowd the floor to party in 2011. The club, owned by Perry Johnson, has been a mainstay in Pine Bluff since the late 1970s and boasts one of the largest such facilities in Arkansas. With a swimming pool, elaborate lighting, a beauty shop, and all of the amenities of a big-city club, people come from all over the state to have fun. (Courtesy of Gallegos Photography.)

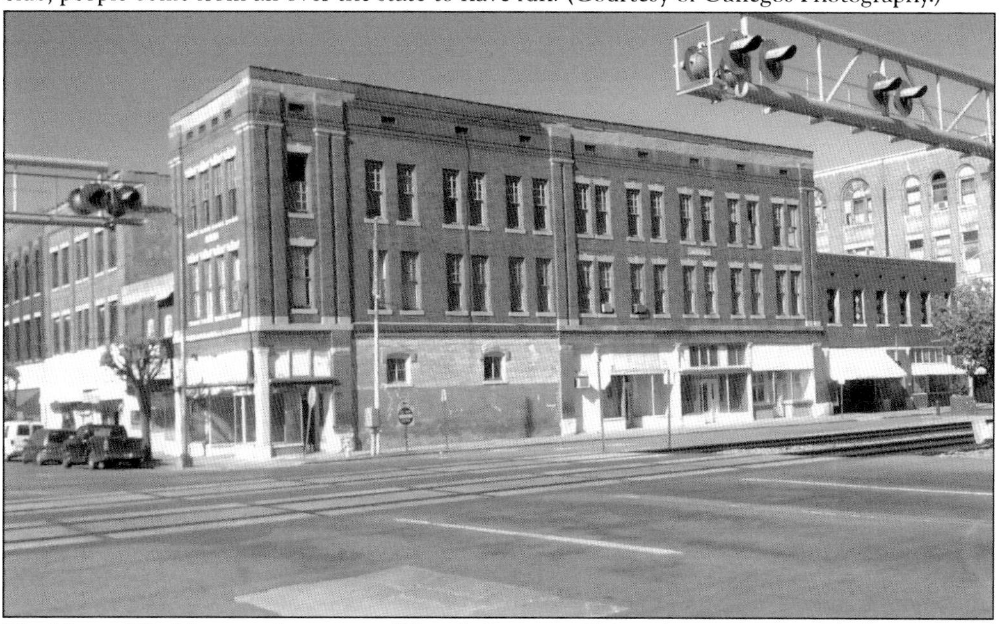

The Howard Building on the corner of Fourth Street and Main Avenue in Pine Bluff maintained a floor that was rented out as a ballroom hall in the early to mid-1900s. This hall played host to such greats as Cab Calloway, Count Basie, Duke Ellington, and other music legends, according to longtime resident George Cooks. The building also housed the offices of many local black businesses over the years, including that of its later owner Judge George Howard Jr. (Courtesy of Jimmy Cunningham Jr.)

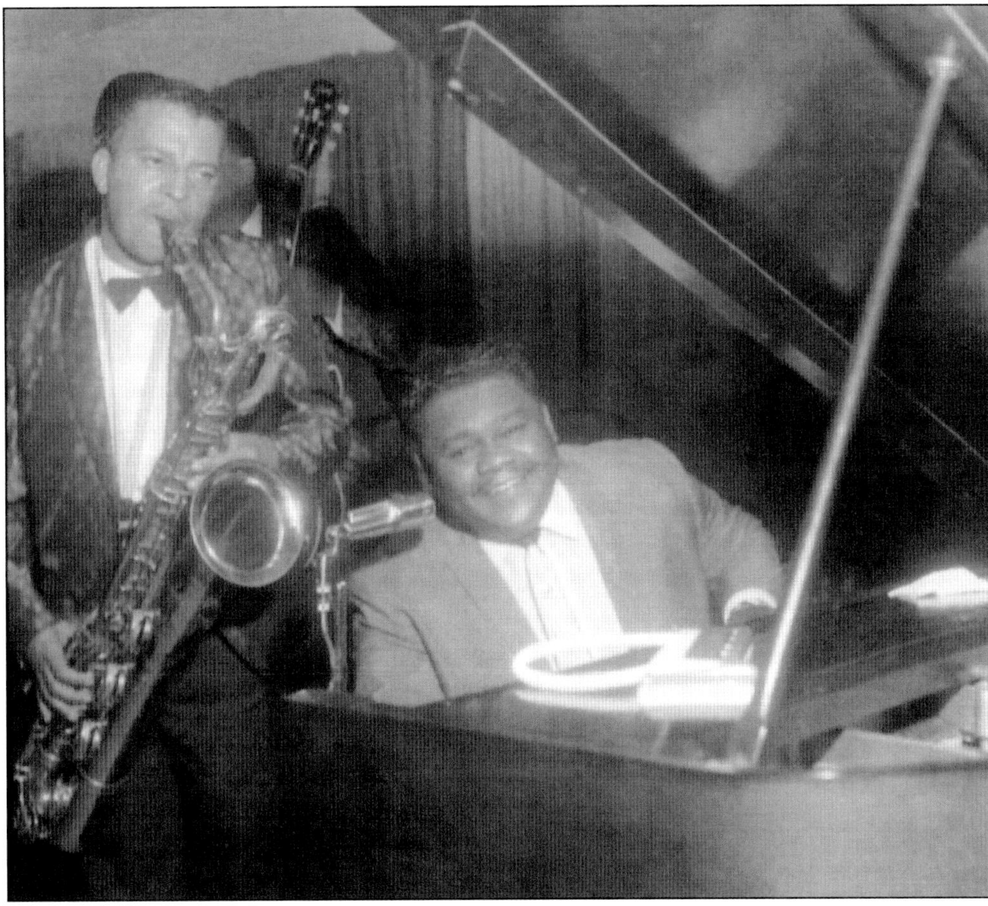

Fats Domino, a popular 1950s and 1960s R&B artist, plays at the Gala Room Club in Pine Bluff, one of many area clubs that hosted the "Chitlin' Circuit," a string of performance venues for black entertainers during the days of segregation. All the acclaimed black celebrities of the segregation era came through Pine Bluff's Chitlin' Circuit such as Ethel Waters, Charlie Parker, Duke Ellington, Louis Jordan, Cab Calloway, Howlin' Wolf, Muddy Waters, B.B. King, Louis Armstrong, the Staple Singers, Ike and Tina Turner, and James Brown, to name just a few. Less mainstream but equally embraced artists like Johnny Taylor, Denise Lasalle, Little Milton, Bobby Rush, Little Johnnie Taylor, Millie Jackson, Tyrone Davis, Bobby "Blue" Bland, Mckinley Mitchell, Z.Z Hill, and others came with even more frequency. They were brought by club owners and promoters like T.L. Bradley, Charlie Baker, Jerry Townsend, Bert Maiden, Bob Hall, Eddie Johnson, Sam Cook, and others. Many of the performance venues in the early years were in places like the Howard Building, the Masonic Building, the Townsend Park "Bic Rec," and juke joint/clubs like Nappy's, Drum's, the Casino, the Jack Rabbit, the Elk's Lodge, and Sturdiks. True to its Delta roots, Jefferson County's local blues/R&B/jazz talent (which sometimes left the area for greater profit) was plentiful and included artists such as James Yancy "Tail Dragger" Jones, Hosea Leavy, Minnie Epperson King, "Pine Bluff Pete," "Queen" Sylvia Embry, Karen Wolfe, "Detroit Johnnie," Cedell Davis, Junior "Cripple Red" Brooks, Earlee Payton and the Blues Cats, Trenton Cooper, Milt Jackson, the Duke Bradley Band, Johnny "Chi" Moore, "Baby Face" Turner, Les Spann, "Hairlong," Junior Collins, Joseph Jarmin, Isaac Scott, N.J. Warren, and many others. Ed Towsend, a graduate of Arkansas AM&N, found success writing several Marvin Gaye songs, including "Let's Get it On," and writing for other artists such as Nat King Cole, Etta James, the Sherilles, and the Impressions. (Courtesy of Special Collections Department, University of Arkansas Libraries.)

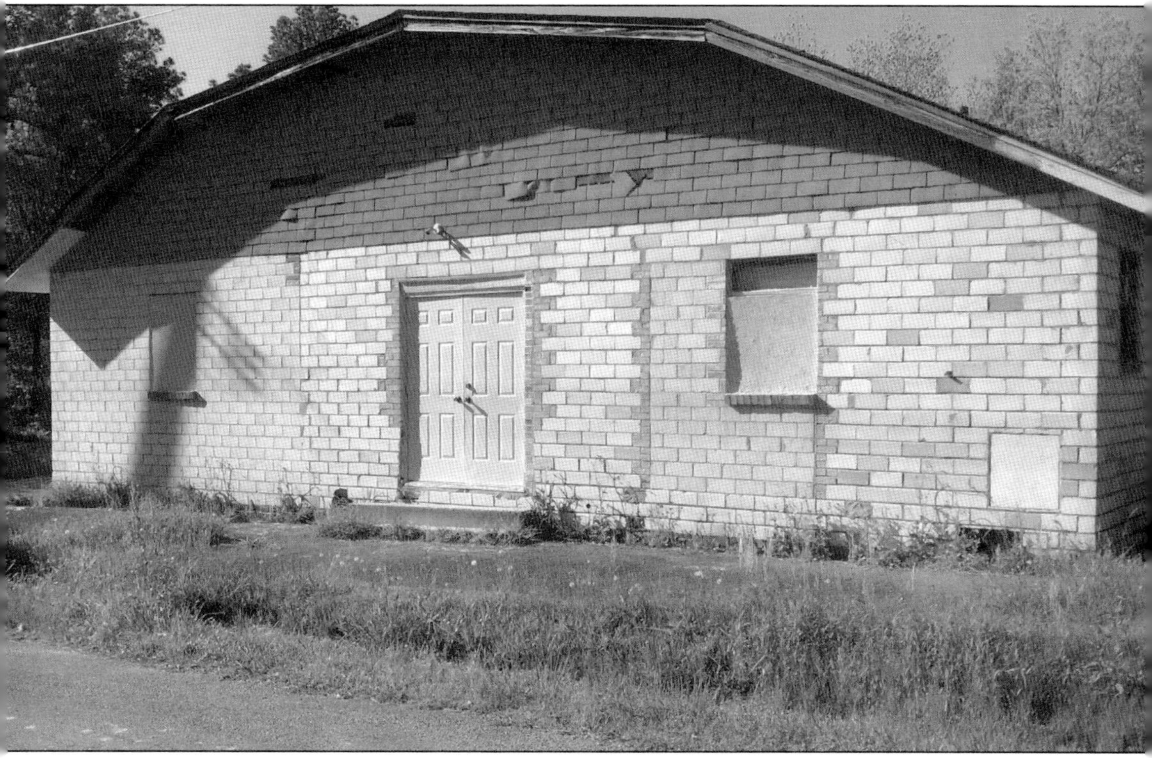

The Pine Bluff Singing Center was organized in 1948 and funded through the efforts of the Pine Bluff Local Quartet Union, a collective of area black quartet groups. Such a facility became necessary in the 1940s when quartets became increasingly popular in Pine Bluff, yet black ministers allowed only sparing use of their churches because of their disapproval of quartets' more animated styles of performance and showmanship, according to Ruth Rice. The Singing Center not only allowed local quartets to gather and sing, but also allowed them to do charity work. Because of the size constraints of the Singing Center, national acts were often booked by the Quartet Union at the Masonic Temple, St. Peter's Catholic School gym, and the Merrill High School gym. Legendary acts performed in Pine Bluff's gospel Chitlin' Circuit, including the Five Blind Boys of Alabama, the Five Blind Boys of Mississippi, the Dixie Humming Birds, the Pilgrim Travelers, the Mighty Clouds of Joy, the Swan Silvertones, the Angelic Singers, the Loving Sisters, Dorothy Love Coates and the Gospel Harmonettes, the Highway QC's, the Harmonizing Four, the Soul Stirrers, and many others. Ruth Rice vividly remembered several occasions in which Sam Cooke and the Soul Stirrers performed at the Merrill High School gym. As the modern era of the 1970s dawned, a new generation of gospel acts came to the area, including Walter Hawkins and the Hawkins Family, Andrae Crouch, Cleophus Robinson, the Gaithers, Shirley Caesar, Willie Neal Johnson and the Gospel Keynotes, Vanessa Bell Armstrong, John P. Kee, Rance Allen, Mattie Moss Clark and the Clark Sisters, and others. Nonetheless, the area was rich with its own array of talented local groups singing at churches, the Singing Center, and on Sunday mornings on live programs such as KCAT's *Gospel Caravan*. These groups included the Spiritual Five, the Williams Singers, the Spiritual Harmonizers, the Gatewood Brothers, the Spiritualettes, Della Anderson and the Glory Bound Singers, the Gloryettes, the Four Larks, the Mighty Supremes, the Singing Constalators, the Beard Singers, the Highland Singers, the Soul Revivals, the True Tones, and many others. Popular choral groups such as the Pine Bluff Male Chorus, the Cosmopolitan Choir, the Young Voices of Faith, the NAACP Youth Choir, the County Wide Mass Choir, and the Men in Black also showcased local talent. (Courtesy of Jimmy Cunningham Jr.)

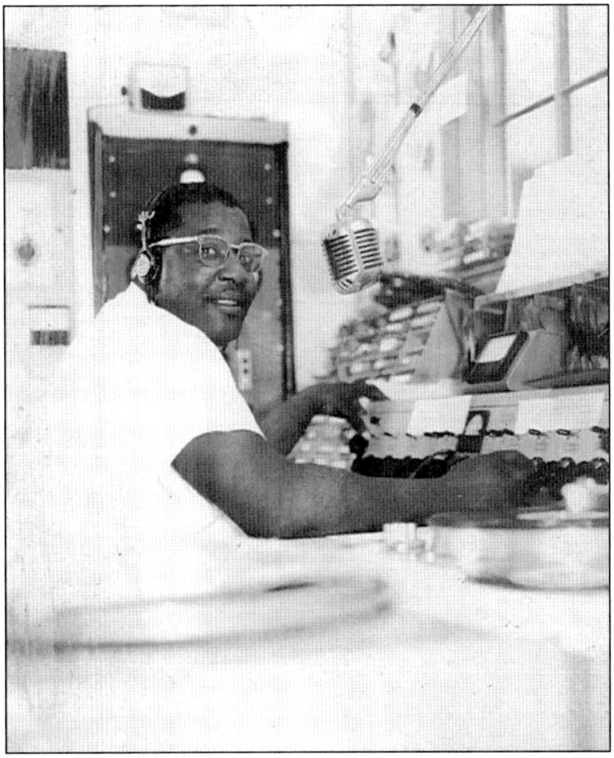

Radio deejay, gospel promoter, and Pine Bluff record store owner Rev. R.L. Summerville (also known as "Mr. Gospel") airs a broadcast at what is thought to be KCAT radio station during the late 1960s. Summerville worked at KPBA, KOTN, KCAT, and KCLA in the 1960s and 1970s spinning black gospel music. He mentored Sid "Spiderman" McCoy in Pine Bluff, who later became the voice for the popular television program *Soul Train* and Johnson Hair Care commercials. Summerville also brought major gospel acts to Pine Bluff as a promoter. (Courtesy of Naomi LaVeaux Summerville.)

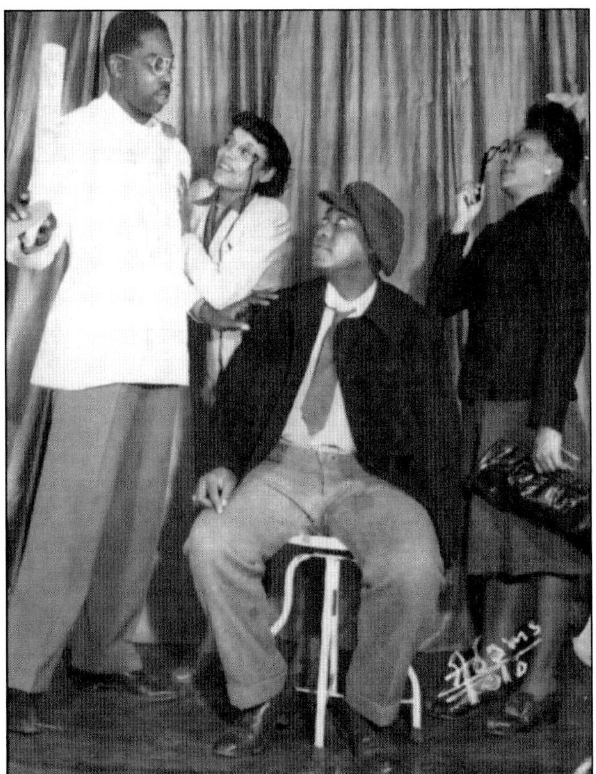

This scene from a minstrel show performed in Pine Bluff during the 1940s conveys humor. The Chitlin' Circuit brought minstrel show performances to places such as Merrill High School's gym, the old Elk's Lodge building, tent sites, and other venues. Sometimes, characters performed in blackface in the very early years, but these shows were still immensely popular among African Americans of the day, particularly before the advent of television. (Courtesy of Juanita Currie.)

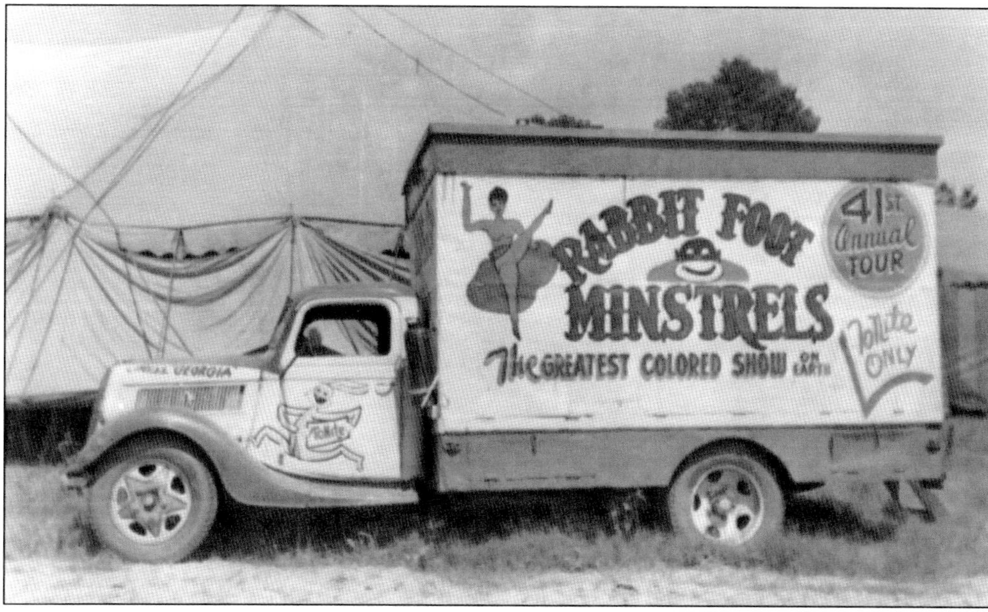

This truck was part of the Rabbit Foot Minstrels fleet, which visited Pine Bluff annually for years from its Port Gibson, Mississippi–based headquarters. The traveling tent show staged an elaborate African American musical variety production that included song, dance, circus acts, and comedy routines for adoring crowds in Pine Bluff and other southern cities. The last documented Rabbit Foot Minstrels show in Pine Bluff was in September 1957. (Courtesy of William H.B. Jones.)

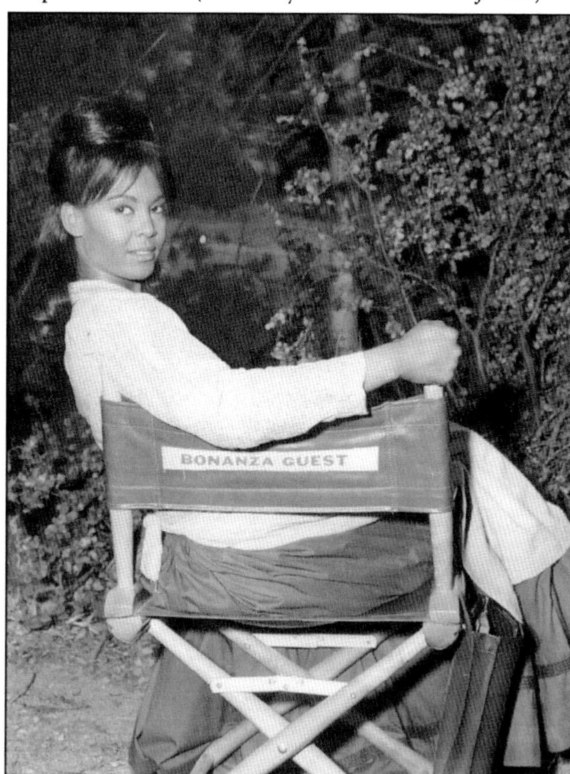

In 1962, Ena Hartman of Moscow became the first African American to receive a talent contract by a national television network, according to the December 1962 issue of *Ebony* magazine. She was discovered in a competition by network executives who saw screen potential. Consequently, she played parts in well-known television series such as *Ironside*, *Bonanza*, *Mission Impossible*, *Adam 12*, and *Star Trek* to name a few. She appeared in at least four movies and was set to play the part of Dorothy Dandridge in a biopic movie alongside Sidney Poitier when negotiations stalled and the production was cancelled. However, Hartman's pioneering work in numerous supporting roles opened doors later for scores of black actors in larger roles. (Courtesy of Jimmy Cunningham Jr.)

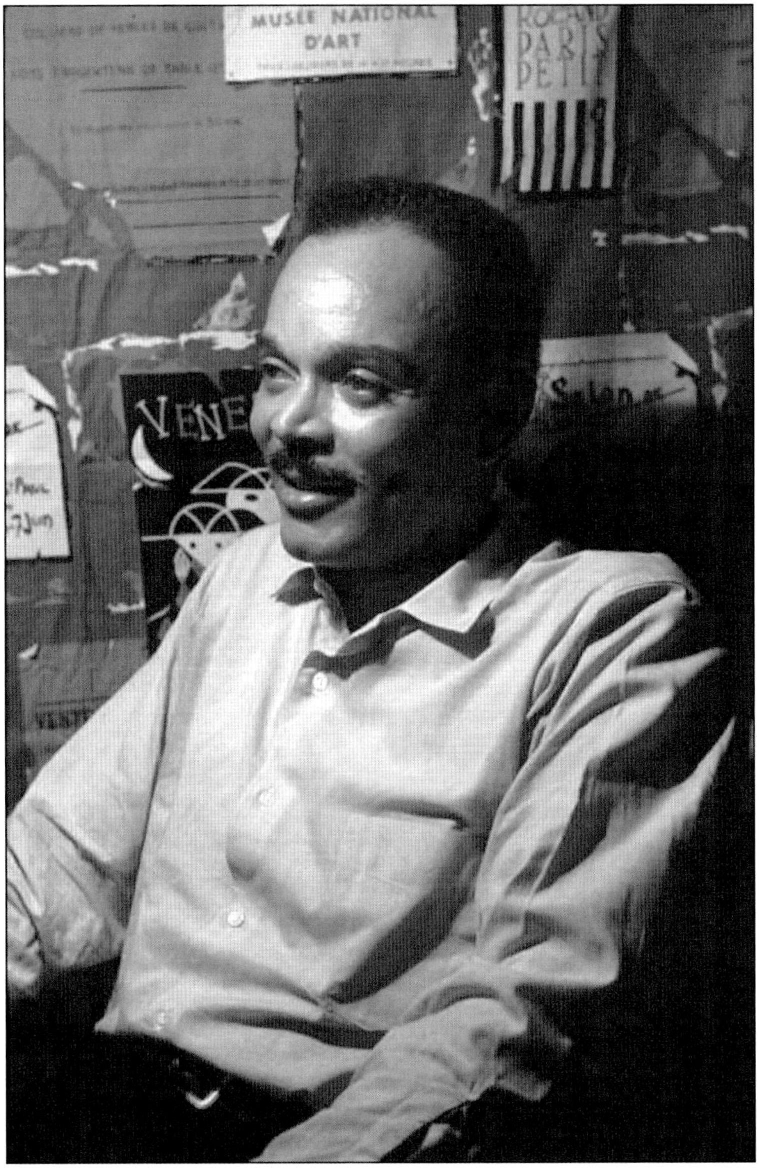

Chester Himes, the first nationally acclaimed African American mystery writer, lived in Pine Bluff during the 1920s. Born in Jefferson City, Missouri, Himes's family moved to Pine Bluff where his father joined the faculty of Branch Normal College. Himes experienced an event while in Pine Bluff that affected him for the rest of his life. A botched chemistry experiment resulted in chemicals blowing up in his younger brother's face. His brother was rushed to the only place in city that had the capacity to treat his severe blinding burns: Davis Hospital. Himes watched his father in tears begging white doctors to treat his son as they matter-of-factly turned him away because he was black. In his autobiography, Himes states that this was the single most painful moment in his life. As a result, blindness and/or racism would be recurrent themes in all his works. Himes received national acclaim with novels such as *Cotton Comes to Harlem* (adapted into a movie starring Redd Fox), *A Rage in Harlem* (adapted into a movie starring Danny Glover and Gregory Hines), *The Real Cool Killers*, and several others. After moving to France, Himes won that country's highest award in literature. (Courtesy of Carl Van Vetchen Trust/Carl Van Vetchen.)

Author, civil engineer, playwright, and Pulitzer Prize–nominee Dr. Mars Hill III was born and raised in Pine Bluff until age 14. At the age of 75, he wrote his coming of age novel, *The Moaner's Bench*, set in fictionalized Pine Ridge, which draws from the many experiences of his childhood in Pine Bluff. This Pulitzer Prize nominated work, Hill's first and only novel, took ten years to write. (Courtesy of Dr. Mars Hill.)

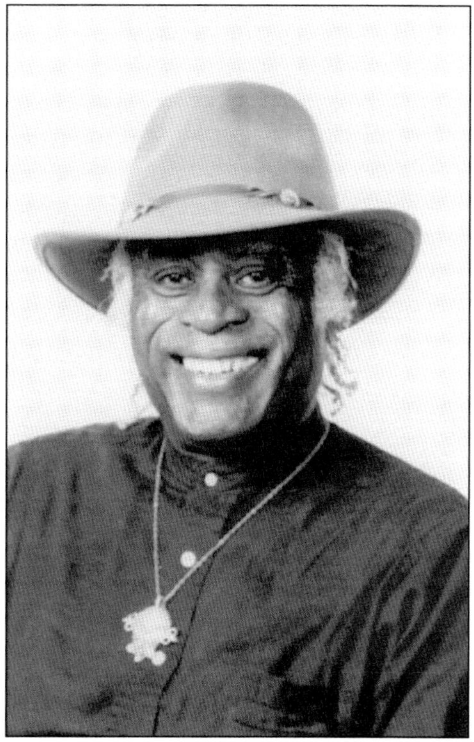

Arkansas Writers' Hall of Famer and best-selling author of 39 novels, Laura Castoro was raised for almost her entire childhood in Pine Bluff. She has published in genres such as historical and contemporary romance, westerns, and contemporary African American fiction. She is the daughter of Dr. David Parker, a former Pine Bluff NAACP leader and dentist, and granddaughter of famed Air Force pioneer Dr. John Parker Jr. (Courtesy of Laura Parker Castoro.)

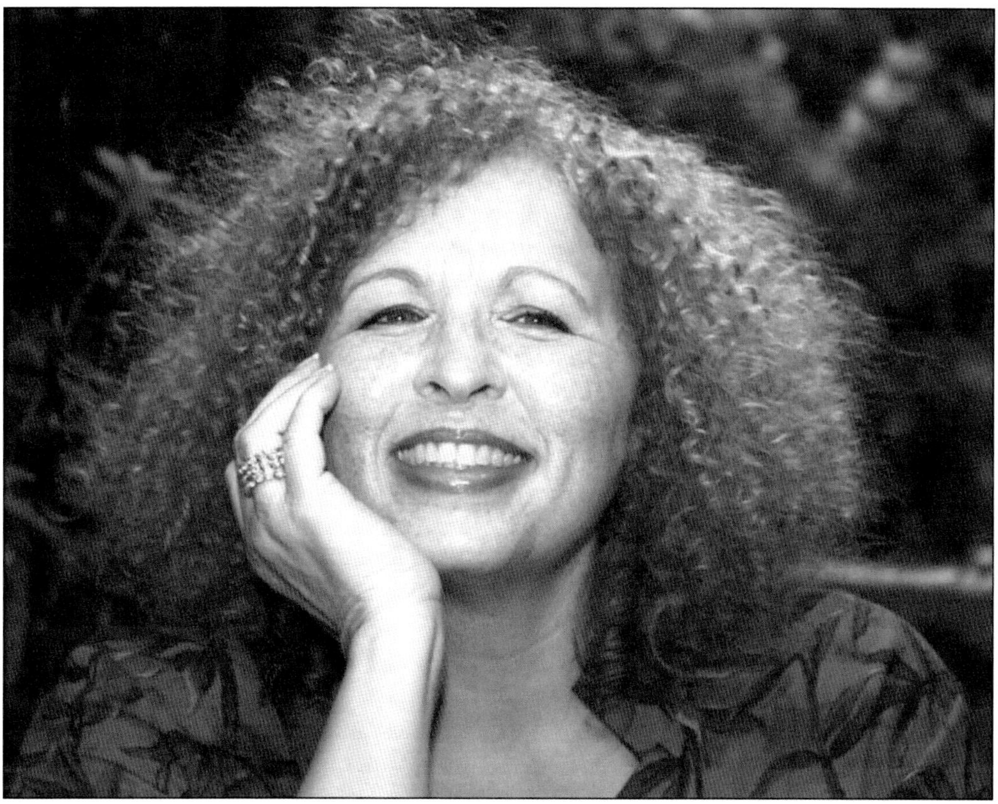

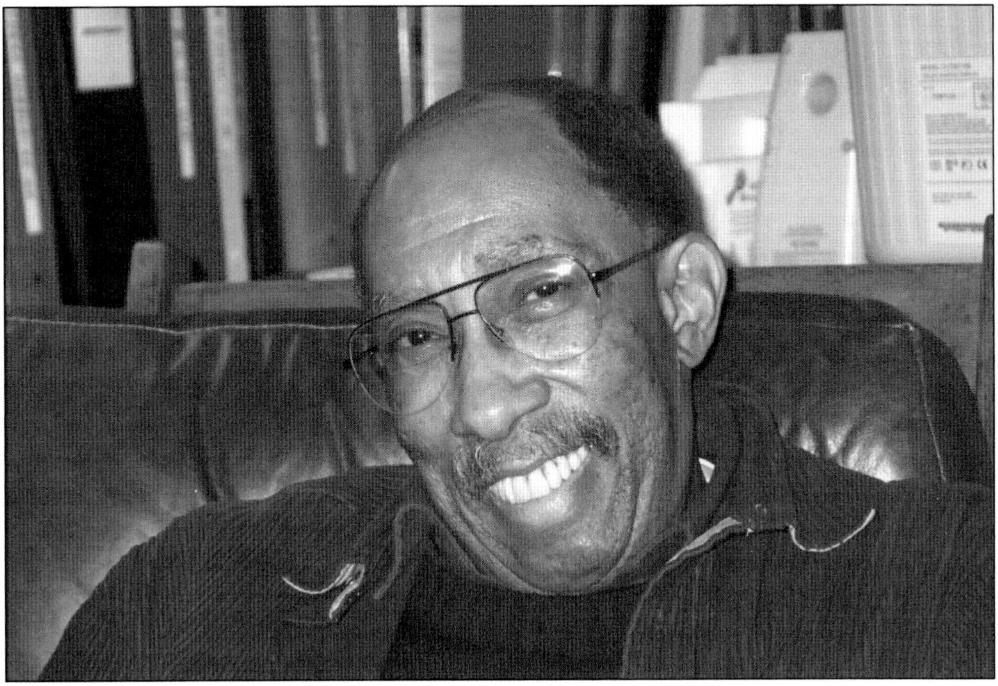

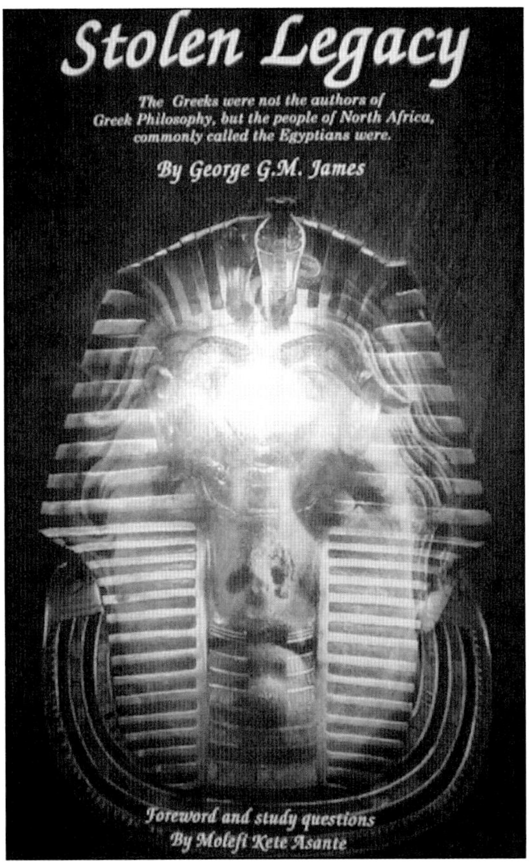

Julius Lester, a folklorist, essayist, professor, author, and winner of the nation's most prestigious children's literature awards, spent his summers as a youth in Pine Bluff staying with his grandmother. Lester's impressions of segregation, color, and family life in the Delta became an important part of the ingredients of his books, essays, and music. Also, Lester's discovery that his grandmother's mixed parentage included Jewish ancestry profoundly impacted him, as he later converted to Judaism. (Courtesy of Julius Lester.)

Guyanan-born Dr. George G.M. James, renowned historian and author, was a resident of Pine Bluff in the 1950s and a faculty member at Arkansas AM&N College. He wrote the classic *Stolen Legacy* in 1954. His work's emphasis on reframing black history's Egyptian origins was a decade before the Black Power movement of the 1960s and three decades before the Afrocentric movement of the late 1980s and 1990s. James's research has influenced scores of black scholars and laymen. (Courtesy of African American Images, Inc.)

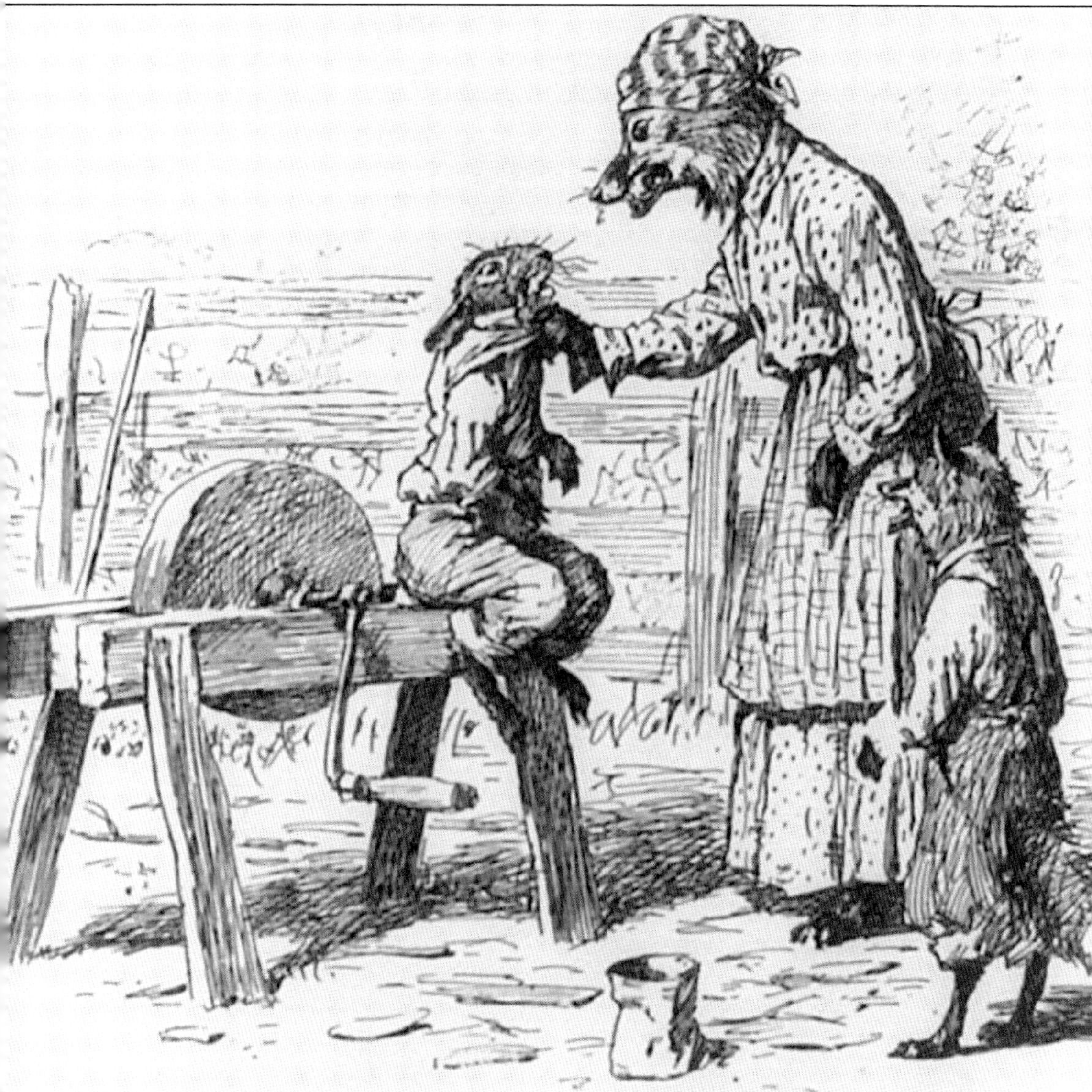

Jefferson County has an incredibly rich record of African American folklore. The Federal Writers Project (1936–1938) documented more personal narratives of former slaves in Jefferson County than any other Arkansas county. Dr. Richard Dorson, considered the father of modern folklore, wrote a seminal book chronicling scores of folktales from Pine Bluff's black community in the 1950s. Alan Lomax, a legendary US folklorist, captured many rare folk songs of prisoners at Jefferson County's Tucker State Prison. Nationally renowned author and folklorist Julius Lester, raised summers in Pine Bluff, parlayed many of the animal folktales of his Brinkley, Arkansas–born father into an astonishing array of children's books. Finally, the lyrics of many of the county's blues artists like Big Bill Broonzy and others represent significant contributions to black folklore. (Courtesy of the Library of Congress.)

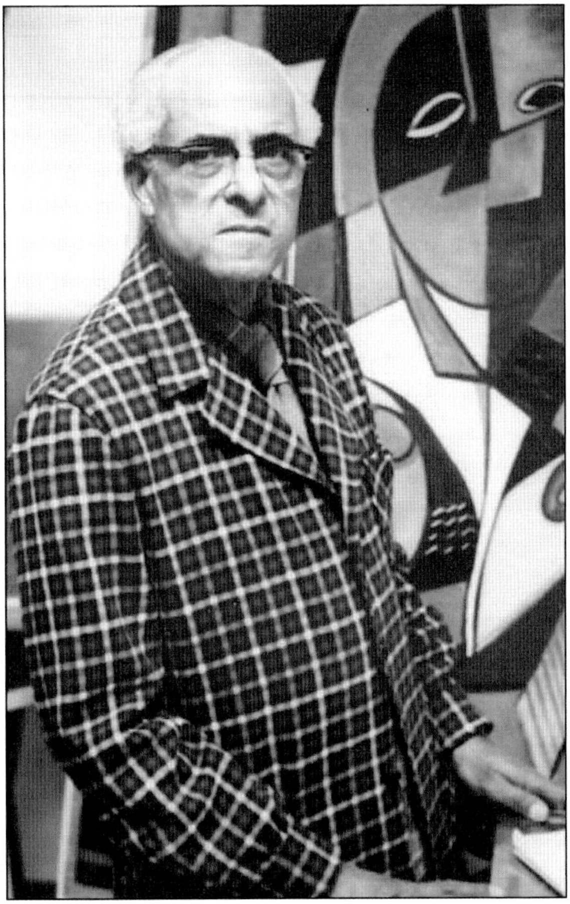

Dr. John Howard, a 40-plus-year resident of Pine Bluff, was the founder and chairman of the art department at UAPB. He studied under Hale Woodruff, one of the great Harlem Renaissance artists. The recipient of numerous awards, Howard produced an incredible array of talented UAPB artists who have achieved regional and national acclaim in their own right such as Harold Dorsey, George Hunt, Henri Linton, Kevin Cole, Jeff Donaldson, and others. (Courtesy of Arkansas History Commission.)

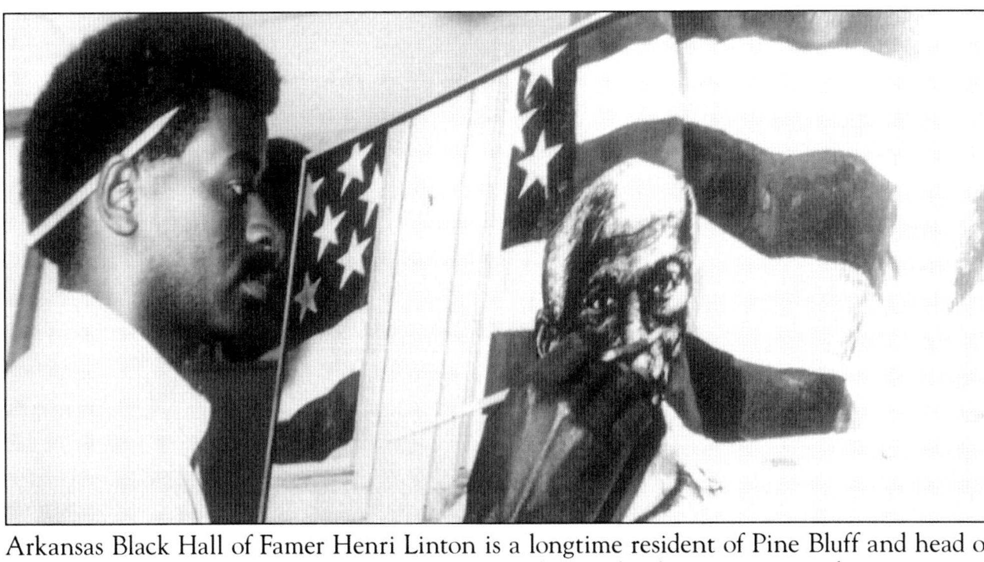

Arkansas Black Hall of Famer Henri Linton is a longtime resident of Pine Bluff and head of the art department at UAPB. He is one of the best-known landscape artists in the state, giving particular focus to scenes from the Delta. He is also considered one of the preeminent historians of UAPB's illustrious legacy. (Courtesy of UAPB Archives.)

Ledell Moorehead-Graham (far right), a faculty member in the art department at Arkansas AM&N, displays her work at an art show in the early 1950s. Because of Moorehead-Graham's unique contributions as an artist and educator, the art exhibition hall at UAPB was named in honor of her. (Courtesy of UAPB Archives.)

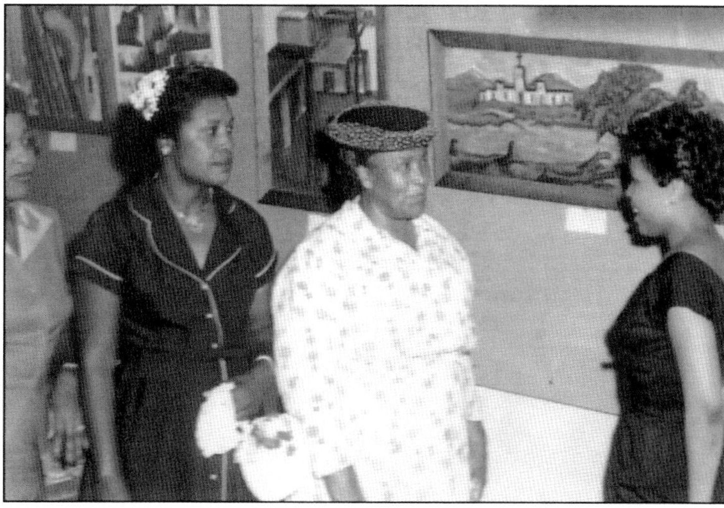

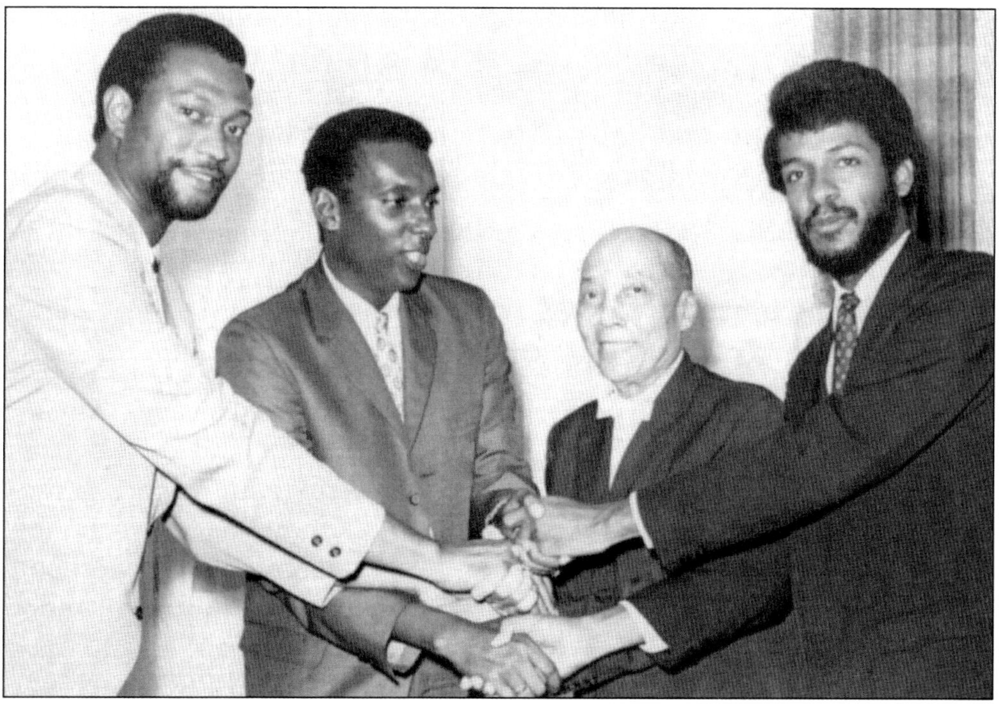

From left to right, Dr. Jeff Donaldson, a native of Pine Bluff, acclaimed Black Arts Movement pioneer, art historian, and critic, shakes hands with activist Stokely Carmicheal, the Honorable Elijah Muhammad, and Cleveland Sellers in 1967. Donaldson was a cofounder of the influential Chicago-based organization, AFRICOBRA (African Commune of Bad Relevant Artists) and later became chairman of Howard University's acclaimed art department. He was also the first African American to receive a PhD in African American art history. (Courtesy of the International Review of African American Art.)

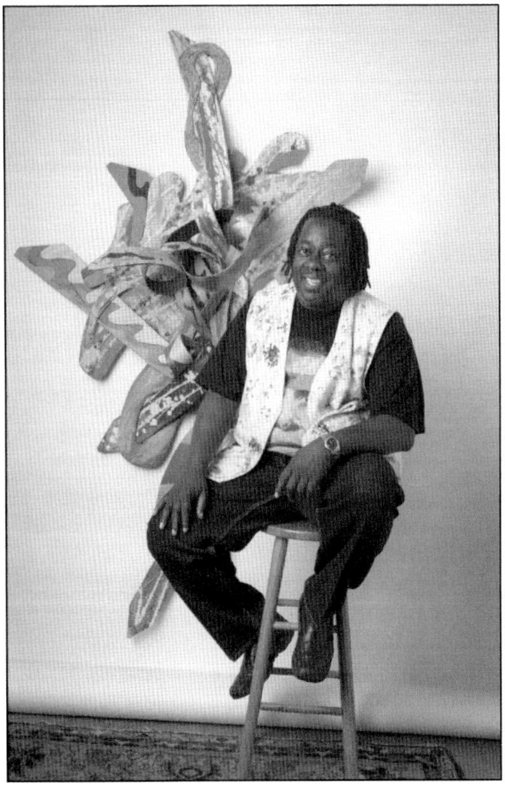

Kevin Cole, a native of Pine Bluff and graduate of UAPB, is one of the South's most acclaimed contemporary visual artists. His 15-story mural in Atlanta was commissioned by the Coca Cola Company for the 1996 Olympics. He has placed more than 1,000 works in collections including the Smithsonian Institution, the Clinton Presidential Library, and the Yale University Art Gallery, among others. Bill Cosby and Michael Jordan are two of the most notable collectors of his works. (T. Meyer photograph, courtesy of Kevin Cole.)

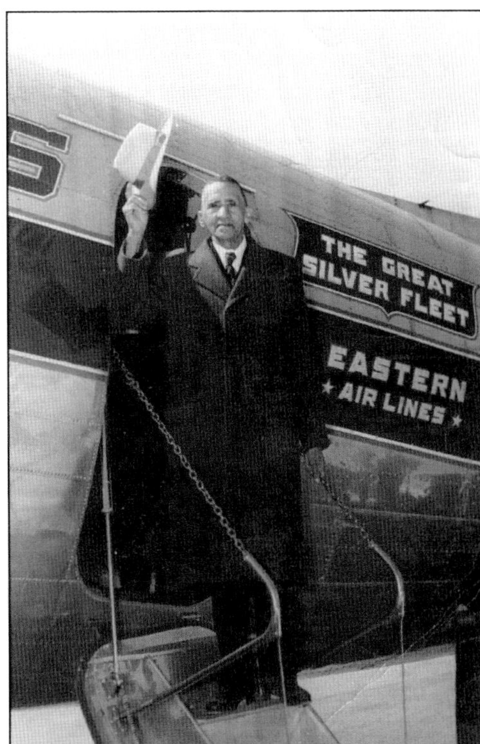

Isaac Hathaway, nationally renowned sculptor and ceramicist, was the only African American ever to design a coin for the US Mint and the first to make death masks and busts of famous African Americans. He was also the first artist to create a ceramics department at a US college. A 22-year resident of Pine Bluff and a member of the faculty at Arkansas AM&N College, Hathaway's works were owned by Pres. Franklin Roosevelt and the automotive industry's Ford family. (Courtesy of Mosaic Templars Cultural Center.)

Three

BUSINESS AND PROFESSIONS

You know, I knowed this town when they wasn't but one store . . . I'm a old woman. I ain't no baby.

—Laura Hart, former Pine Bluff slave
WPA Slave Narratives

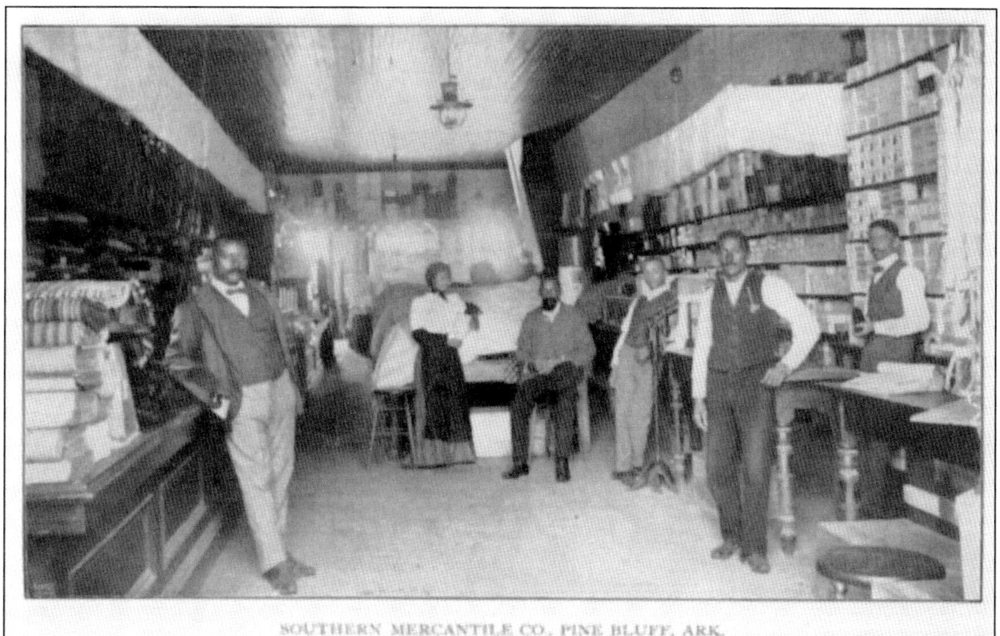

The Southern Mercantile Company, formed in 1898, was a successful Pine Bluff business owned by Marion Perry Sr. (far left), Ferd Havis (not pictured), and Wiley Jones (not pictured) with capital stock of $50,000 (2011 value: $1.3 million) according to a 1903 *Cleveland Journal* article. Note the astonishing statistics of Pine Bluff's early black wealth and business development found in the introduction of this book. (Courtesy of New York Public Library.)

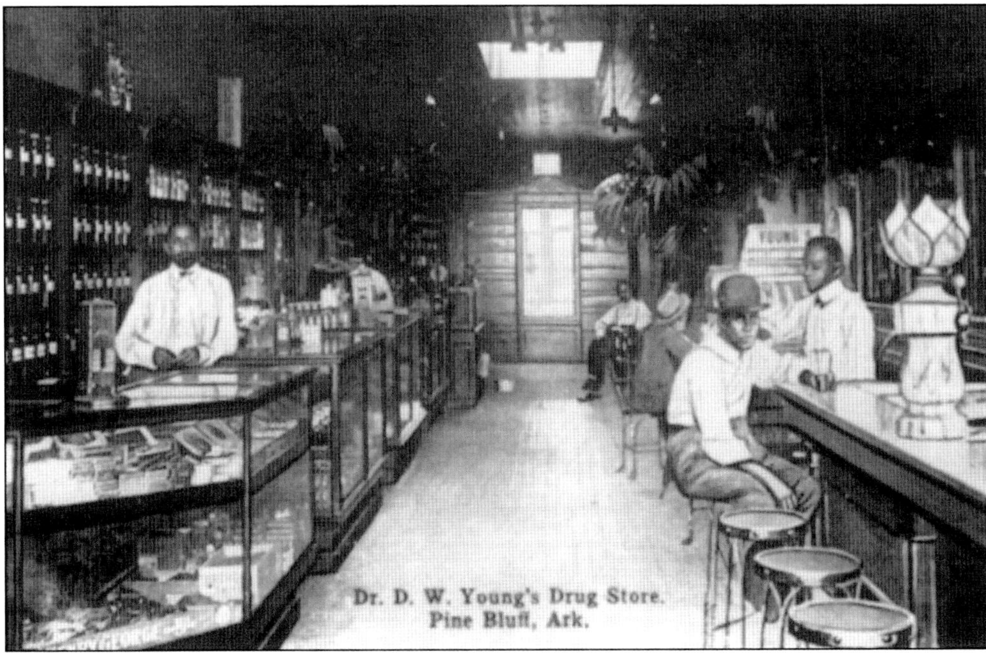

Around 1900, Dr. D.W. Young's drugstore was a thriving business with patrons from all over the county. Dr. Young (left) was the first black graduate of Northwestern University's School of Pharmacology and settled in Pine Bluff to serve the growing population there. (Courtesy of Paul Purdue.)

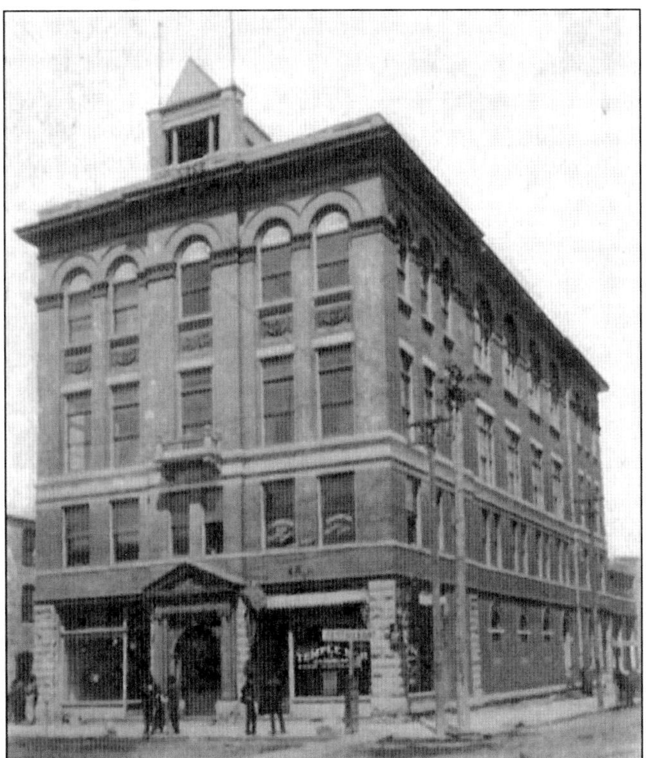

When the Masonic Temple was constructed in 1904, it was the largest building in Pine Bluff. The structure, erected and financed by African American masons throughout Arkansas at a total cost of $50,000 (modern equivalent of $1.3 million), housed local businesses and served as a meeting center for masons. Over the years, the building maintained offices for many of the city's black professional class and also served as a vital social/cultural venue. (Courtesy of Paul Purdue.)

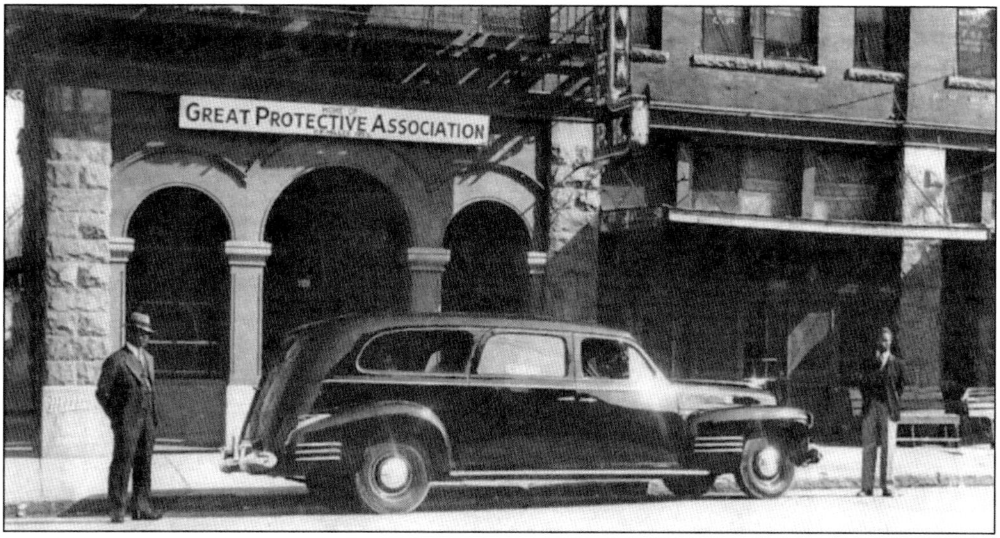

P.K. Miller Funeral Home and the Hotel P.K. stand here in the 1930s on the corner of Third Avenue and Alabama Street in Pine Bluff. Miller migrated from Mississippi to Wabbaseka. He later moved to Pine Bluff and opened a funeral home, hotel, theater (the Vester), and a real estate company. Upon his death, his wife, also named Vester, successfully ran the enterprises. The person on the far right is a young U.S. Brown Sr., who began working for Miller and later formed Brown Funeral Home. (Courtesy of Myrtus Henry.)

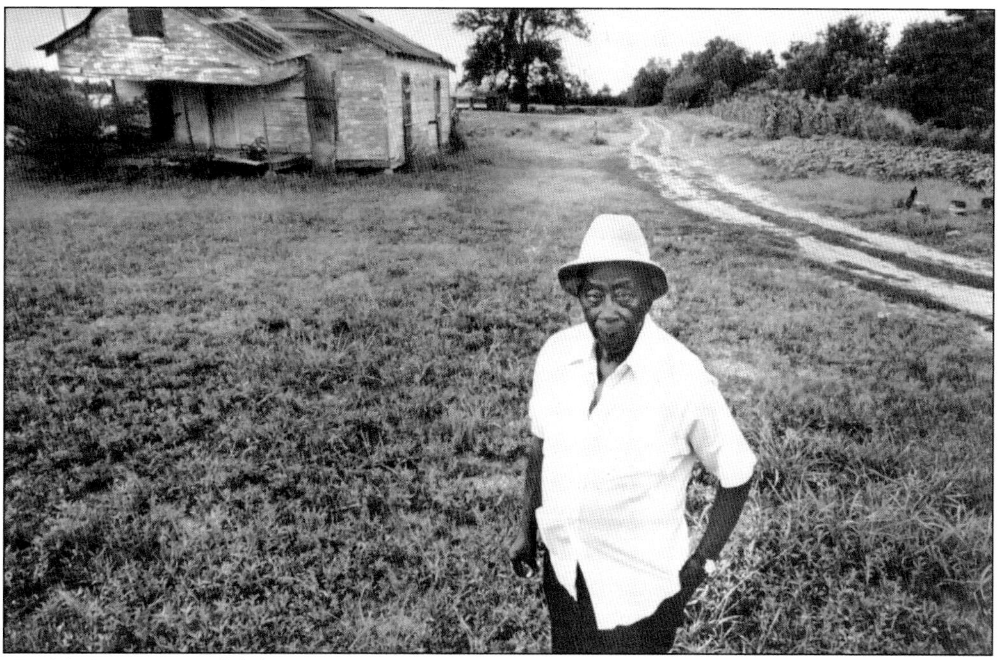

"Daddy Bruce" Randolph, a native of Pastoria, stands near his old 1920s restaurant building outside of Pine Bluff during the 1980s. By 1961, Randolph had moved to Denver, Colorado, and opened a barbeque restaurant. Eventually, he started a tradition of feeding hundreds in need at Thanksgiving in Denver and Pine Bluff while maintaining his restaurant. His work galvanized volunteers and continues through the foundation bearing his name. (Karl Gehring photograph, courtesy of *The Denver Post*.)

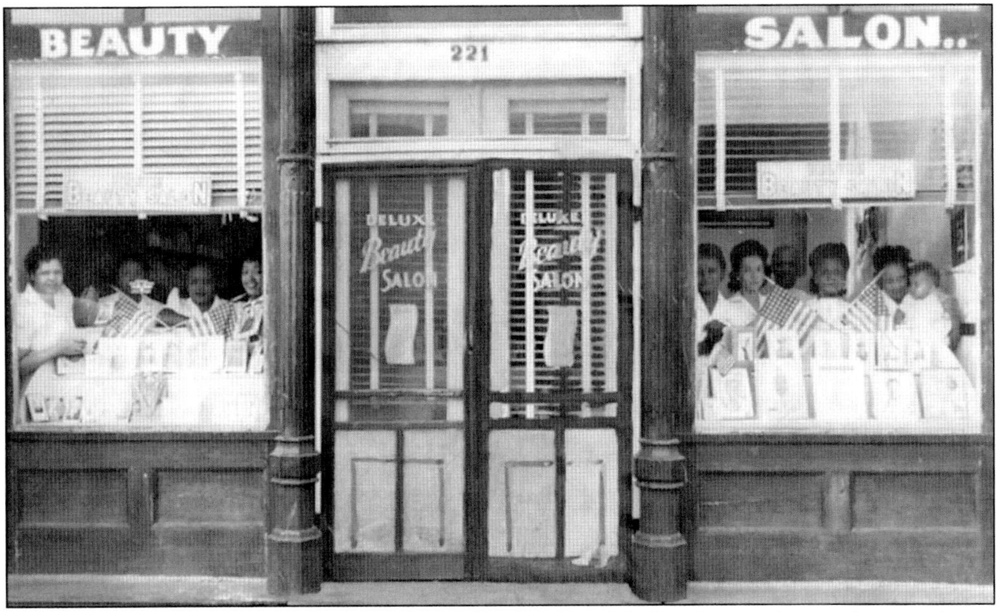

Students of the Deluxe Beauty and Barber School in Pine Bluff gather at the windows in this c. 1949 photograph. Georgia Young owned the school, which trained scores of African American hairdressers and barbers from all over Arkansas. (Courtesy of Juanita Currie.)

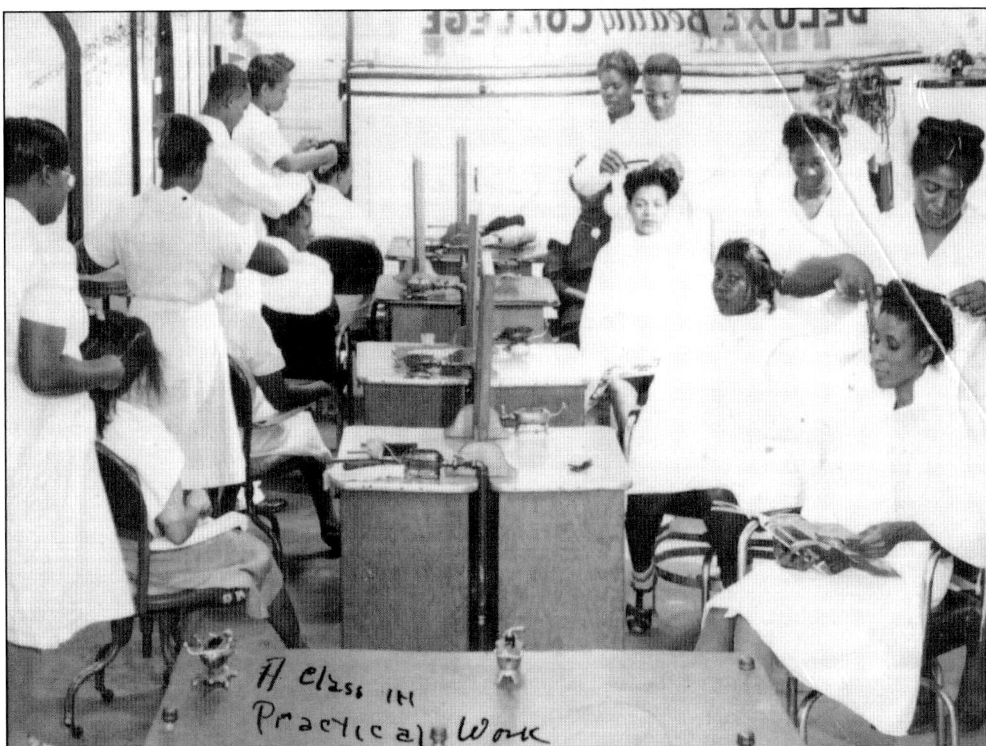

America's future beauticians take a practical class in hairstyling during the 1940s. Customers of the beauty school paid lower rates for styling in exchange for allowing beauticians in training to work on their hair. (Courtesy of Juanita Currie.)

Barber students cut hair at the Deluxe Beauty and Barber School during the late 1940s in Pine Bluff under the guidance of Lee Treadwell. Many of the students enrolled were returning World War II veterans. (Courtesy of Juanita Currie.)

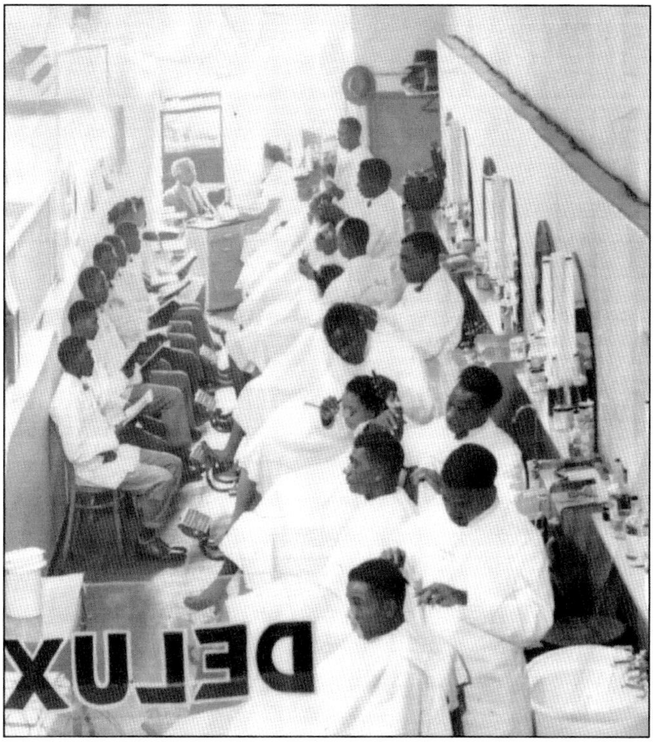

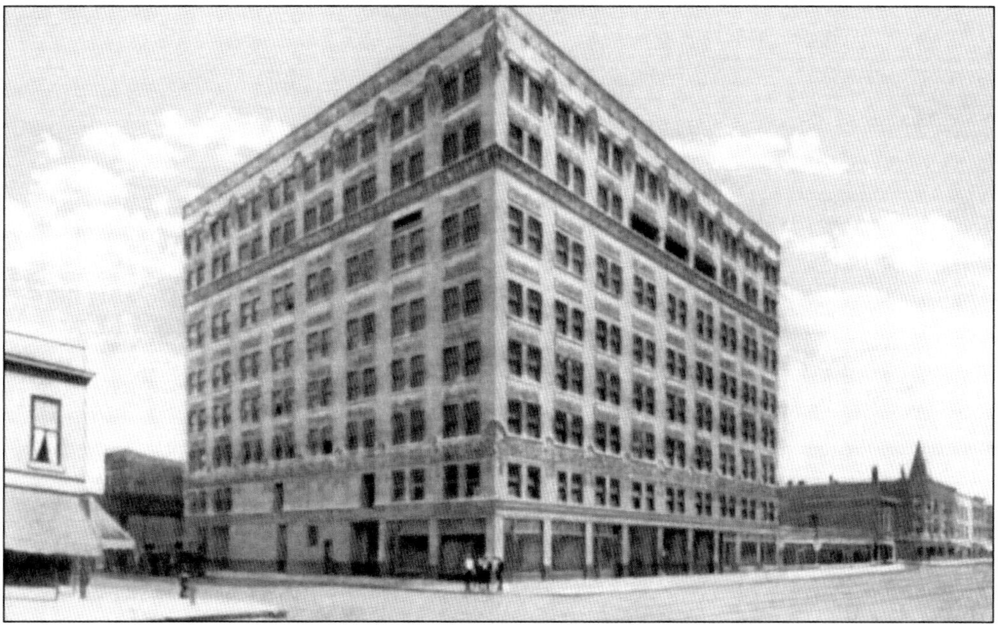

The chief engineer for Chicago's eight-story National Pythian Temple, billed in 1927 as the largest and most expensive structure built by blacks, was former Pine Bluff resident Charles Duke. Duke was the first black to receive an engineering degree from Harvard University and also designed other noted structures. Duke's father, Jesse, also a resident of Pine Bluff and editor of two local black newspapers—the *Echo* and the *Harold*—worked with activist Ida B. Wells in her anti-lynching campaigns. (Courtesy of Illinois Digital Archives.)

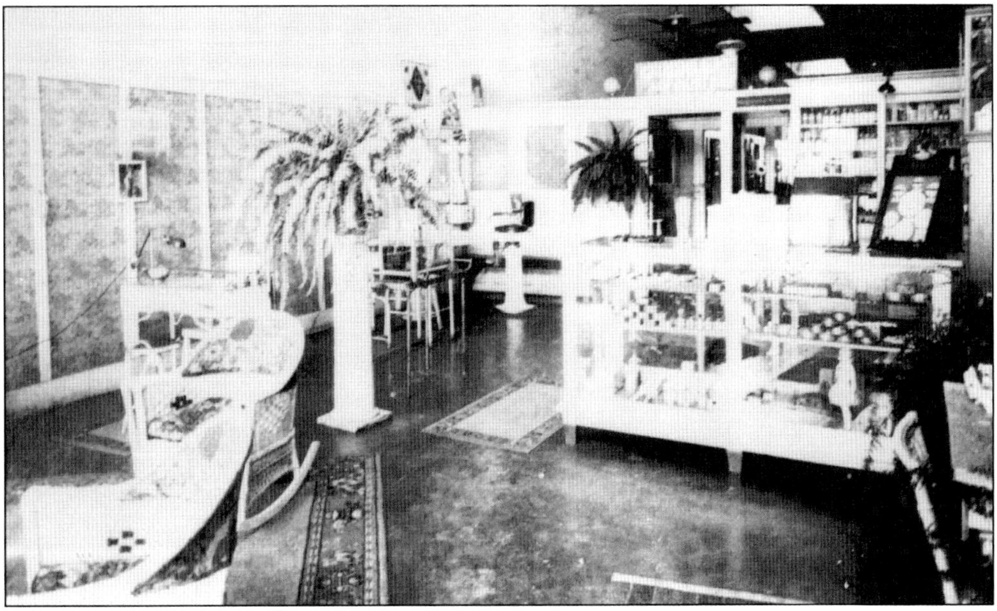

Nettie Hollis Johnson's beauty shop opened as the first such shop in Pine Bluff in 1906. This 1920 picture shows her neatly arranged interior that featured all black operators serving white women exclusively. Her entrepreneurial spirit was fed by working in her mother's store, the Hollis Grocery Store, where she did clerking and bookkeeping. (Courtesy of Arkansas History Commission.)

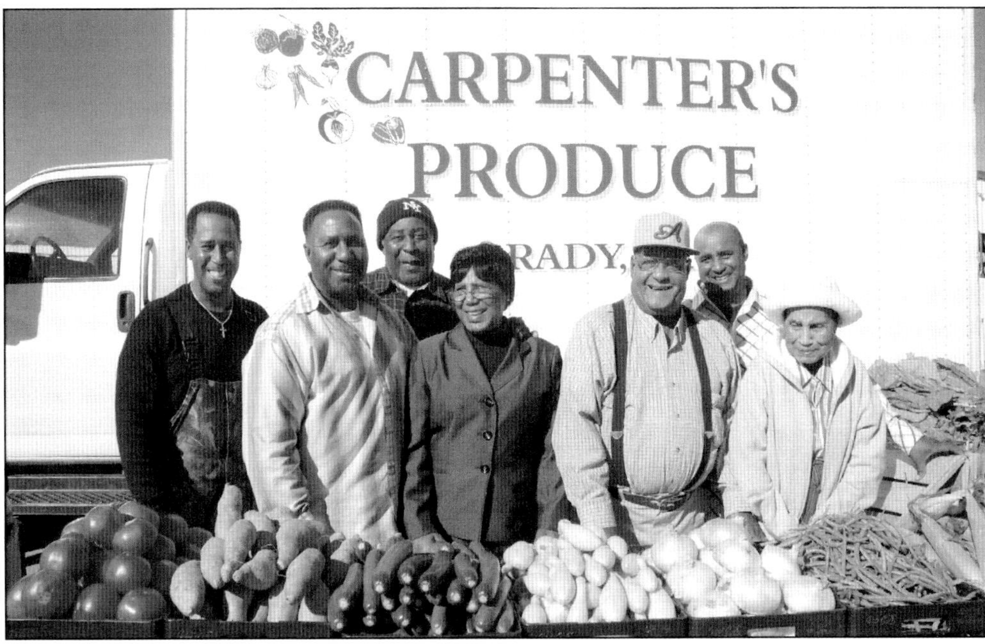

The Carpenter family of Grady maintains a thriving produce store and fish market in Pine Bluff. With 1,200 acres of Lincoln County land and 35 employees, they provide produce to the general public, Wal-Mart, Kroger, and other national food chains. The patriarch, Abraham Carpenter Sr. (third from right) was recently inducted into the Arkansas Black Hall of Fame. Whether at the Pine Bluff Farmer's Market or local civic events, the Carpenter family is known and admired throughout Jefferson County. (Courtesy of Arkansas Farm Bureau.)

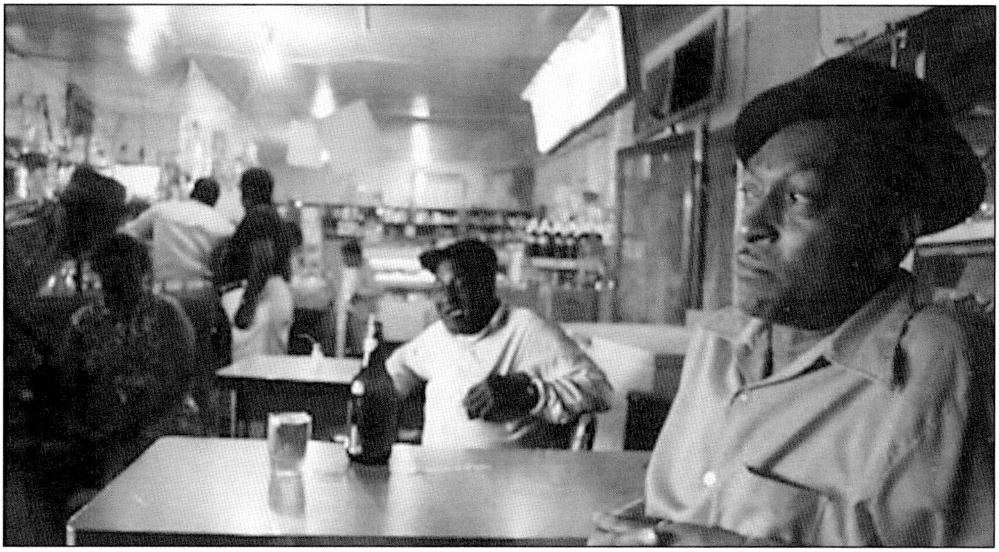

Patrons enjoy a drink in the 1980s at Anner's Place, a corner grocery store/diner located adjacent to Townsend Park in a section of Pine Bluff known by locals as "the Backwoods." Anner's Place was a favorite spot for kids who had just finished swimming at the park and wanted treats like Lemonheads, Bazooka bubblegum, cookies (two for a penny), a peppermint stick in a pickle, Jungle Juice, Now & Laters, or a candy necklace. Adults loved the delicious southern-style dinner plates. (Courtesy of Special Collections Department, University of Arkansas Libraries.)

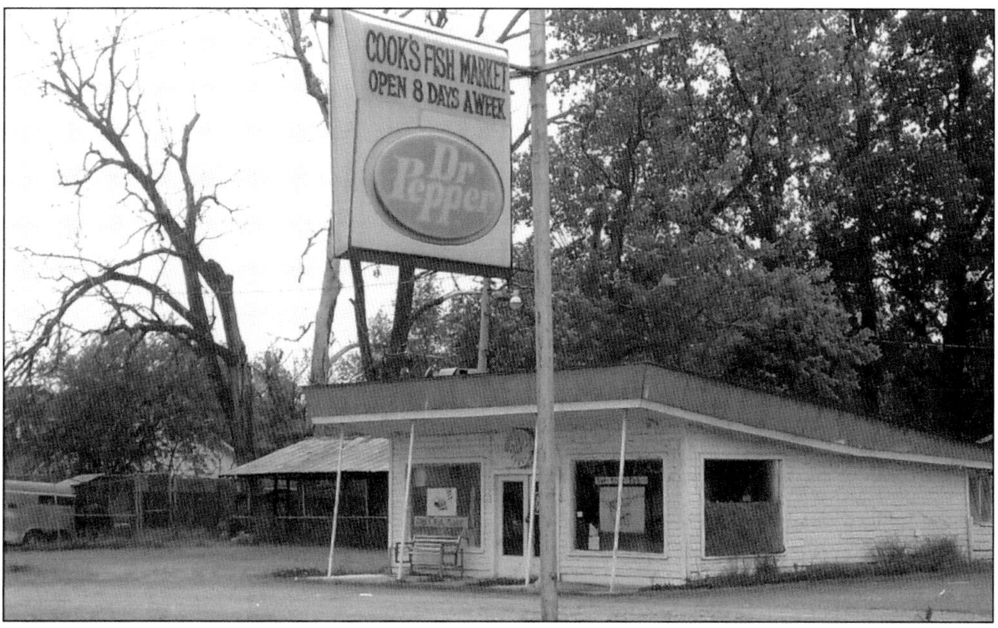

While Cook's Fish Market was not African American owned, it was frequented by a predominately black population from all over the county. Countless people made the trek from Pine Bluff and the surrounding area across the Free Bridge to get the best-seasoned fried catfish, buffalo, or gar in the entire Delta. Kids could watch the alligator kept in a pen or view the deer and the monkeys in the fenced area behind the store. (Courtesy of Jimmy Cunningham Jr.)

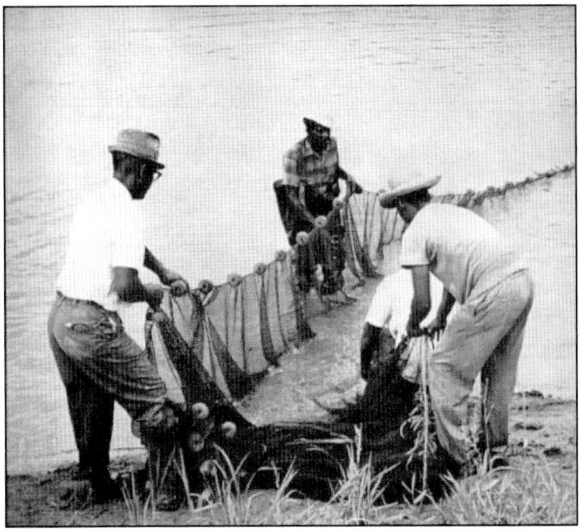

Workers tend fish nets at Evans and Son's catfish farm. In 1968, this black-owned 45-acre catfish farm in Moscow, the brainchild of Dr. Earl E. Evans, maintained 13 ponds, employed 14 people, and was featured in the national news media. It had the state's only operating catfish processing plant at the time. (Courtesy of Special Collections Department, University of Arkansas Libraries.)

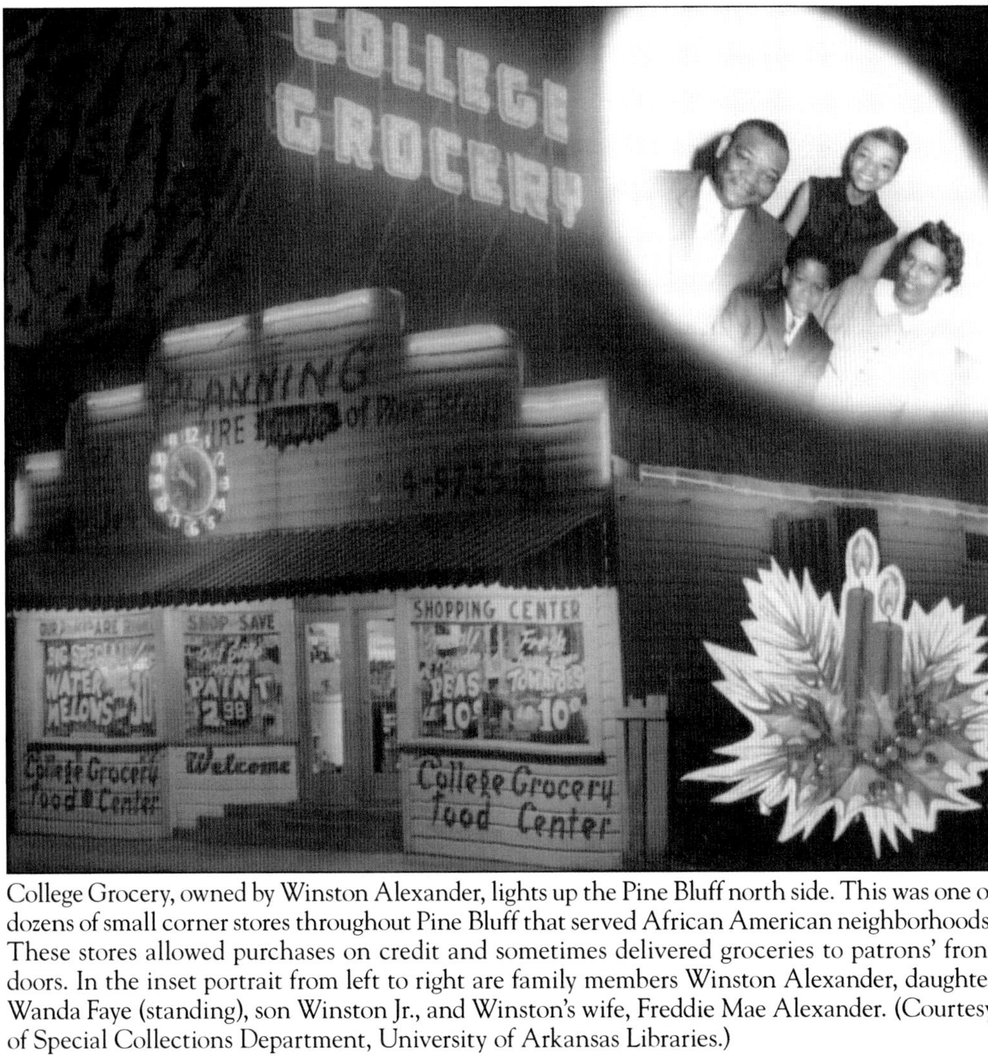

College Grocery, owned by Winston Alexander, lights up the Pine Bluff north side. This was one of dozens of small corner stores throughout Pine Bluff that served African American neighborhoods. These stores allowed purchases on credit and sometimes delivered groceries to patrons' front doors. In the inset portrait from left to right are family members Winston Alexander, daughter Wanda Faye (standing), son Winston Jr., and Winston's wife, Freddie Mae Alexander. (Courtesy of Special Collections Department, University of Arkansas Libraries.)

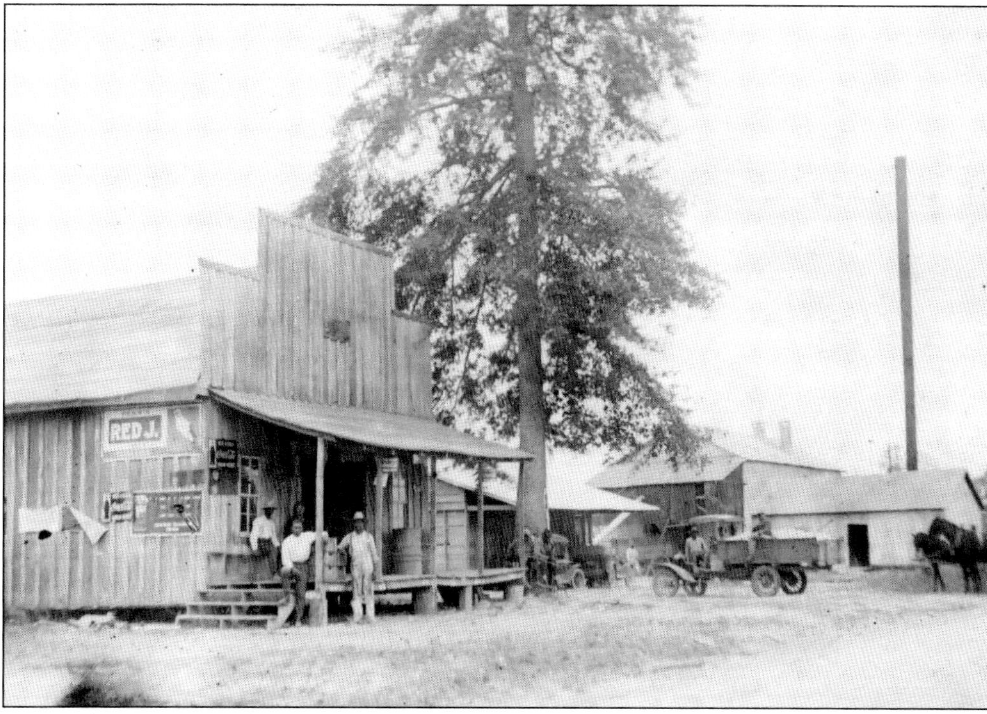

U.G. Dalton Jr.'s general store and mill in Moscow stand side by side in the 1920s. According to Dalton's daughter Dr. Mildred Henry, the family fought to keep their businesses as members were forced to maintain armed night watch to thwart attempts of destruction by racist white locals. Vigilantes went as far as trying to set a church on fire one windy night so that the flames would blow onto the adjacent general store and burn it down. Eventually, the Daltons left Moscow and moved to Pine Bluff. (Courtesy of Arkansas History Commission.)

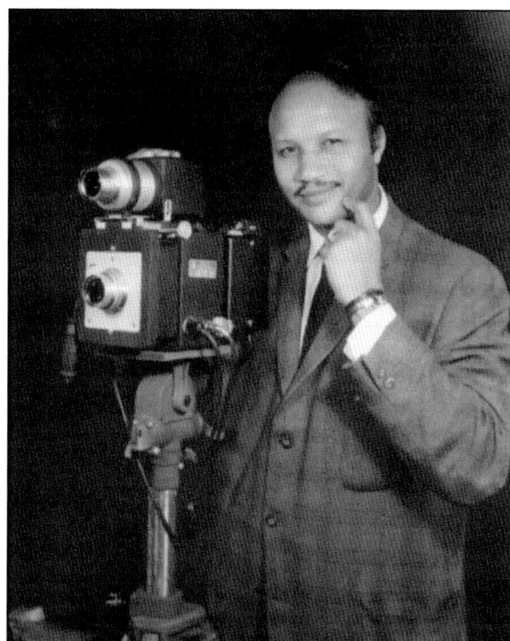

From the 1940s to the 1990s, Geleve Grice's immense portfolio established him as the foremost Arkansas photographer of this era. Grice, a Tamo native and longtime Pine Bluff resident, shot thousands of images largely capturing African American life in the Delta and south Arkansas. His photographs have appeared in national and statewide media outlets. His work is featured in *A Photographer of Note* by Dr. Bob Cochran and throughout this publication. (Courtesy of Special Collections Department, University of Arkansas Libraries.)

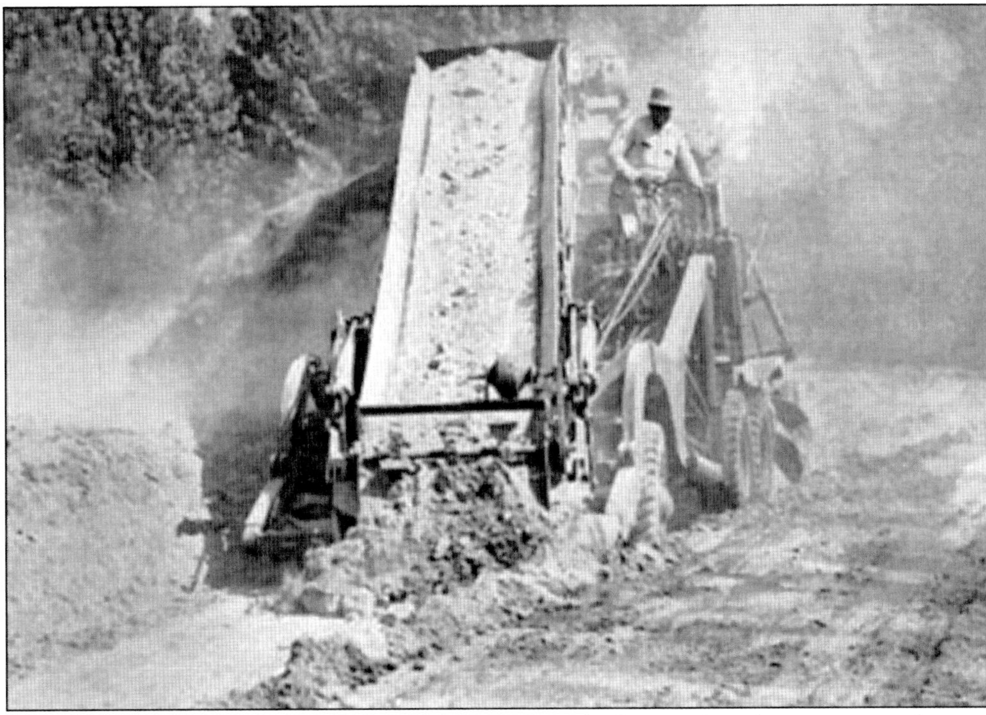

Emmanuel Moore of Pine Bluff manipulates his newly designed earth-moving machine in 1964. He developed it at a cost of $95,000, and it delivered the average cubic yards of dirt at a rate twice that of the conventional machines of the day. His invention led to requests from all over the world for his new product. (Courtesy of Special Collections Department, University of Arkansas Libraries.)

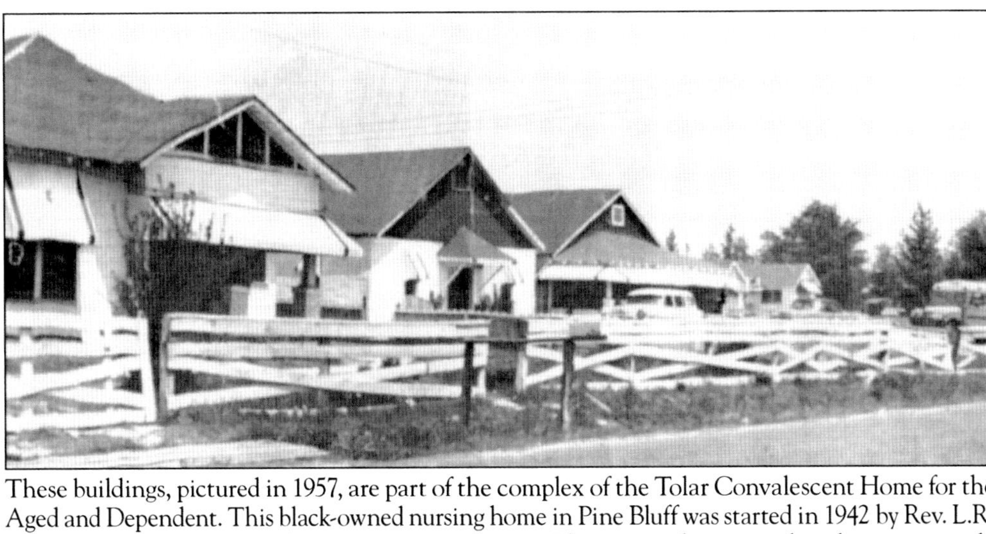

These buildings, pictured in 1957, are part of the complex of the Tolar Convalescent Home for the Aged and Dependent. This black-owned nursing home in Pine Bluff was started in 1942 by Rev. L.R. Tolar, a woman passionate about community service. The nursing home employed approximately nine health-care workers at the time and maintained up to 25 patients. The grounds had several buildings not shown in this image, including a church. (Courtesy of Juanita Currie.)

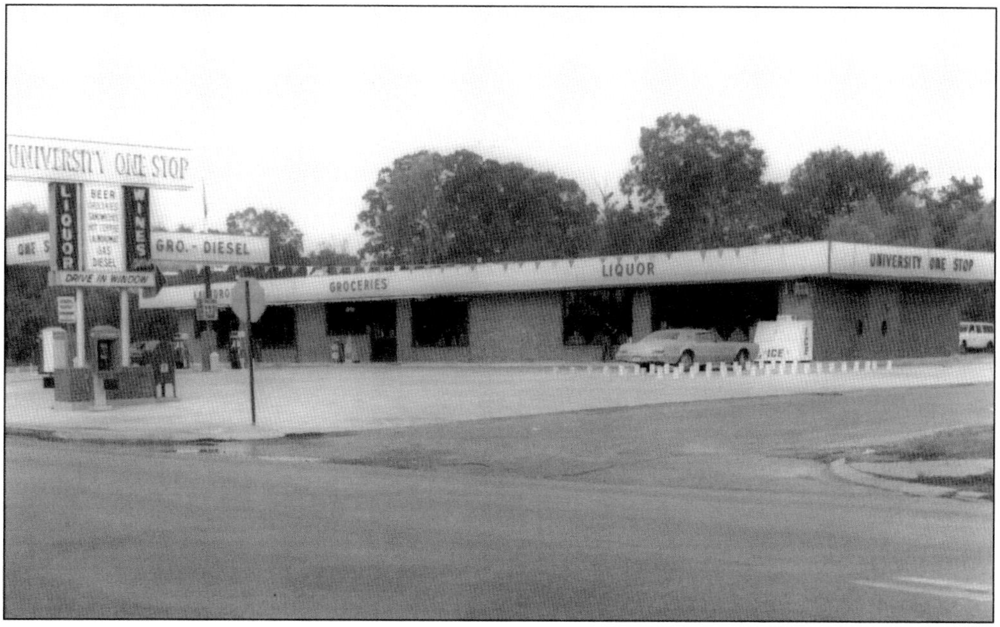

University One Stop beckons patrons from University Drive in the 1980s. It was the creation of Pine Bluff's Elmer Dancy Sr., who astutely combined a laundromat, convenience store, and a liquor store. To this combination, he later added a radio station and an oil company (located at another site). Dancy proved to be one of the most adventurous and respected black businessmen of this era. (Courtesy of Karen Dancy Dickson.)

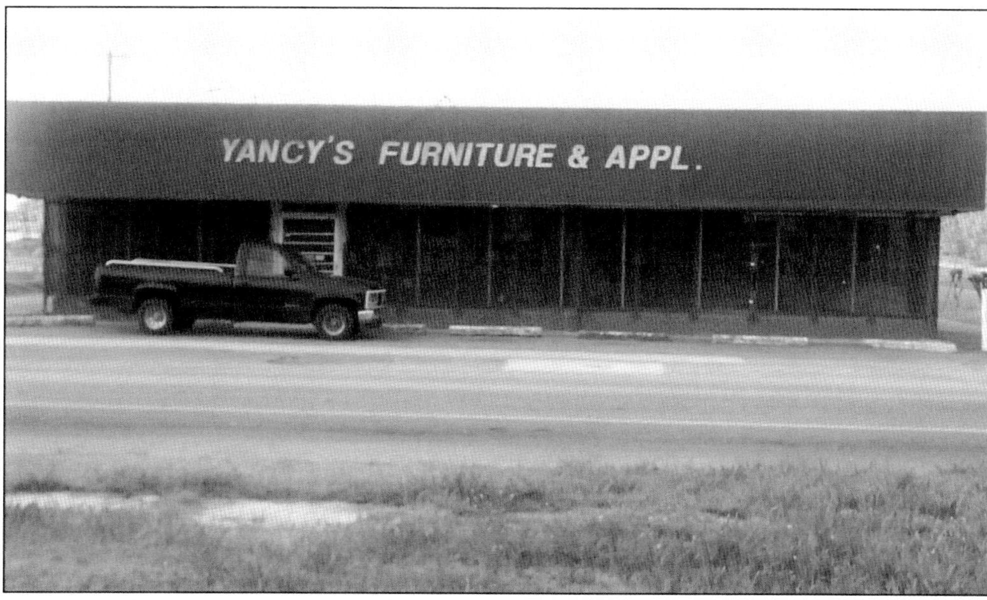

One of the oldest black businesses in Pine Bluff, Yancy's Furniture and Appliances was established in 1945 by Lewis Yancy. The store has weathered challenges from an inability to receive products because companies did not want to be seen delivering to a black business to being initially shut out of the furniture seller's market. Still, their persistence has rewarded them and sustained their family for years. Since the death of Yancy, his wife, Queen, has successfully continued their tradition. (Courtesy of Jimmy Cunningham Jr.)

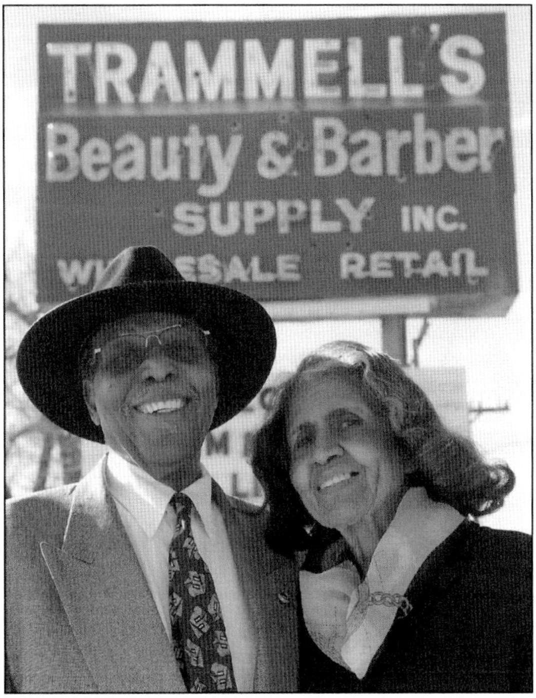

Trammell's Beauty & Barber Supply invites patrons new and old. Theodora Trammell (right) started in the 1950s with a highly successful Pine Bluff beauty shop that catered to local and statewide patrons. However, her need to constantly purchase beauty supply goods from Little Rock prompted her business-savvy husband, Clincy Trammel Sr. (left) to open a local beauty supply store. The store has been so successful that it employs family members and maintains a fiercely dedicated following today. (Courtesy of Ralph Fitzgerald.)

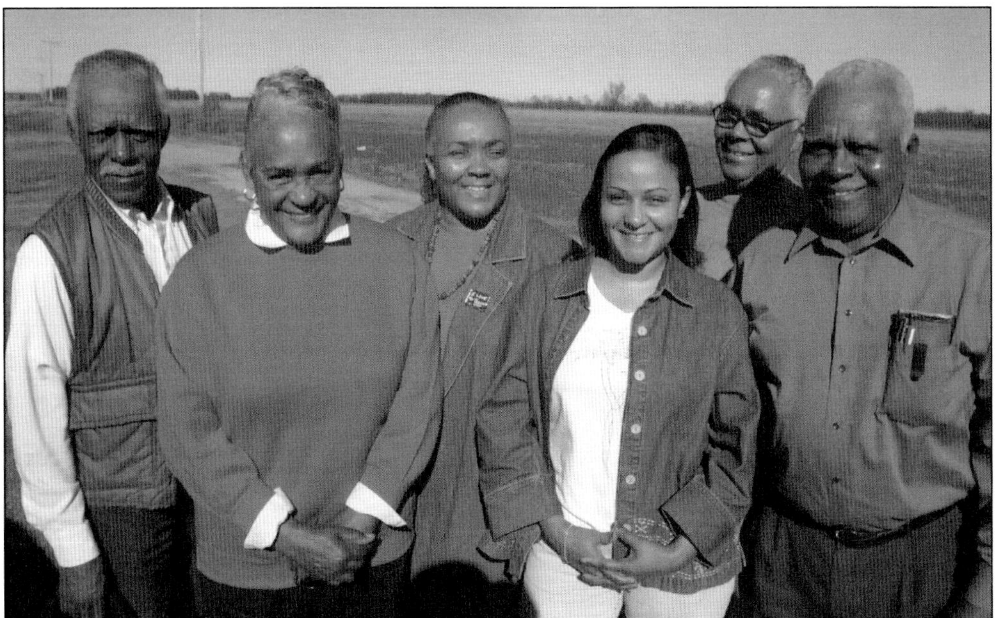

Members of the Edwards family pictured here include, from left to right, Jasper Edwards, Dr. Josetta Wilkins, Dr. Joanna Edwards, Angela Wilkins, Janice McDonald, and Jean Edwards. They stand proudly on the Jefferson County land that has been in their family since the late 1800s. They remember picking cotton as toddlers and walking over seven miles one-way to school, often in the rain, and learning to milk cows, shell peas, and shuck corn. They took the 40 acres originally owned by their grandfather sometime after slavery and turned it into a prosperous 570-acre farm business called Laura J's–Edwards, Inc. (Courtesy of University of Arkansas System, Division of Agriculture.)

Four

Military and Civil Defense

Oh, yes, I remember lots about the [Civil] war . . . It would be so dark you couldn't see the sun even. That was from the smoke from the fighting. You could just hear the big guns going b-o-o-m, boom, all day.

—Margert Ulm, former Humphrey slave
WPA Slave Narratives

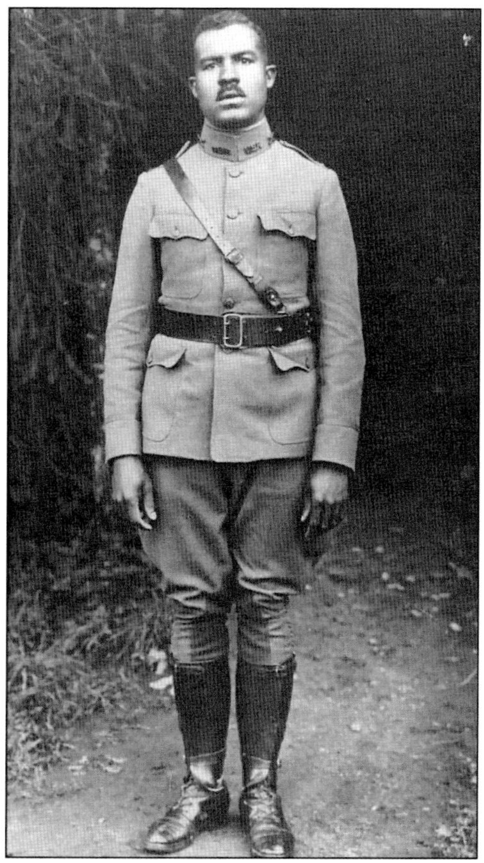

Marion Perry Jr. of Pine Bluff was one of four African Americans to graduate in the US Army's 17th Provisional Training Battalion as a second lieutenant during World War I. Following the war, Perry became a lawyer and married the granddaughter of financial tycoon Madame C.J. Walker, helping to run the family's Indiana-based business after the founder passed. Perry later moved back to Pine Bluff and worked as an attorney, co-owner of the family funeral home, and president of Olympic Life Insurance. In his later years, he became known as a community historian, meticulously maintaining rare records, images, and documents related to Pine Bluff's history and that of his family. (Courtesy of A'Lelia Bundles.)

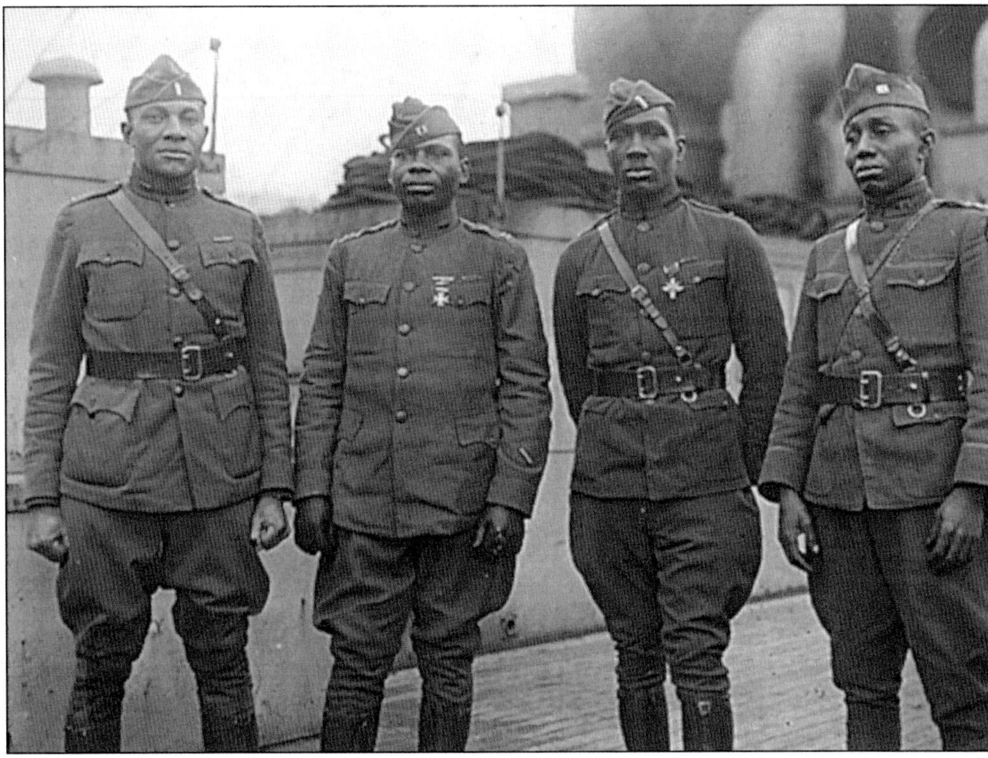

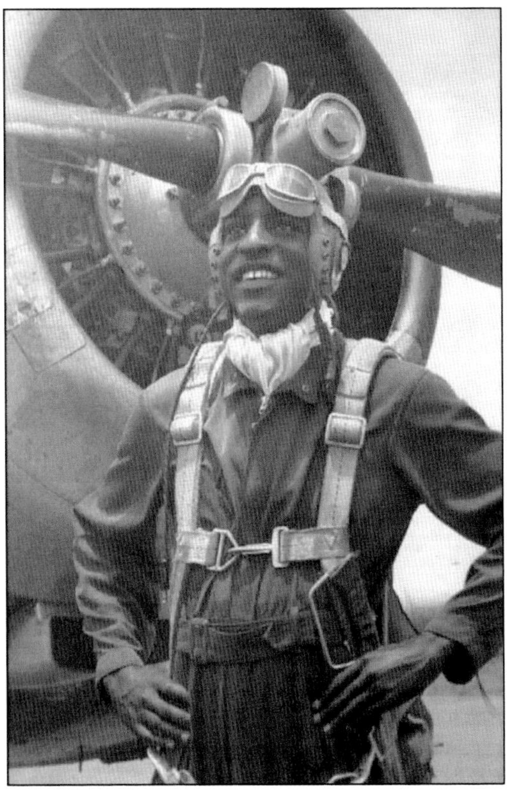

Captain E. White (far right) of Pine Bluff along with other World War I officers from the 366th Infantry Regiment (known as the Buffalo Soldiers) is on board the ship the *Aquitania*. Others serving in Buffalo Soldier units who were natives or residents of Pine Bluff include Gaston Williams and Willie Harris, both of whom served in World War II; Isaac Johnson, grandfather of Eunice Pettigrew, who entered service in 1867; and Mordecai Yeizer, who served from 1879 to 1881. (Courtesy of National Archives and Records Administration.)

Dr. Granville Coggs, a native of Pine Bluff, was a member of the 332nd Fighter Group (known as the Tuskegee Airmen) and the 477th Bombardment Group of the US Army Air Corps during World War II. He earned badges for aerial gunner, aerial bombardier, and multiengine pilot. Coggs later became a successful radiologist and invented two biopsy devices. An avid athlete, he has run the 100-, 200-, and 400-yard track events in the Senior Games since 1997. (Courtesy of Dr. Granville Coggs.)

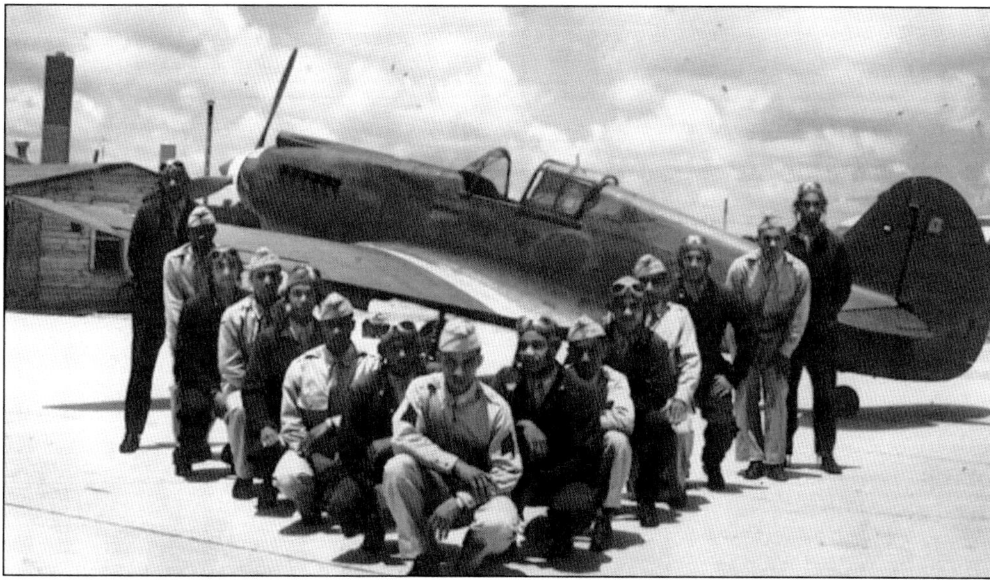

Herbert V. Clark, a native of Pine Bluff (fourth from left) served as a member of the 99th Fighter Squadron (Tuskegee Airmen) of the US Army Air Corps during World War II. He was part of the first class of black pilots trained in Tuskegee. Clark was shot down while flying over Germany on August 16, 1944. He evaded capture and led a small group of Italian partisans until he returned to the 99th on May 7, 1945. (Courtesy of US Air Force.)

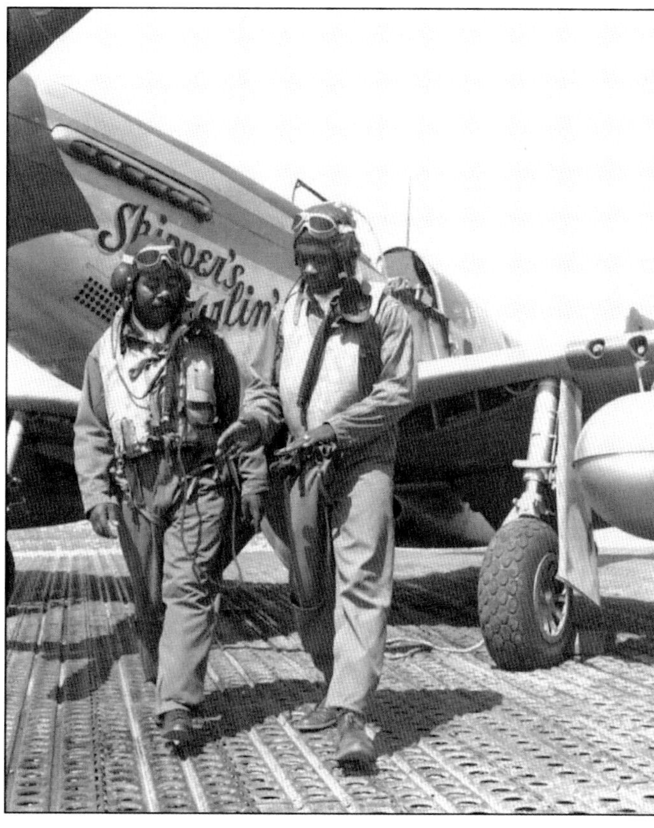

Roy Lagrone (right), a native of Pine Bluff, was a member of the 332nd Fighter Group (Tuskegee Airmen) of the US Army Air Corps during World War II. He discovered his love for flying when, as a teenager, a barnstorming pilot took him up for a ride. He later became art director of Rutgers University Medical School. His art, depicting black military pilots, has been showcased at the Pentagon, the National Museum of the US Air Force, and other venues. (Courtesy of the National Museum of the Air Force.)

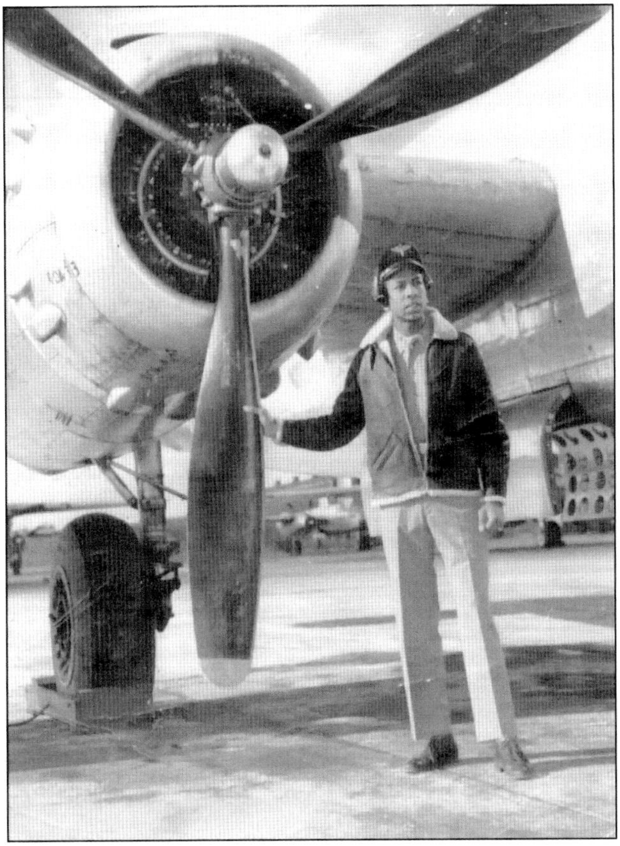

Ben "Flaps" Berry, a native of Pine Bluff, was a member of the 332nd Fighter Group (Tuskegee Airmen) of the US Army Air Corps and a World War II B-25 pilot. In spite of his family being forced out of Pine Bluff by the Ku Klux Klan in the 1930s because of his father's complaints about sharecropper treatment, Berry's life has soared. He later became an aerospace engineer and a member of the technical staff for the Apollo, Space Shuttle, and International Space Station programs. He is also the designer of the first computerized "fly by wire" flight control system. (Courtesy of US Air Force.)

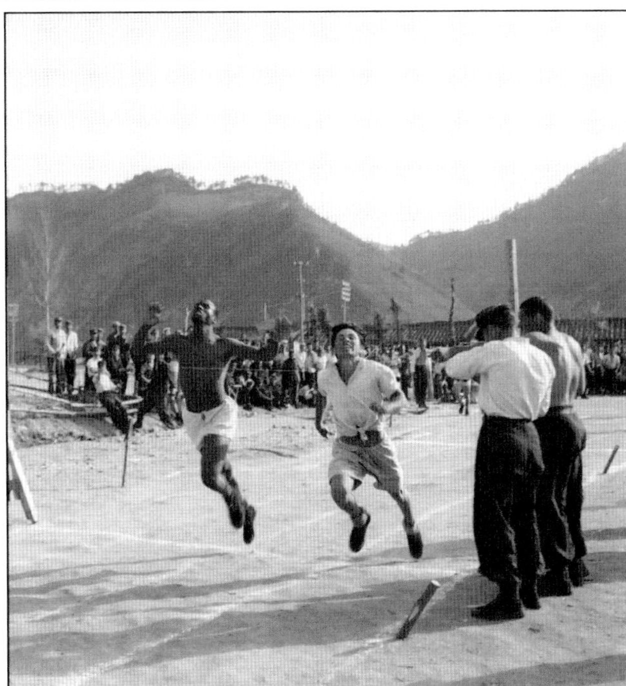

Sgt. Willie Clinton (left) of Pine Bluff surges ahead of Pfc. Raymond Almendarez in a makeshift sporting event at a North Korean POW camp in June 1952 during the Korean War. The picture was taken by Frank Noel, an Associated Press photographer who was also a prisoner at the camp in Ching-Song, North Korea. (Frank Noel photograph, courtesy of AP Images.)

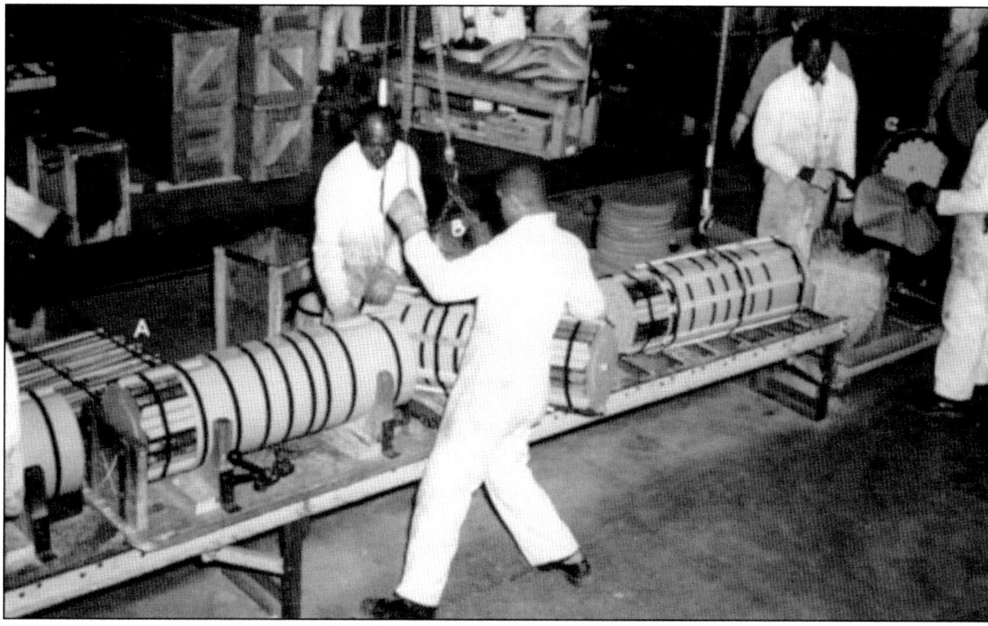

Workers carry out their tasks on a Pine Bluff Arsenal assembly line during the 1940s. The hiring of blacks at the Pine Bluff Arsenal was a direct result of the manpower shortage created by World War II and by directives from President Roosevelt's Fair Employment Practices Committee. Black women also benefitted from the new job opportunities. Ann Marie Young earned the highest civilian award given by the War Department when she saved the lives of co-workers after a 1943 explosion there. (Courtesy of Pine Bluff Arsenal.)

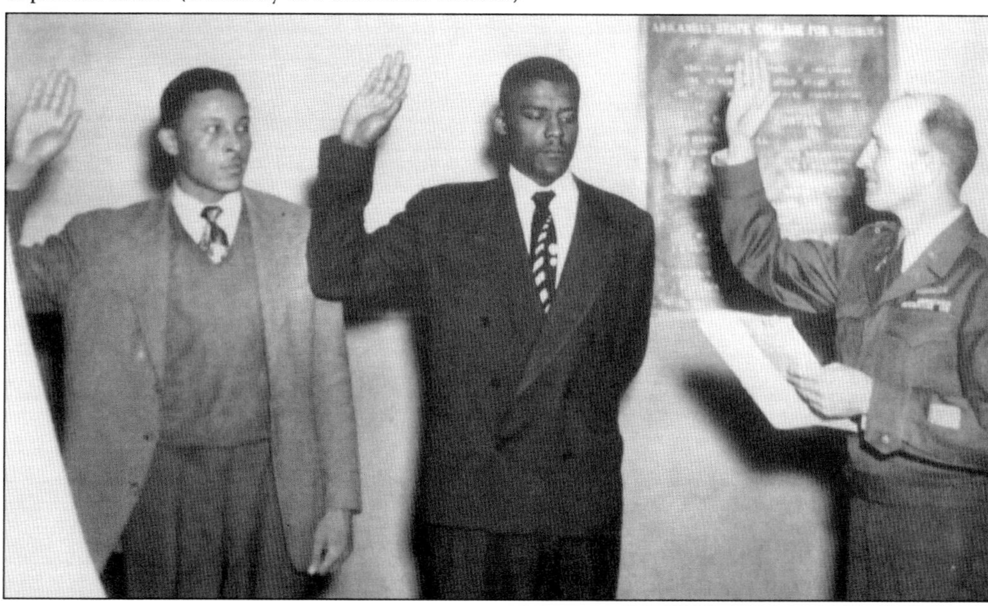

Henry Pennymon is shown in what is believed to be an early 1950s Arkansas National Guard military induction ceremony. Pennymon was a veteran of World War II and a football star at Arkansas AM&N College. He later became director of alumni relations at UAPB. He was noted as the black community's quintessential historian in Pine Bluff with an amazing recollection of names, places, and events. (Courtesy of UAPB Archives.)

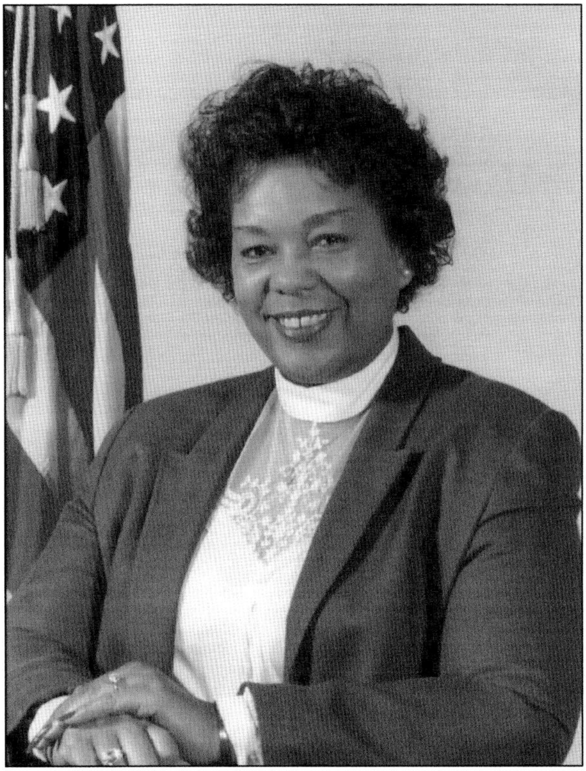

Raye Montague, a Pine Bluff resident since age nine, revolutionized the naval industry in 1971 as a manufacturing engineer after producing the US Navy's first computer-generated rough draft of a ship. When Pres. Richard Nixon gave a two-month deadline for a rough draft of FFG-7 frigates, she was called upon because of her rare computer experience and her advanced engineering expertise. She designed the ship in an unprecedented 18 hours, forever changing naval vessel development. In 1972, she received the US Navy's Meritorious Civilian Award, the Navy's third highest honorary award. (Courtesy of Raye Montague.)

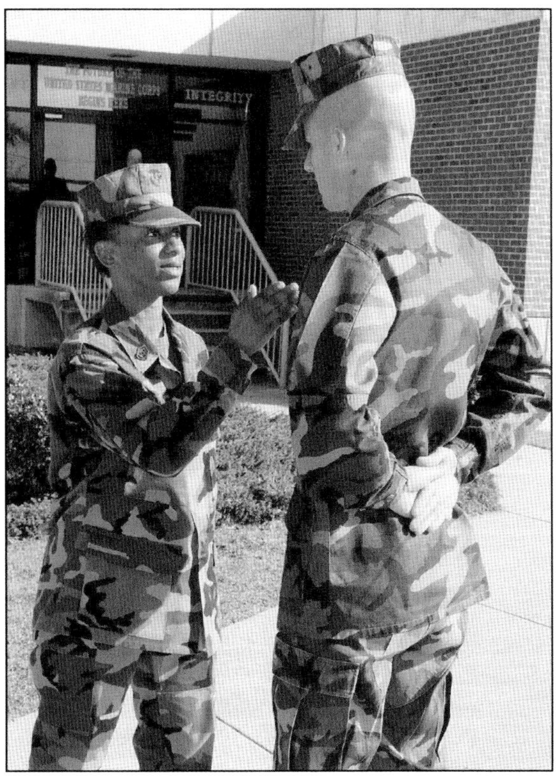

US Marine Corps sergeant major Stephanie Murphy, a native of Pine Bluff, was the first female drill instructor to serve at the US Naval Officer Candidate School. In 2008, she deployed in support of Operation Iraqi Freedom. Her 20-plus year military career has included honors such as the Meritorious Service Medal, Navy and Marine Corps Commendation Medal, the Navy and Marine Corps Achievement Medal, and many others. (Courtesy of US Department of Defense.)

Five

Community Life

Yes'm I believes in haints [ghosts] . . . My mama seen my daddy after he been dead a long time. He come right up through the crack by the fireplace . . . They had to sing and pray in the house 'fore my mama would go back.

—Lydia Jones, former Pine Bluff slave
WPA Slave Narratives

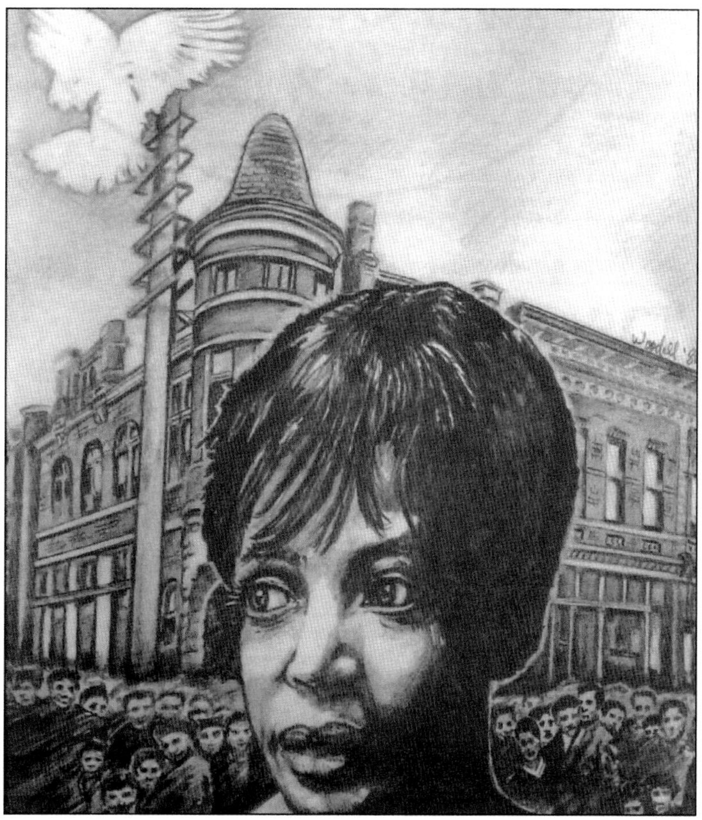

Ellen Burnett Jefferson created a wild uproar in Pine Bluff when she told of a dream that God would destroy the city on May 29, 1903, by 5:00 p.m. if residents were not at least six miles outside of the area. The *New York Times* reported that about 8,000 blacks (about 90 percent of the black population) hurriedly left town, many selling their homes and personal property by the doomsday date. Lost labor in Pine Bluff alone amounted to an estimated $200,000 (2010 equivalent of $4.8 million). While the area experienced a savage storm on the predicted day, no citywide destruction occurred. (Courtesy of *Arkansas Times*.)

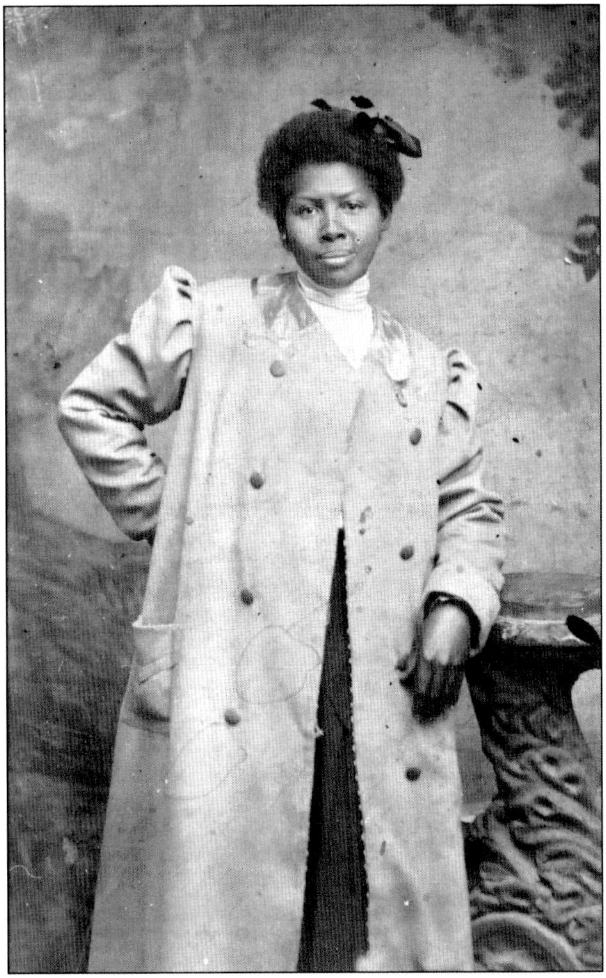

Ellen Franklin Mazique exudes self-confidence in this c. 1905 picture taken not long after her graduation from Merrill High School. She later became an exemplary teacher and elementary school principal in Wabbaseka. Mazique was also the mother of Lillian Mazique Johnson, a well-known Pine Bluff teacher. (Courtesy of Arkansas History Commission.)

Black and white workers at the Bluff City Lumber Company, pictured here around 1900, helped maintain an industry that was an integral part of Pine Bluff's economy. Historically, lumber-producing sawmills were as numerous as cotton gins. Because of Jefferson County's geographic position as a gateway from the Delta into the Arkansas Timberlands, it has always benefitted from both the agriculture and timber industries. (Courtesy of Library of Congress.)

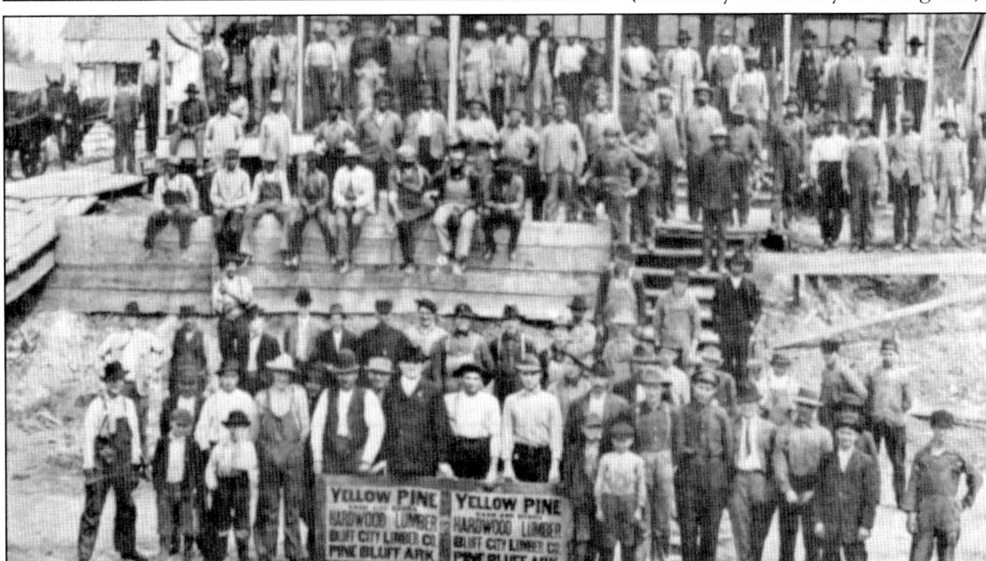

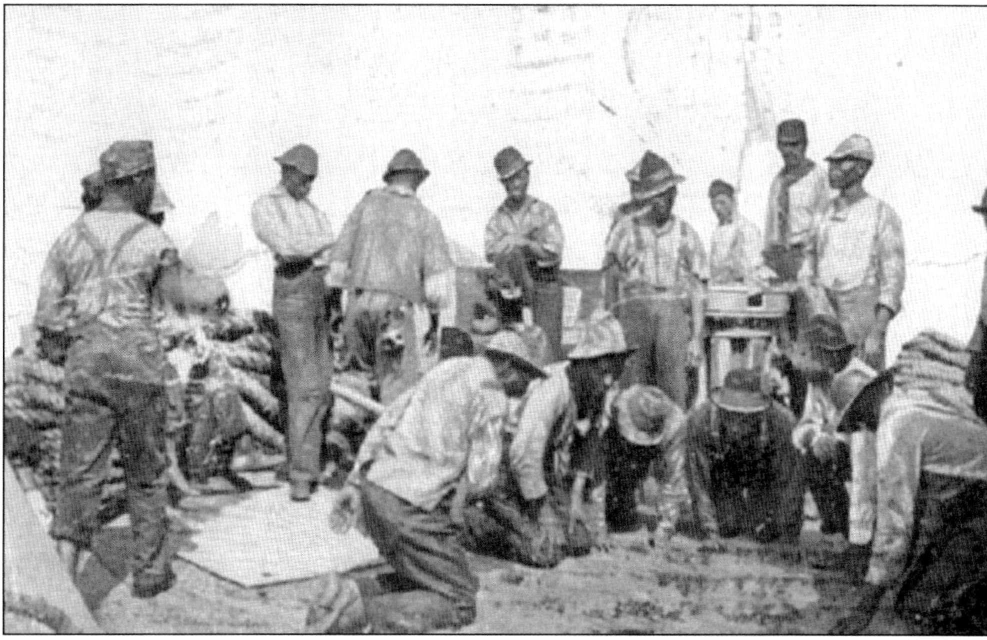

A group of men shoot craps in 1907 while onlookers watch. A 1904 ordinance in Pine Bluff stated that "any person who shall be guilty of betting any money on . . . Brag Bluff, Poker, Seven-up, Three-Up, Twenty-One, Thirteen cards, the Odd Trick, Forty Five, Whist, Boston or any other game . . . shall on conviction, thereof, be fined in any sum not less than five nor more than ten dollars." (Courtesy of Paul Purdue.)

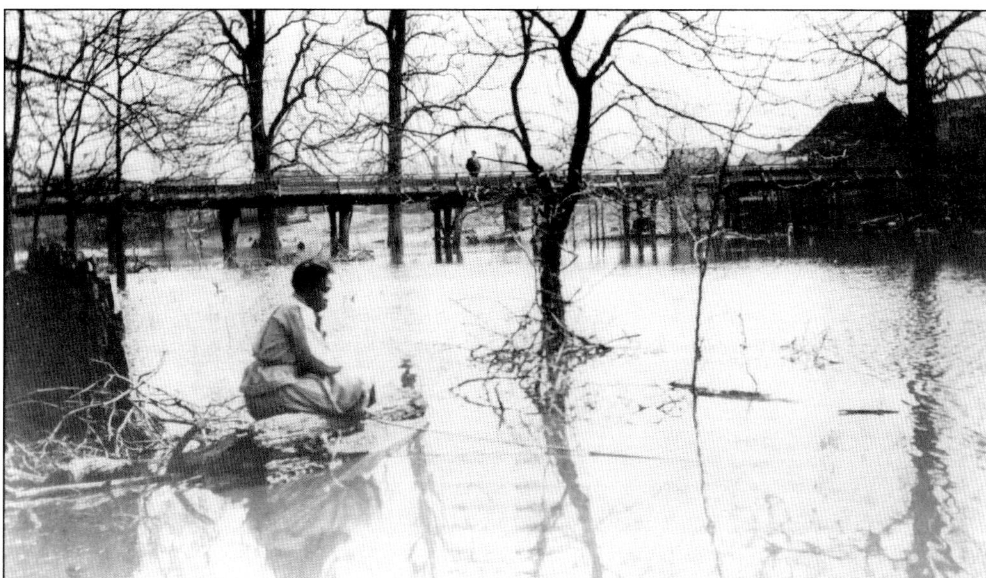

A lady fishing in Altheimer around 1900 illustrates a favorite pastime. Whether using cane poles, rods and reels, or trotlines, Jefferson County residents have always savored the challenge of catching a "mess" of catfish, crappie, bream, perch, gar, bass, buffalo, or other kinds of fish. (Courtesy of Arkansas History Commission.)

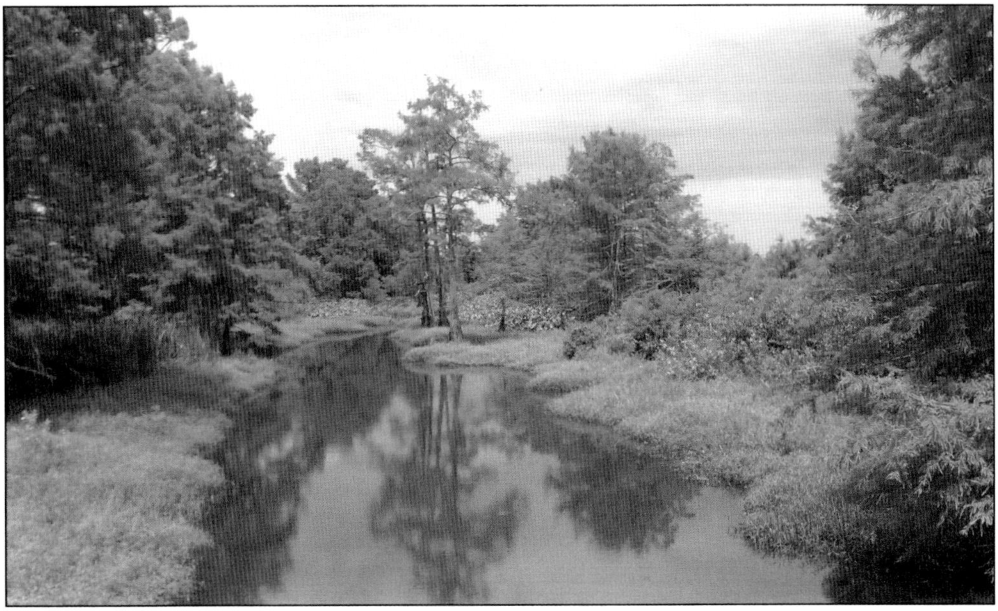

Bayou Bartholomew is the longest bayou in the world, the second most diverse stream in North America, and the dividing line between the Delta and the Timberlands regions. According to accounts in Rebecca Huskey's *Bartholowmew's Song*, black moonshiners owned numerous liquor stills throughout the bayou area just south of Pine Bluff during the early 20th century. The underground market thrived until World War II when shortages of sugar made it hard to continue. (Courtesy of Jimmy Cunningham Jr.)

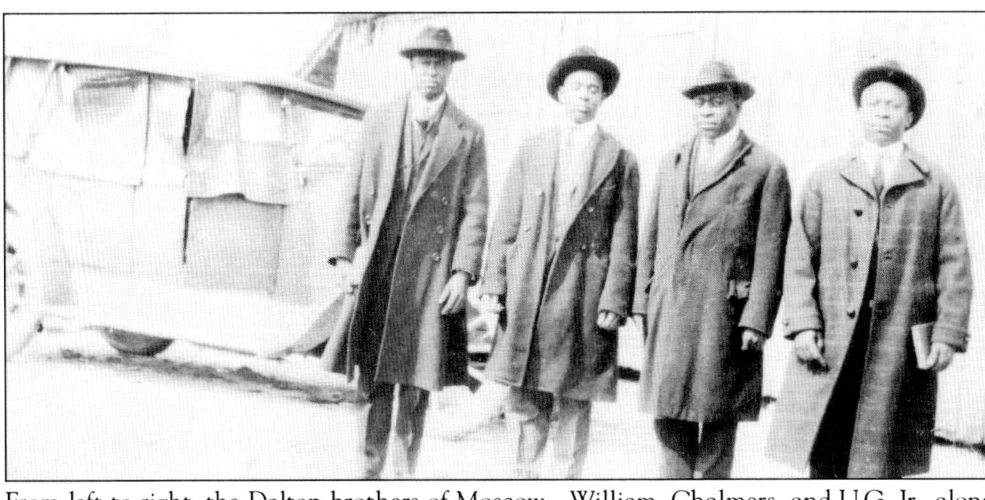

From left to right, the Dalton brothers of Moscow—William, Chalmers, and U.G. Jr., along with their cousin William Crawford—pose in a 1920 photograph with their finely adorned car. (Courtesy of Arkansas History Commission.)

Henry Rogers and son Felton of Moscow offer a dapper look at hog killing time in 1910. The meat from these hogs would be salted and cured for preservation. To further extend the life of the meat, it would often be smoked in a smokehouse. (Courtesy of Arkansas History Commission.)

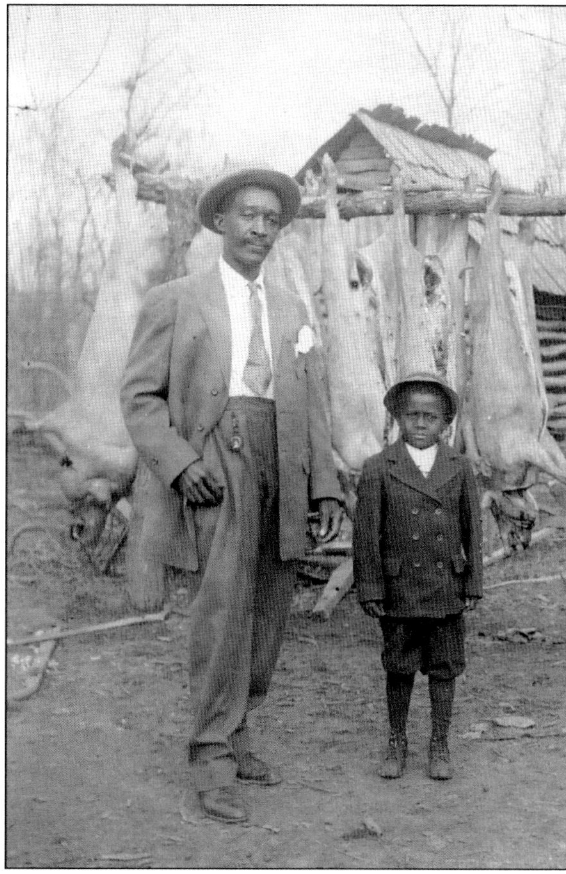

Dorothea Smith, Negro home demonstration agent for Jefferson County, leads a corn-canning demonstration for women and girls in 1930. Agents such as Smith were key in showcasing emerging home economics strategies for families living in rural areas. (Courtesy of US National Archives and Record Administration.)

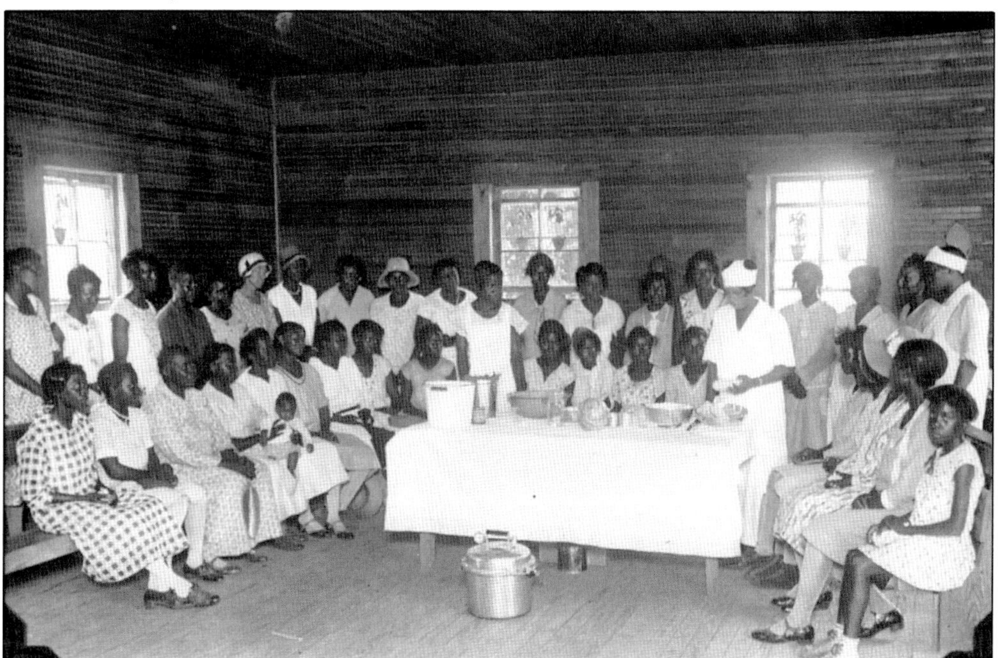

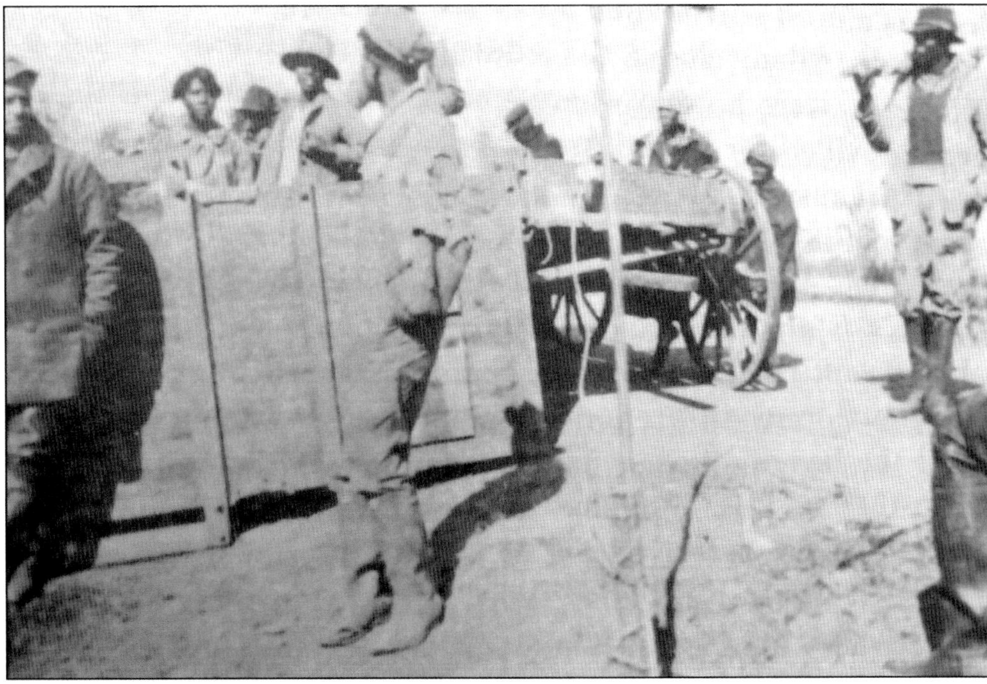

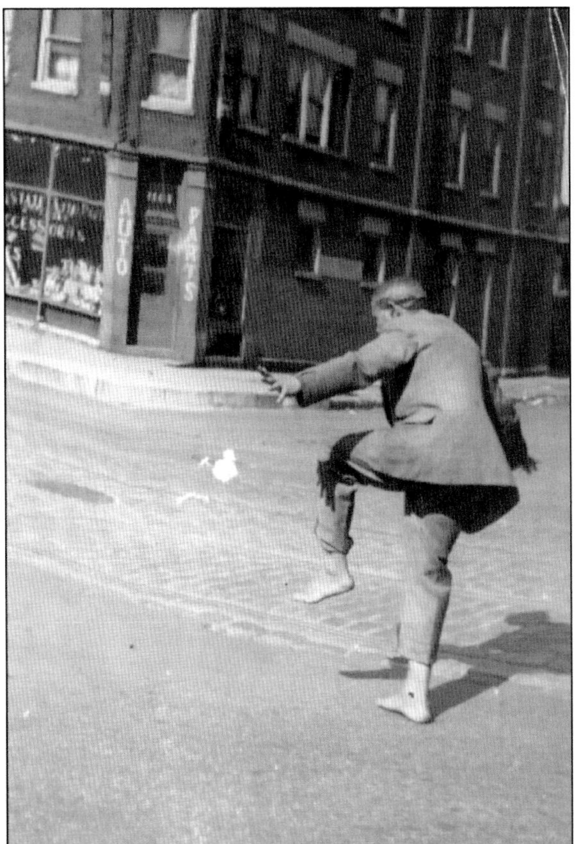

Residents evacuate to a levy in Pine Bluff during the infamous 1927 flood. Many African Americans were evacuated to the Free Bridge and levy by the Arkansas River, where they had to wait for days for waters to recede as they faced precarious living conditions. (Courtesy of Wilson Photographic Studio.)

A colorful man strikes an interesting pose in this 1937 Pine Bluff photograph. For years, Pine Bluff's black community has produced characters whose humor, skills, and/or persona have made them local legends. Some of these people, some known only by their nicknames, include "Nubby," "Waving Willy," "Little Leg Emma," "Tarzan," "Rooster," "Honey Hush," "Black Knight," "the Peanut Man," "Possum," "Momma Red," "Booty Green," "Forty-Fo'," "Cannonball," "No Nose," "Momma Hot," Edward Pennington (also known as "the Running Man"), and a Miss Juanita. (Courtesy of Special Collections Department, University of Arkansas Libraries.)

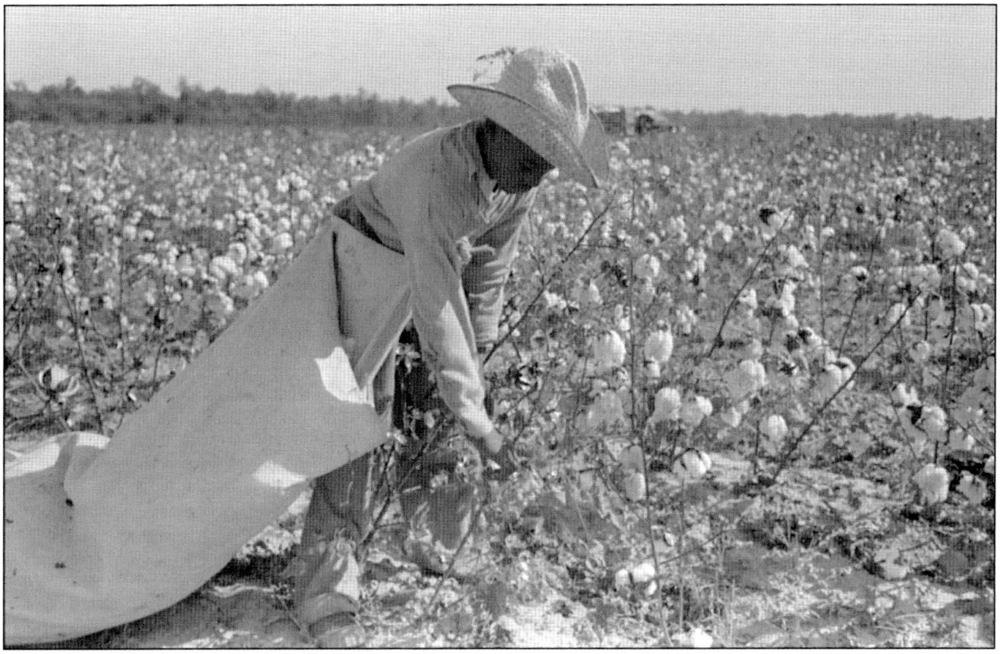

A young boy in the Lake Dick area near Altheimer picks cotton in 1938 for 75¢ per 100 pounds. With such low wages, this youngster needed to pick more than his weight to make over one dollar in a day. Youth of this era worked in the fields around the school calendar, which maintained split sessions in the summer and fall to accommodate cotton chopping and picking times. (Courtesy of Library of Congress.)

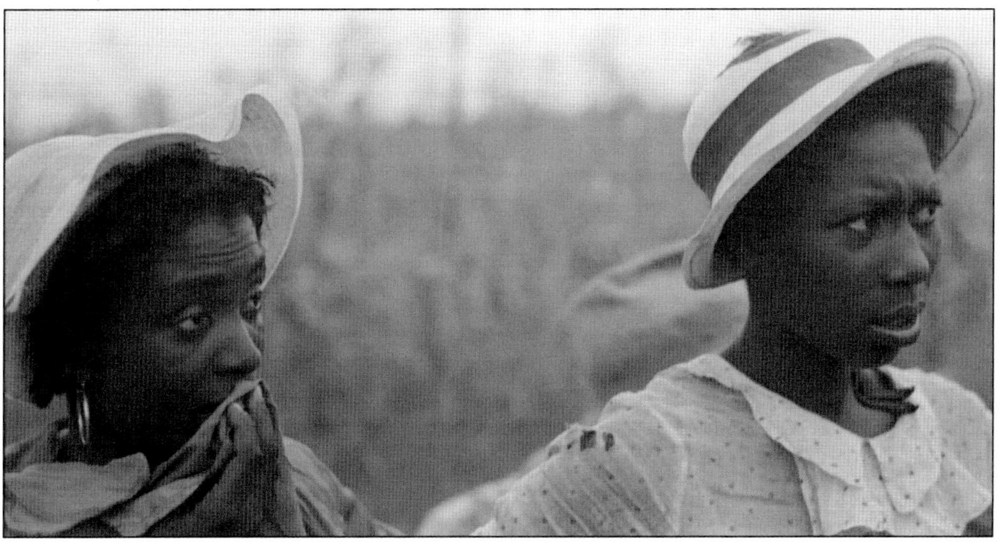

Two women in the cotton fields near Lake Dick are in disbelief over something in 1938. Twenty years prior, black women in Pine Bluff were in disbelief that they were being underpaid for picking cotton even though cotton prices had tripled. They decided not to work and instead relied on a federal allotment for World War I spouses. White planters were livid and convinced the city to pass a resolution to jail them if they did not work. However, the resolution did not receive the federal support it needed for enforcement and was reluctantly shelved by city officials. (Courtesy of Library of Congress.)

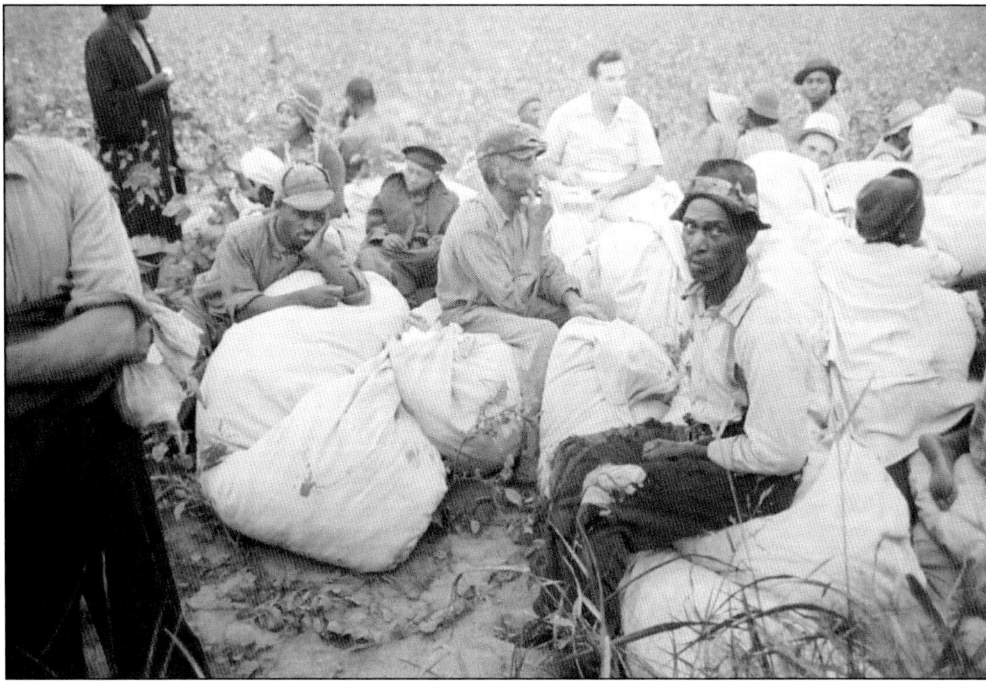

After a long day in the Jefferson County cotton fields, workers wait patiently as cotton sacks are weighed. A good cotton picker could bag 350 to 400 pounds of cotton a day. (Courtesy of Library of Congress.)

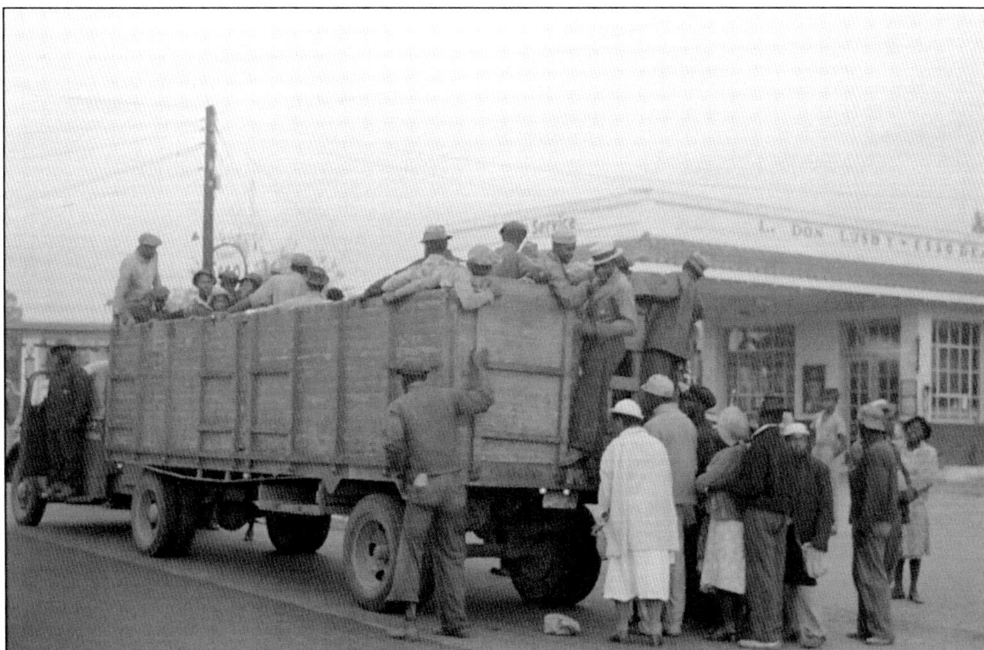

Several places in Jefferson County were pick-up spots for workers who wanted to earn money in the cotton fields. This stop in 1938 was on the north side of Pine Bluff, just off Cedar Street (University Drive) and Pullen Street. (Courtesy of Library of Congress.)

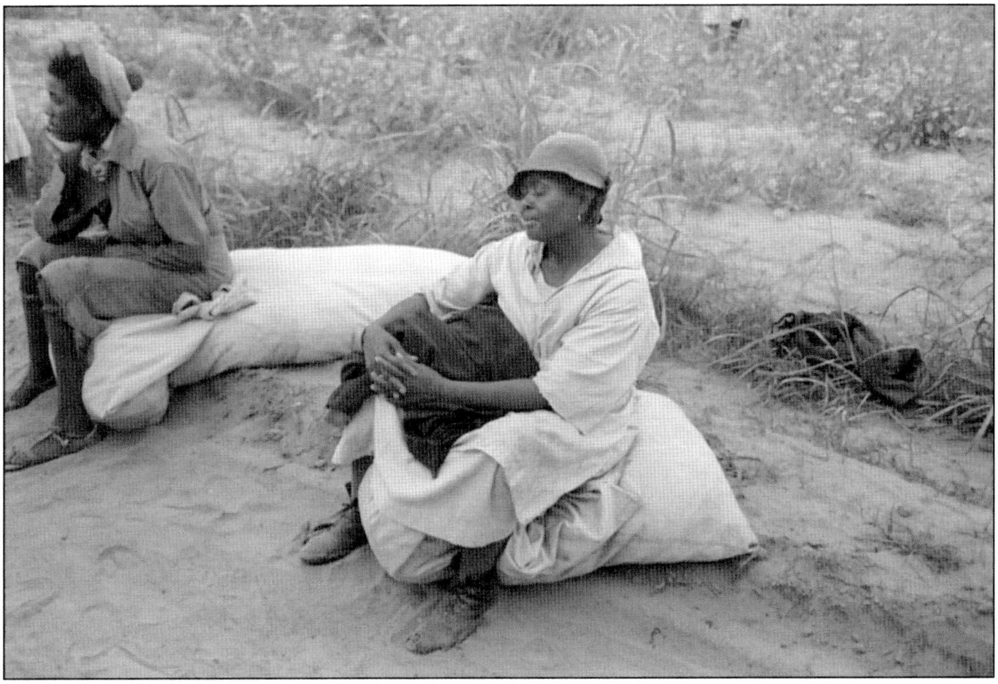

The combination of stifling southern heat and backbreaking work in the Lake Dick–area cotton fields take their toll on this laborer as she turns her cotton sack into a makeshift seat. (Courtesy of Library of Congress.)

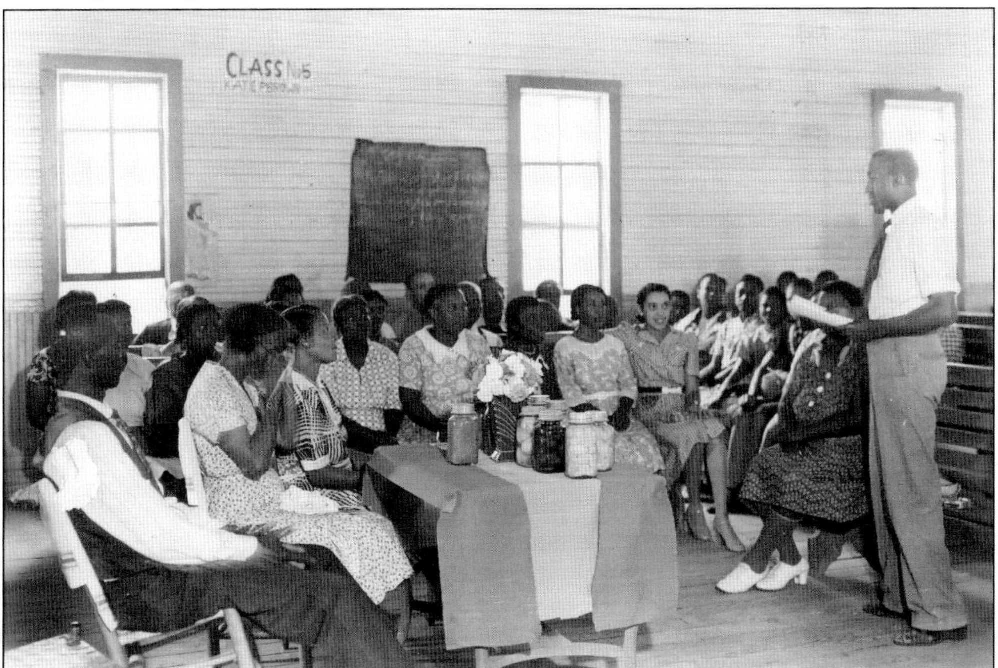

Negro Agricultural Agent C.D. McKindra addresses the Jefferson County Negro Agricultural Committee in 1940. (Courtesy of Special Collections Department, University of Arkansas Libraries.)

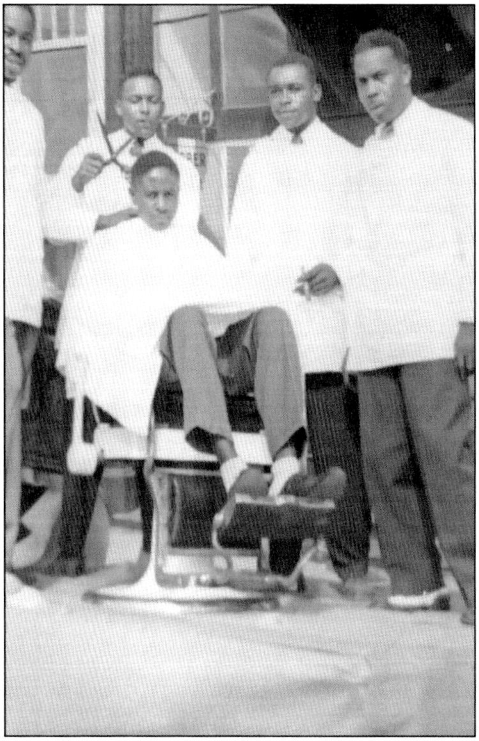

A young barber prepares to cut hair in Pine Bluff during the 1940s. Barbershops in Jefferson County have served as places where black men could get conks, pompadours, bangs, afro blowouts, New Yorkers, shags, hi-top fades, Jheri curls, parts, or other hairstyles. Yvonne Treadwell, a former barbershop owner, remembered when black barbers met in 1960 and debated raising their haircut prices from "six bits" (75¢) to $1. Many barbers said their patrons would not pay such an outrageous price. (Courtesy of Juanita Currie.)

Baseball legend Jackie Robinson signs autographs at a 1949 Arkansas AM&N football game as college professor Albert Baxter (fourth from left) watches the field action, and 11-year old Jimmy Cunningham Sr. (far left, partially obscured by the man's hat) stares in awe at the sports icon. (Courtesy of UAPB Archives.)

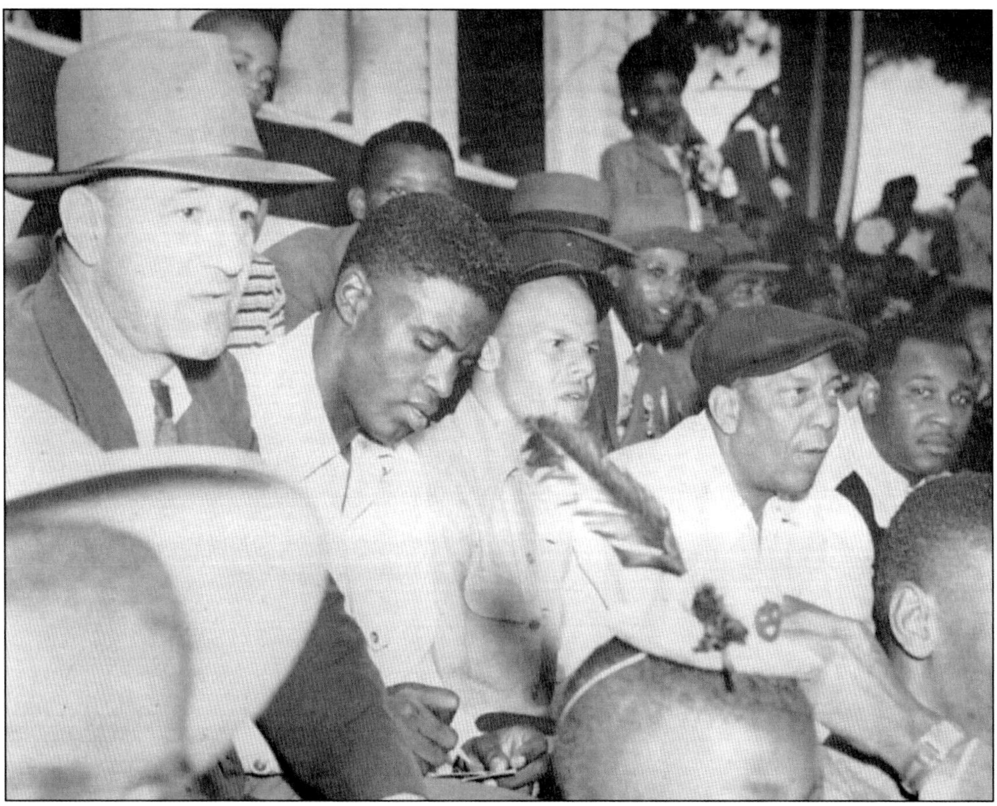

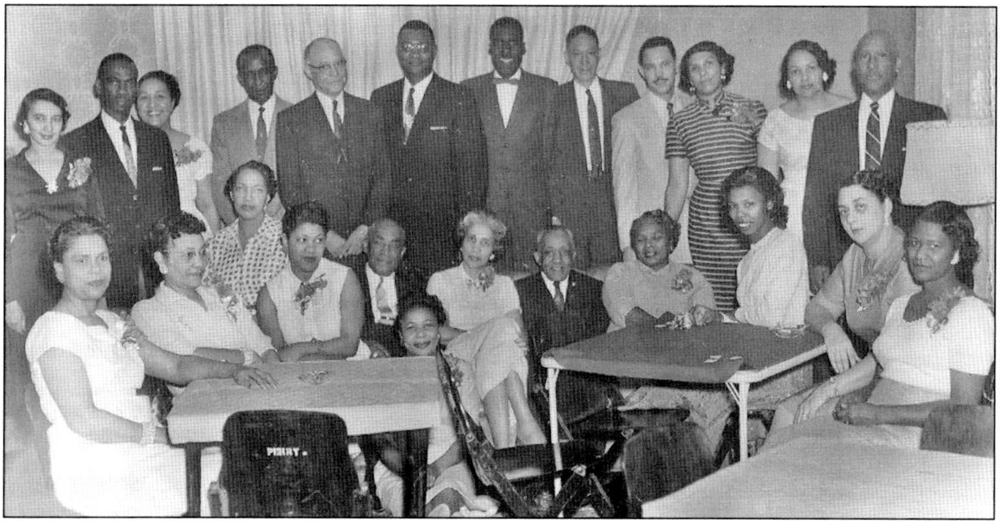

Members of the IQ Bridge Club (ladies) and the 20th Century Club (men) in Pine Bluff represented social organizations that included the most educated professionals in the city. Typical of this group were people like Dr. Cleon Flowers (second row, seventh from left), known as the "Godfather of Arkansas Medicine" and the first doctor in the nation to deliver Siamese twins at home, and Della Phipps (first row, fourth from left), longtime registrar at Arkansas AM&N College. (Courtesy of Myrtus Henry.)

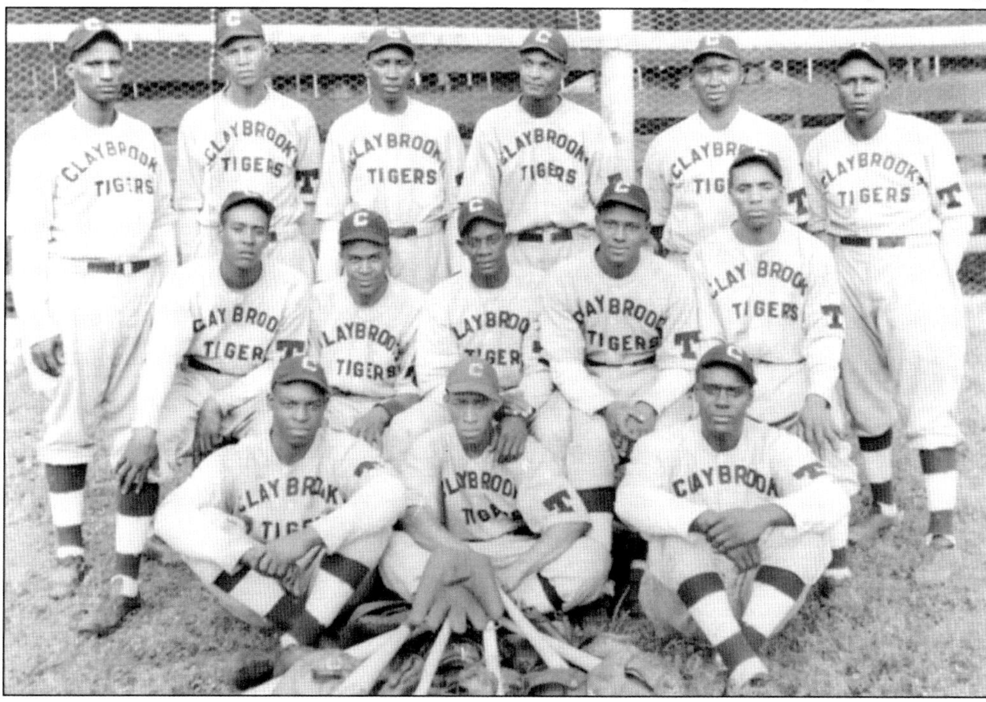

The Claybrook Tigers, a black-owned, semiprofessional baseball team based in Crittendon County, Arkansas, includes Wabbaseka's fast-pitching Theolic "Fireball" Smith (second row, left) shown here around 1935. Smith later went on to play three decades as an All Star for three Negro League teams. Charles Johnson and J.C. McHaskell (neither pictured) are the other known Negro League baseball players from Pine Bluff. These men blazed the trail for people like Pine Bluff's Torri Hunter, who signed a $26 million contract in 2012 with the Detroit Tigers. (Courtesy of Dr. John Haddock Jr.)

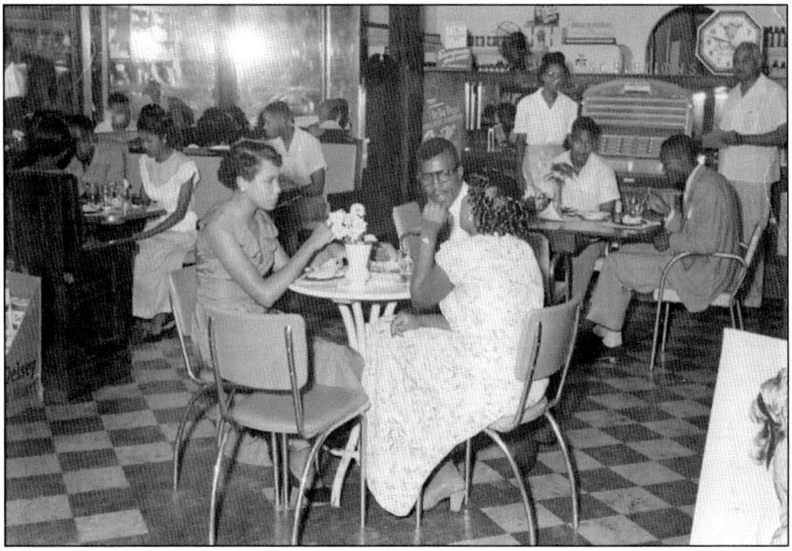

Lunchtime at Dr. D.W. Young's pharmacy in the 1940s always drew neatly dressed Pine Bluff patrons who enjoyed the great meals and service. (Courtesy of Juanita Currie.)

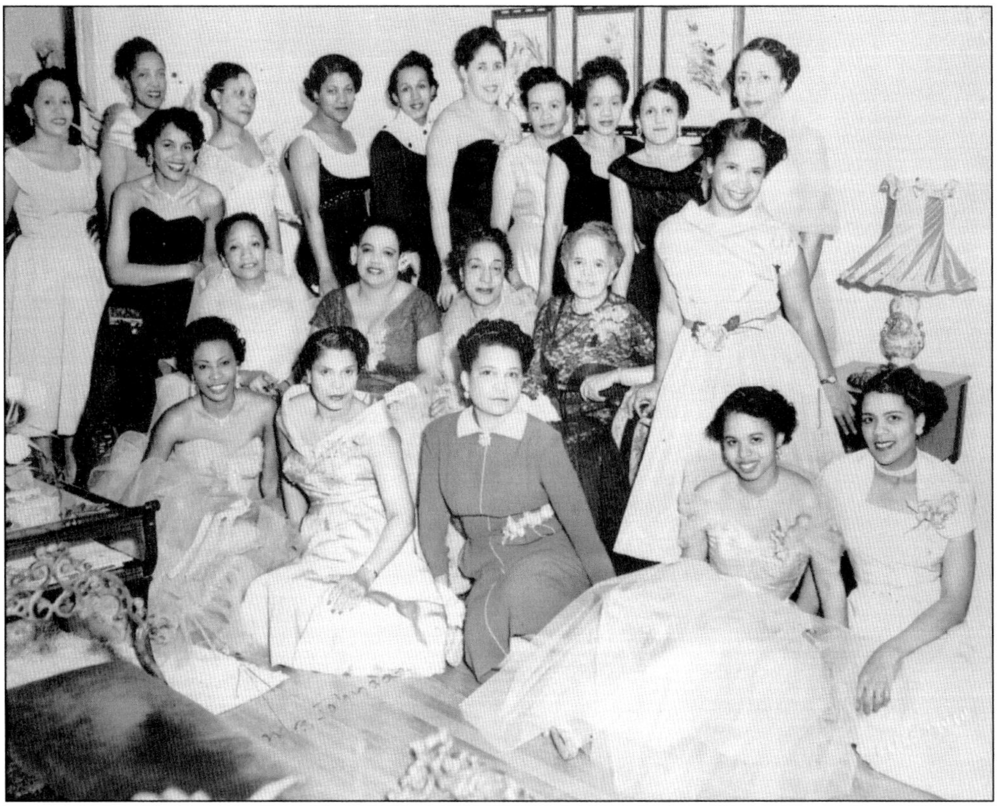

Pine Bluff graduate chapter members of Alpha Kappa Alpha Inc. don warm smiles here in 1953. Other Greek organizations such as Alpha Phi Alpha, Delta Sigma Theta, Phi Beta Sigma, Kappa Alpha Psi, Zeta Phi Beta, Sigma Gamma Rho, and Omega Psi Phi have always been an integral part of Pine Bluff's black middle class. Their community work, charitable contributions, and mentoring have served countless residents. (Courtesy of Arkansas History Commission.)

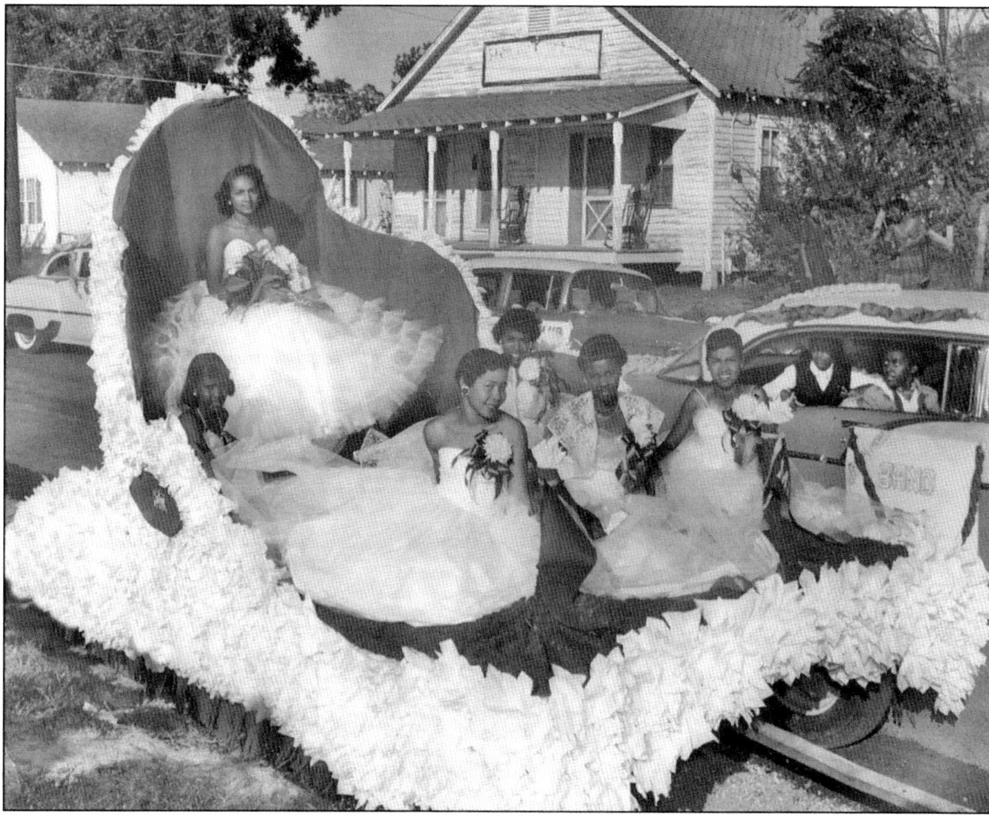

Members of the 1957 Merrill High homecoming court, including homecoming queen Paola Harrell, ride proudly on a float. (Courtesy of Paola Harrell.)

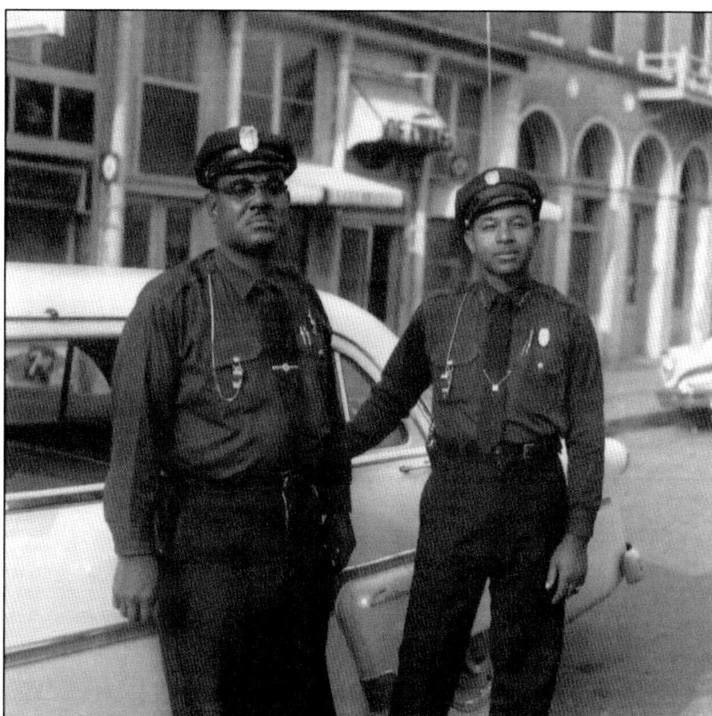

Officer Bradley and AM&N chief of security Willie Perkins stop on Pine Bluff's Third Street in the early 1960s. (Courtesy of Special Collections Department, University of Arkansas Libraries.)

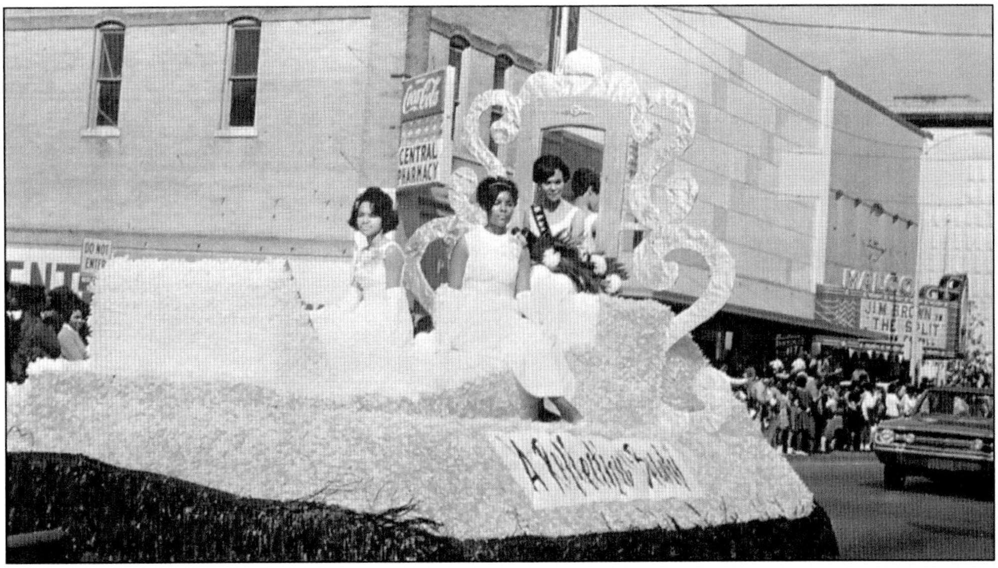

A 1969 Arkansas AM&N College homecoming parade featuring beautiful campus queens brings in spectators from all over the county. Homecoming has become a time-honored tradition in Pine Bluff, serving as a huge annual community reunion. Former alumni and non-alumni alike converge on the area to partake in revelry and renew social ties. (Courtesy of Karen Dancy Dickson.)

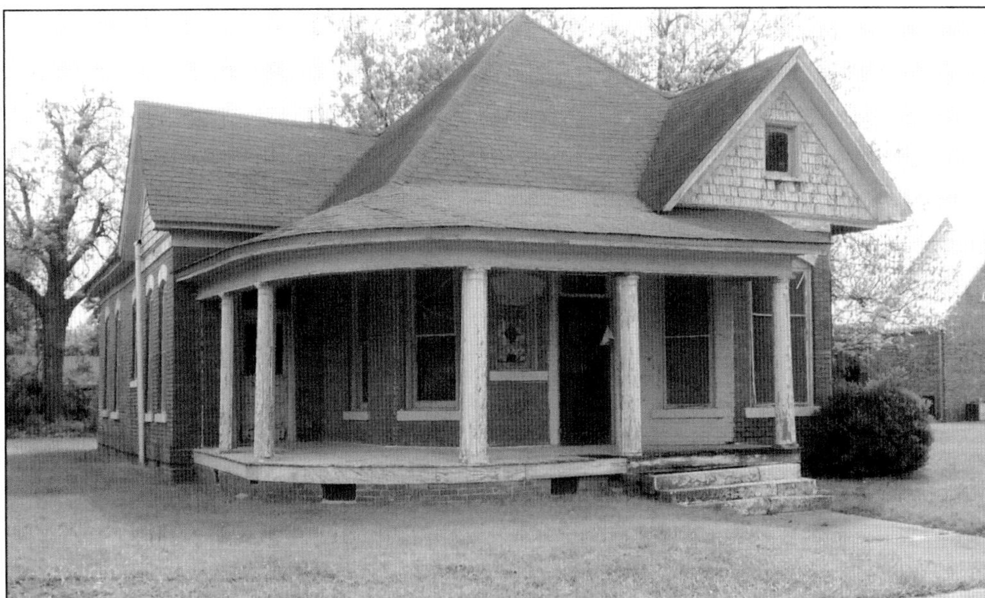

Dr. John Walker Parker Sr., Pine Bluff dentist, NAACP organizer, co-owner of the Moving Picture Theater, and prominent civic leader, built this home around 1909. The Parkers maintained family life here and housed distinguished visiting blacks who came to the area. Walker's son Dr. John Walker Parker Jr., a Pine Bluff native, later became the first African American head of general surgery in the US Air Force. His grandson Dr. David Parker became a prominent dentist and civic leader in Pine Bluff. (Courtesy of Jimmy Cunningham Jr.)

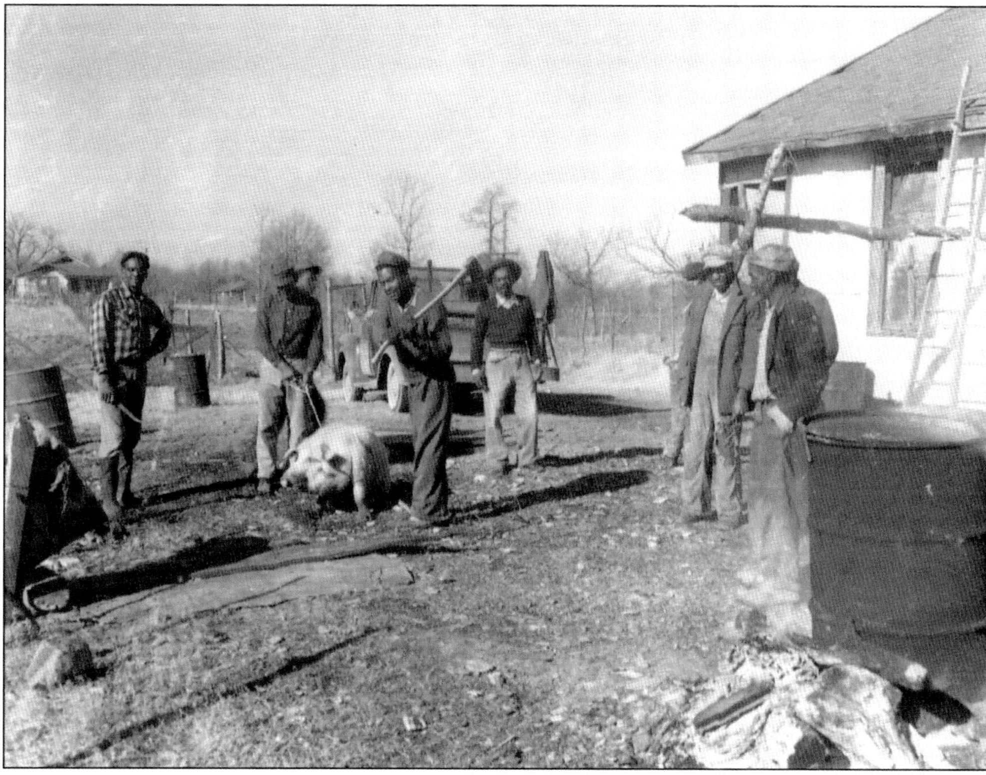

Men prepare for a hog killing in Jefferson County in 1950. Butchering a hog on small area farms was typically an event that illustrated communal values. Neighbors often assisted and were given a share of meat for friends and others in the community. (Courtesy of Special Collections Department, University of Arkansas Libraries.)

A mid-1960s Arkansas AM&N football game allows this fan in vogue eyewear to sport her look. Homecoming games were often times in which fashion could almost overtake football. Over the years, dress modes have become more casual, but prior to the late 1950s, a young woman was not considered completely attired at a homecoming game unless she wore a hat, gloves, and a dress. (Courtesy of Special Collections Department, University of Arkansas Libraries.)

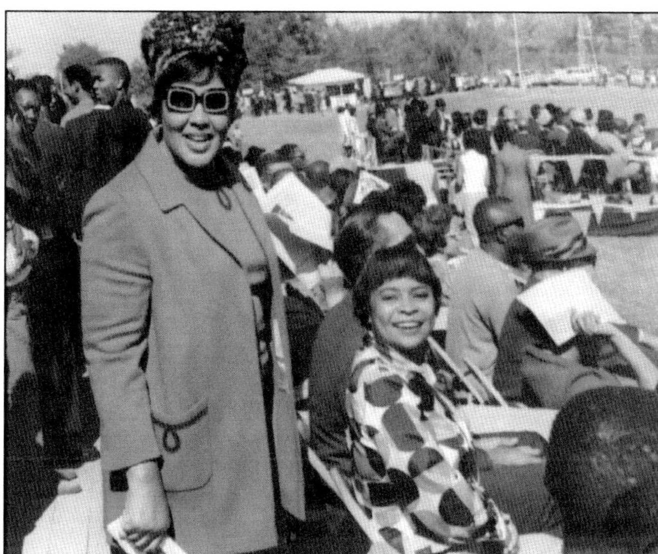

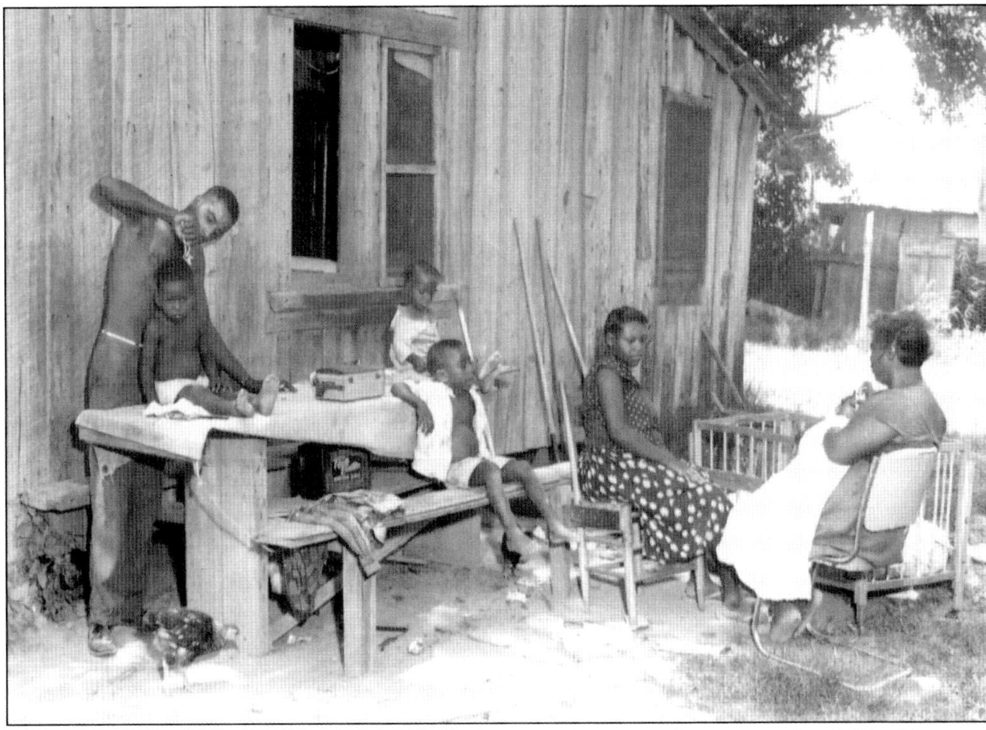

A family relaxes in the shade near Pine Bluff as a young boy gets a haircut in the 1950s. (Courtesy of Special Collections Department, University of Arkansas Libraries.)

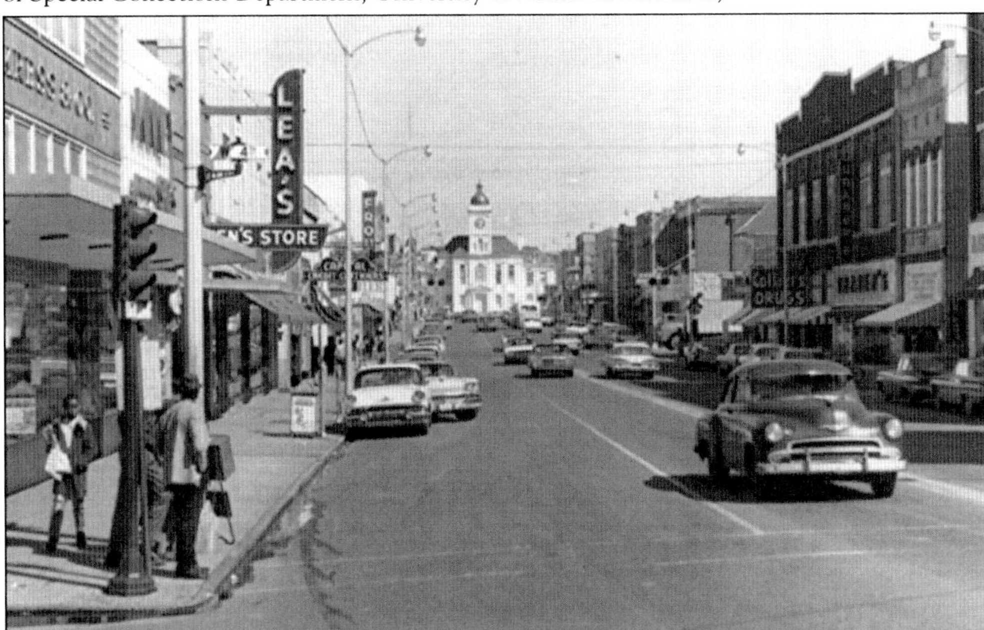

Downtown Pine Bluff is vibrant in this 1960 image. Around this time, many people from the county and other parts of southeast Arkansas visited downtown often in cars, but occasionally, rural residents arrived in horse- or mule-hitched wagons. It was a big deal for many to "go to town" and purchase essentials or just mingle, particularly on weekends. (Courtesy of Paul Purdue.)

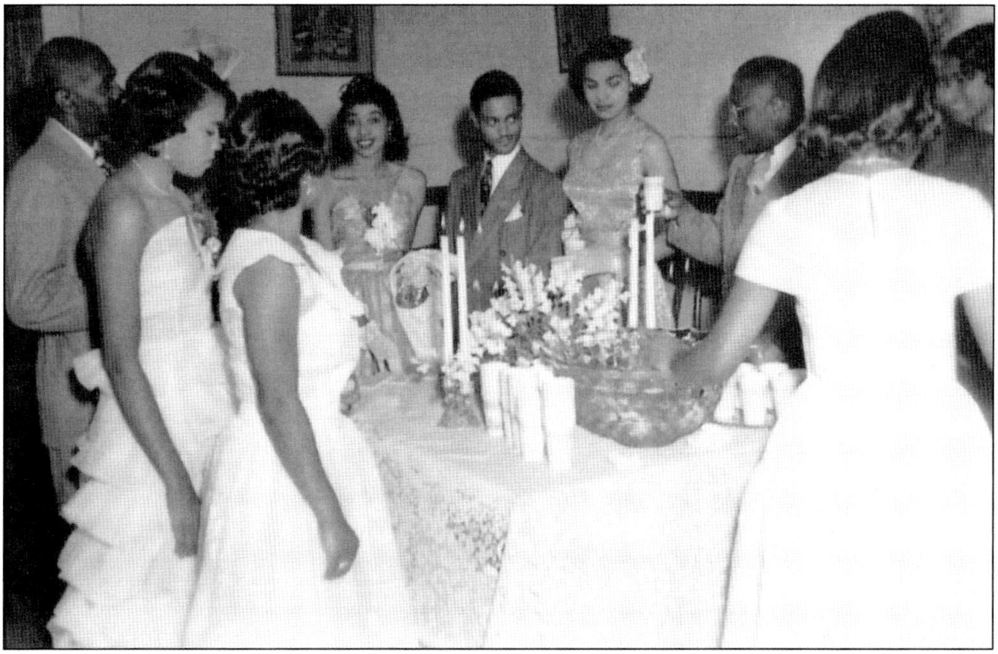

A 1960s formal reception in Pine Bluff employs the social graces common in the black middle class. The story of Jefferson County is the story of some of the most refined, educated blacks in the United States living and interfacing with some of the most hardworking, down-home African Americans anywhere in the country. Out of this eclectic mix, the county has forged its character. (Courtesy of Special Collections Department, University of Arkansas Libraries.)

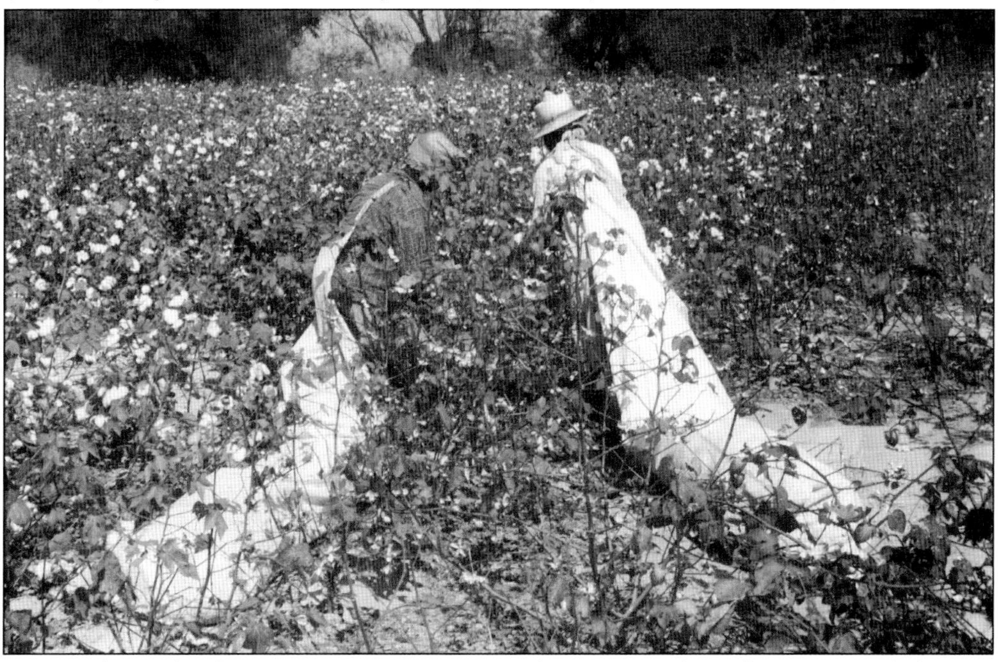

Even as the civil rights movement was sweeping the nation with its dynamic social changes, scenes like this 1963 image in Jefferson County were still reminiscent of an era from 100 years past. (Courtesy of Arkansas History Commission.)

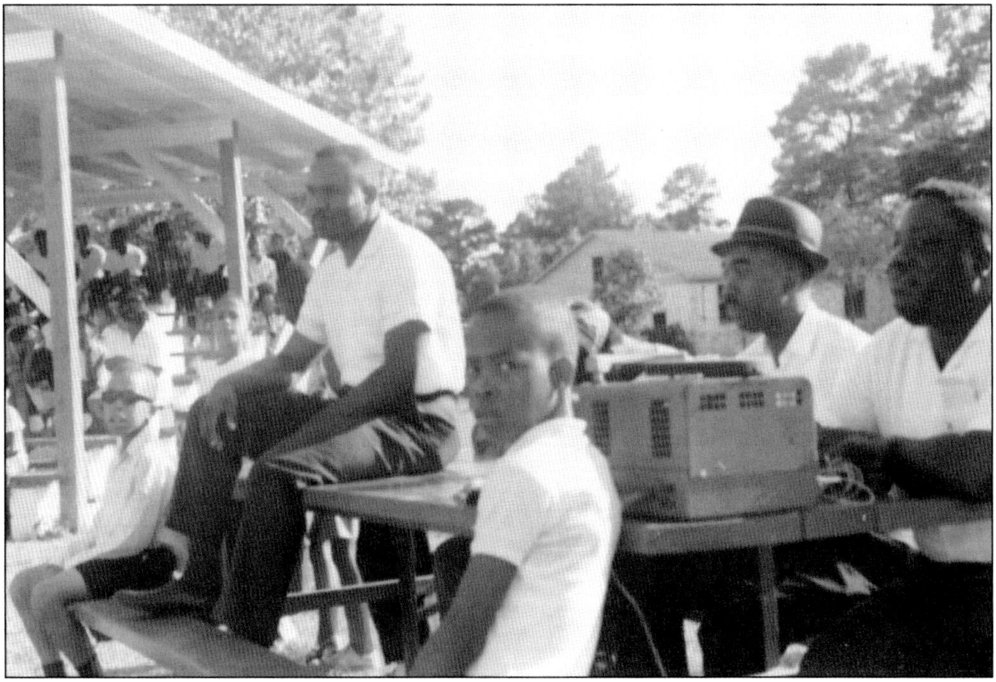

Spectators view a baseball game in 1964 at Townsend Park in Pine Bluff. The park, built for African Americans as a counterpart to the larger public park for whites (Oakland Park), was a center for recreational and social activities. Boasting baseball, swimming, and basketball facilities along with two multipurpose buildings (the "Little Rec" and the "Big Rec"), Townsend Park had widespread appeal in the black community. (Courtesy of Arkansas History Commission.)

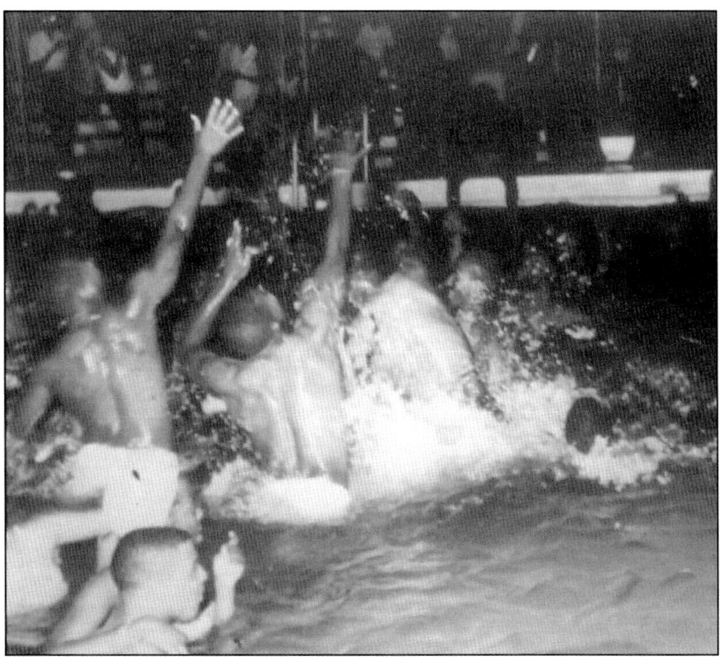

Young people have fun at a Townsend Park night pool party while onlookers watch from the stands in 1967. This city pool attracted scores of black youth during the summer months. The park and its pool were the hang out spots for setting up dates, cruising, meeting friends, observing fashions, listening to music on transitor radios and eight-track tape players, or just relaxing. (Courtesy of UAPB Archives.)

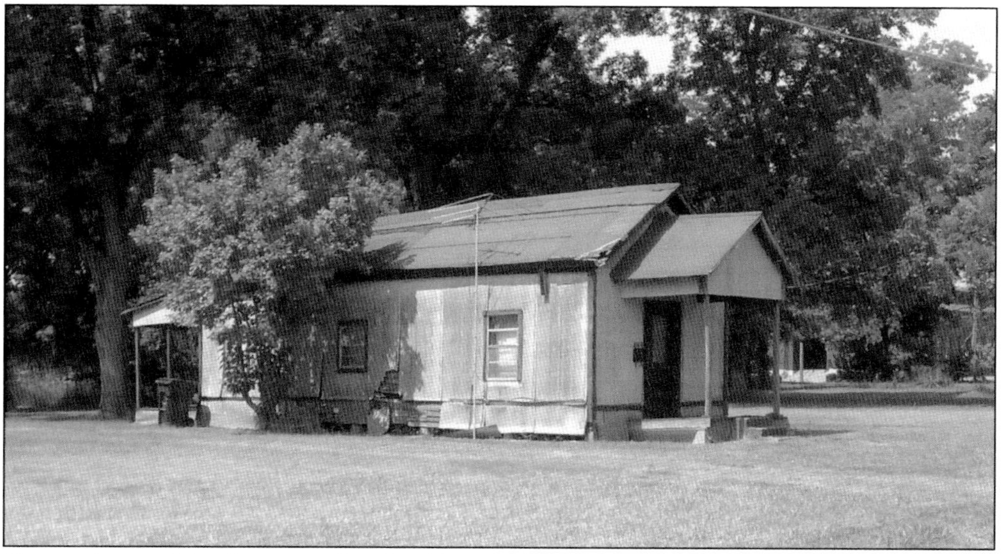

Shotgun houses like this one in Pine Bluff, probably built around the 1920s, were once common sights in African American neighborhoods throughout the county. Today, they are being bulldozed rapidly as many have fallen into disrepair. Their architectural style has been traced from Africa to Haiti to New Orleans, and renewed interest in other parts of the South has made their preservation a cultural priority. (Courtesy of Jimmy Cunningham Jr.)

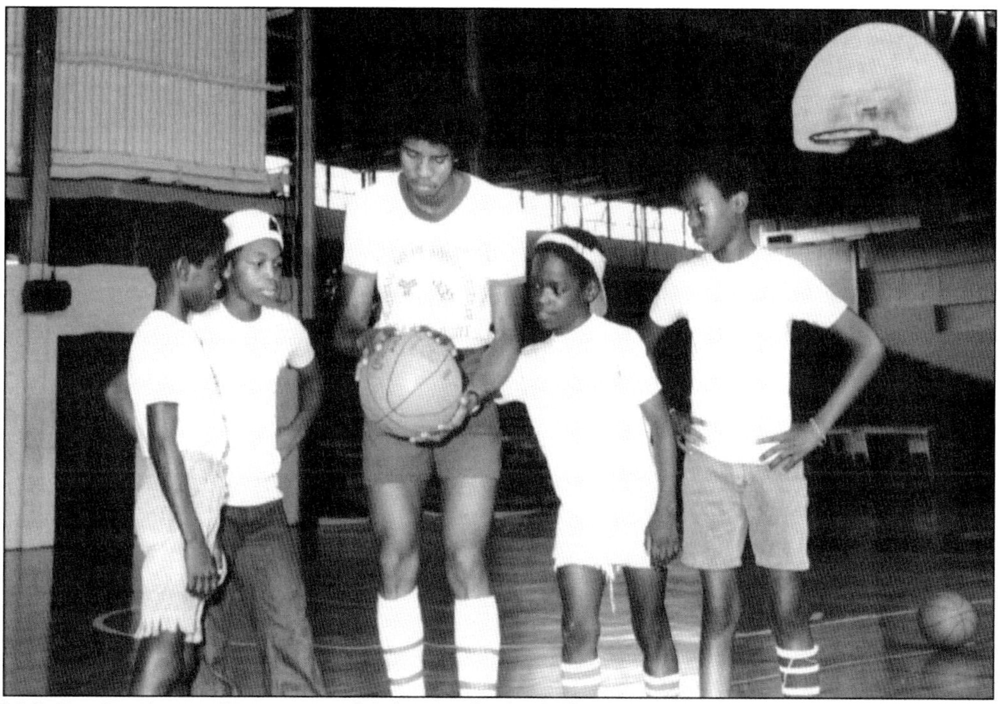

U.S. Reed, a former University of Arkansas basketball star, shows a group of Pine Bluff youth basketball techniques during a late 1970s session of the National Youth Summer Sports Program. This program, hosted at UAPB, provided hundreds of youth with exposure to an assortment of athletic and social skills along with personal mentoring over the years. (Courtesy of Special Collections Department, University of Arkansas Libraries.)

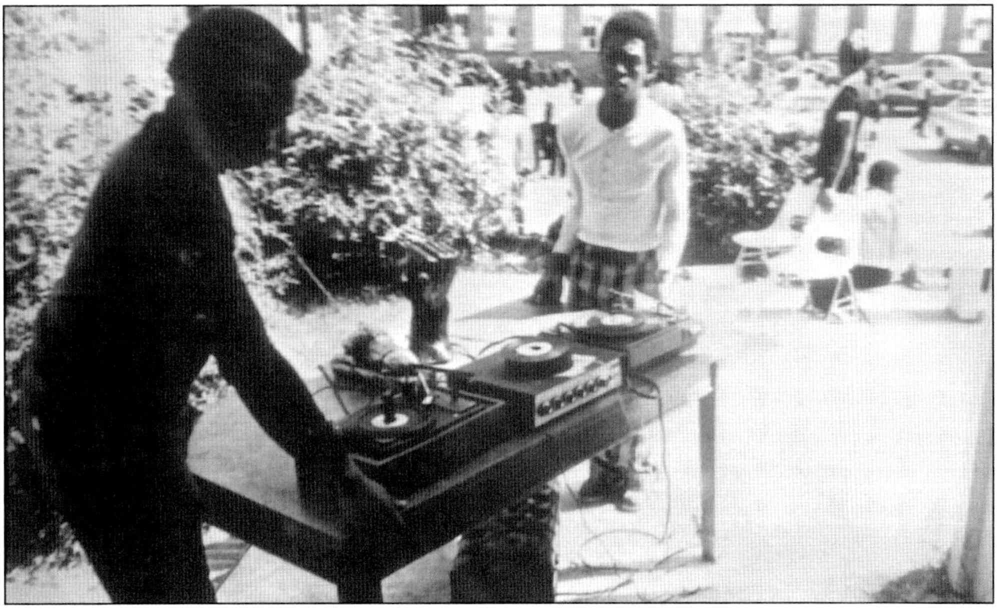

Two college students at UAPB prepare to deejay in 1975. Deejays like Gary "Drack" Wilson, Troupadour Crump, Michael Morgan, and others rocked parties all over the county. Favorite party spots during the 1970s and 1980s for black teens were the Townsend Park Big Rec, the American Legion building, the skating rink, and the Pine Bluff Convention Center lobby, among others. Early 1980s battle dance groups such as the Human Tornados and the 2nd Street GQers were also popular at such venues. (Courtesy of UAPB Archives.)

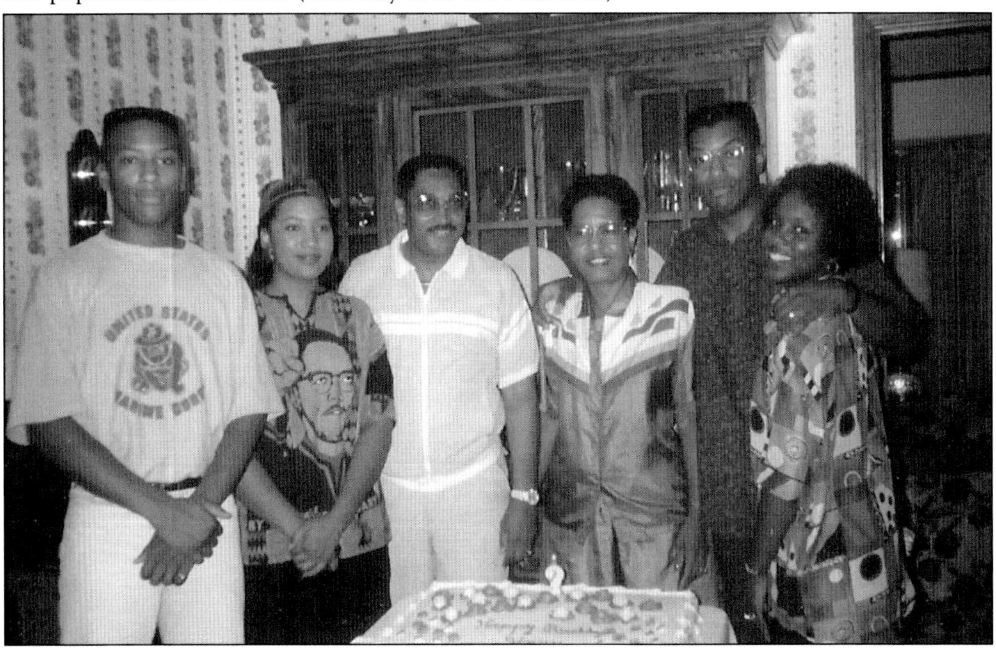

The Cunningham family celebrates a birthday sometime around 1991. Members include, from left to right, Marc, Camuriel (or "Chick"), Jimmy Sr. (the first African American podiatrist in Pine Bluff), Donna (longtime teacher at Dial and Jack Robey Junior High Schools), and Jimmy Jr. and his wife Alicia. (Courtesy of Donna Cunningham.)

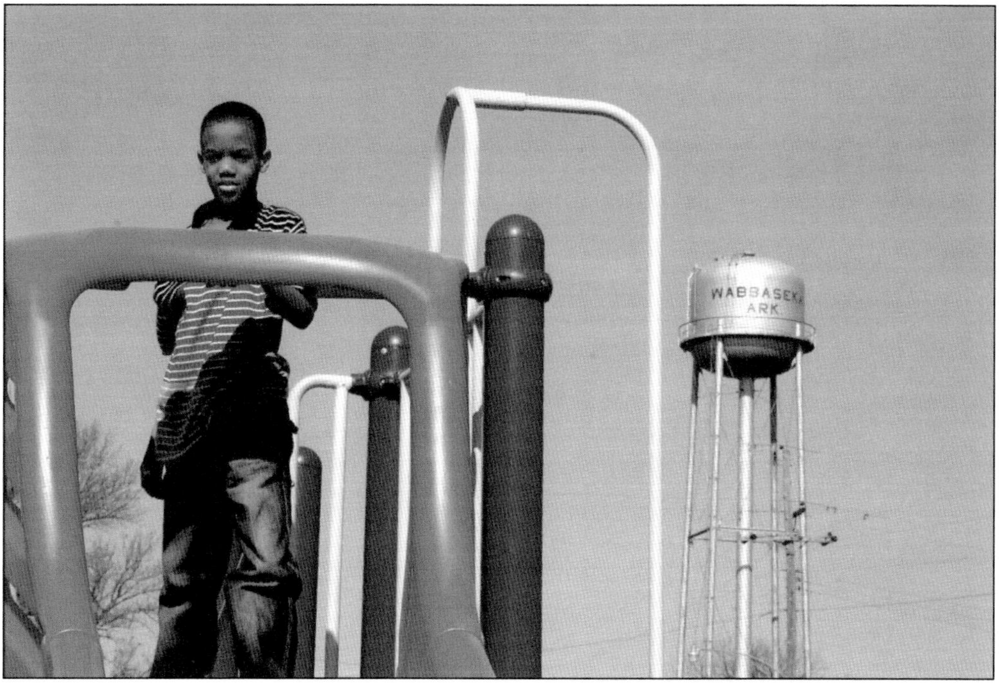

A young Wabbaseka boy takes in his surroundings near the water tower. The area around Wabbaseka, Humphrey, and Stuttgart is considered the duck hunting capital of the world. Each year, thousands of hunters converge on the marshy prairies to bag ducks and geese flying south. (Courtesy of Jerry Sims.)

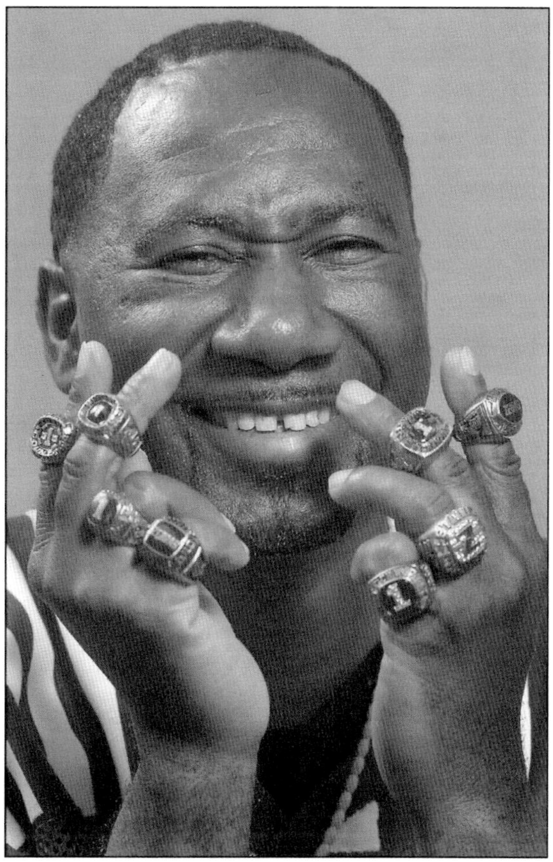

Greg Walker shows off his many Pine Bluff High School championship rings. Walker has been one of the school's most ardent football fans, having served as the team manager for over 25 years both as a student and as a graduate. His passion at games is overwhelming. In spite of any developmental challenges, Walker has been an inspiration for student athletes and community admirers. (Courtesy of Ralph Fitzgerald.)

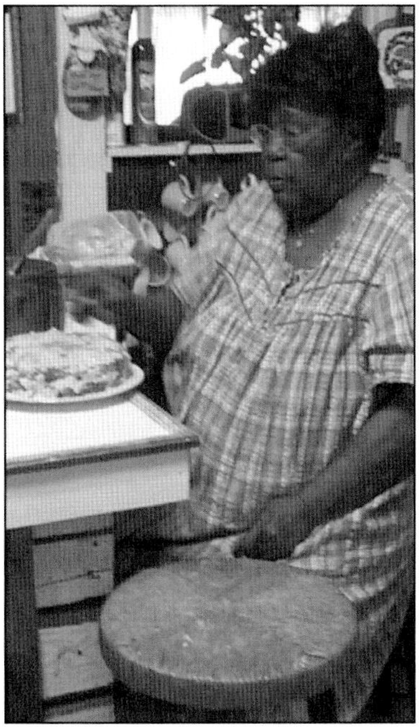

Eva Mae "Big Momma" Burks prepares Sunday dinner in Pine Bluff. Locals have been gravitating to her home for years after church, partaking in food and fellowship. Burks is known for her down-home specialties such as chitlins, black-eyed peas, sweet potatoes, collard greens, catfish, neckbones, butterbeans, hog head souse, macaroni and cheese, fried chicken, steamed cabbage, homemade rolls, oxtails, pound cake, peach cobbler, tea cakes, and other favorites. All her guests and family know that her "soul food" is just as good when it appears in the form of her endless wisdom and insights about life dispatched from her trademark recliner chair. (Courtesy of Jymmeka Moore.)

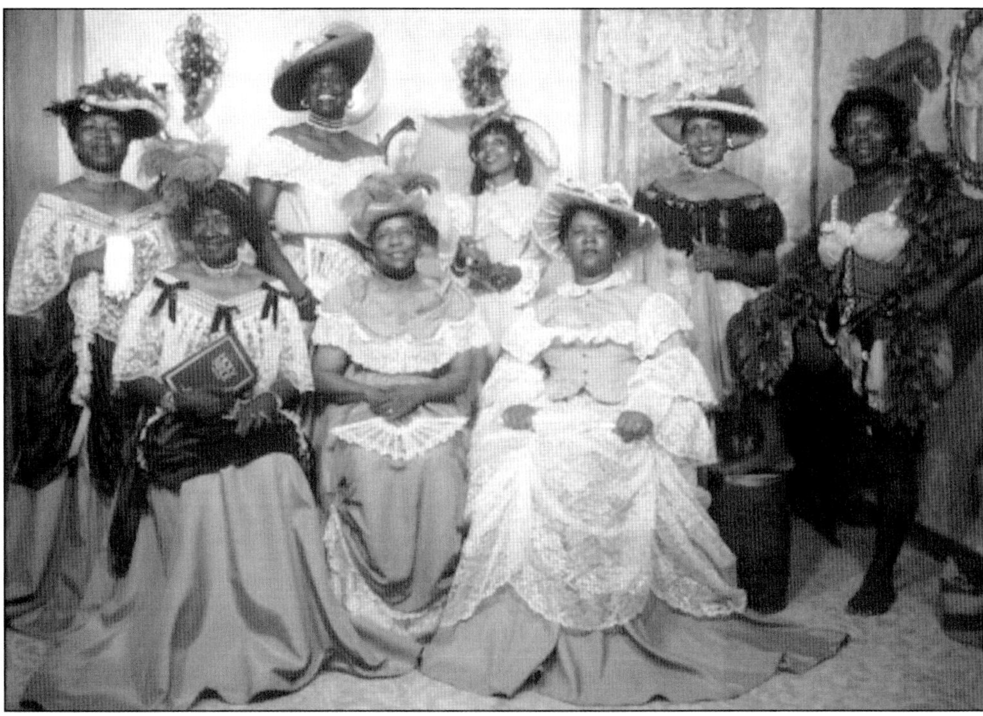

Flowers' power is evident here in the 1990s as some of the Flowers family women dress in vintage 19th-century attire along with friends. Flowers family members include Martha Flowers (first row, left), Dr. Martha Flowers (second row, second from left), Joyce Flowers (second row, third from left), and Mary Flowers (second row, fourth from left). The Flowers family of Pine Bluff enjoys a legacy of excellence in medicine, pharmacology, education, politics, law, and a variety of other fields. (Courtesy of John Flowers.)

Six

Race, Civil Rights, and Civic Leadership

I know I run out in the yard where there was eighty Yankee soldiers and I pulled out my shirt tail and ran down the road kickin' up the dust and sayin', "I'm free! I'm free!"

—Tom Haynes, former Pine Bluff slave
WPA Slave Narratives

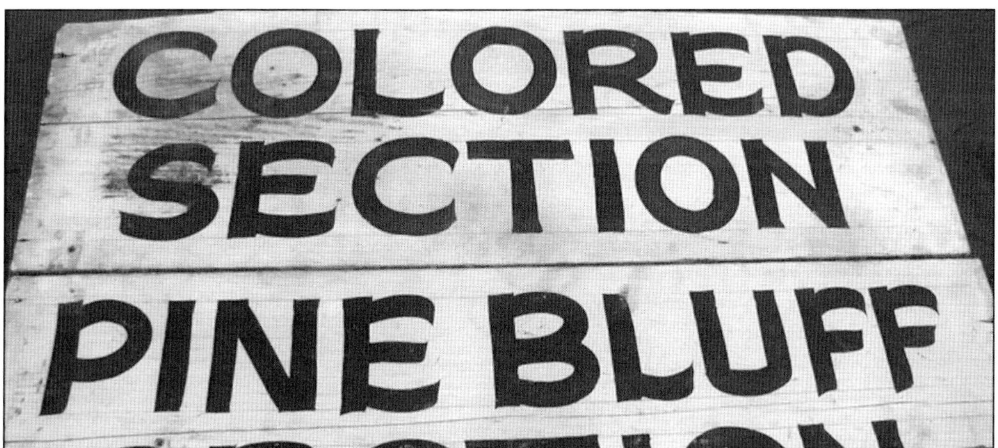

A Pine Bluff segregation era sign is pictured here. The practical effects of segregation for Sgt. Lester Simons meant being chased during 1940s Army training exercises near Pine Bluff by armed white farmers demanding his black unit stop marching on the "white" highway and move to a water-filled ditch with snakes. For Dora Caldwell, it meant being unable to touch handkerchiefs she wanted to buy while inside Newberry's Store. For jazz great Dizzy Gillespie, it meant having a white man smash a bottle across his head in Pine Bluff for refusing to play a request of "Darktown Strutter's Ball." For maid Vinella Byrd, it meant not being allowed to clean her hands in the same wash pot as the white Pine Bluff family for whom she worked. (Courtesy of Stonegate Antiques.)

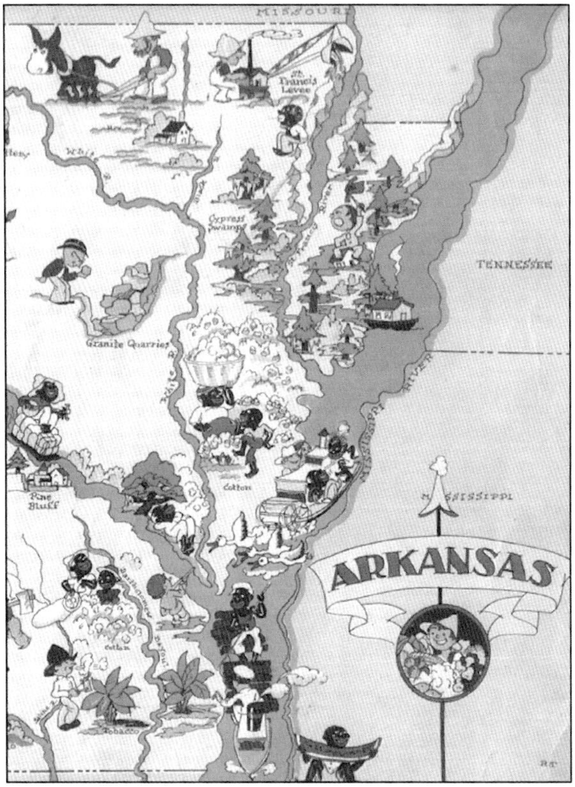

A 1935 map showing the Arkansas Delta, including Pine Bluff, is replete with racist caricatures. Stereotypes depicting a carefree, blissful world for African Americans in a section of the state with such extreme discrimination and hardship actually spoke volumes about efforts to sanitize the appearance of southern exploitation and justify social and economic paternalism. (Courtesy of Hearthstone Legacy Publications.)

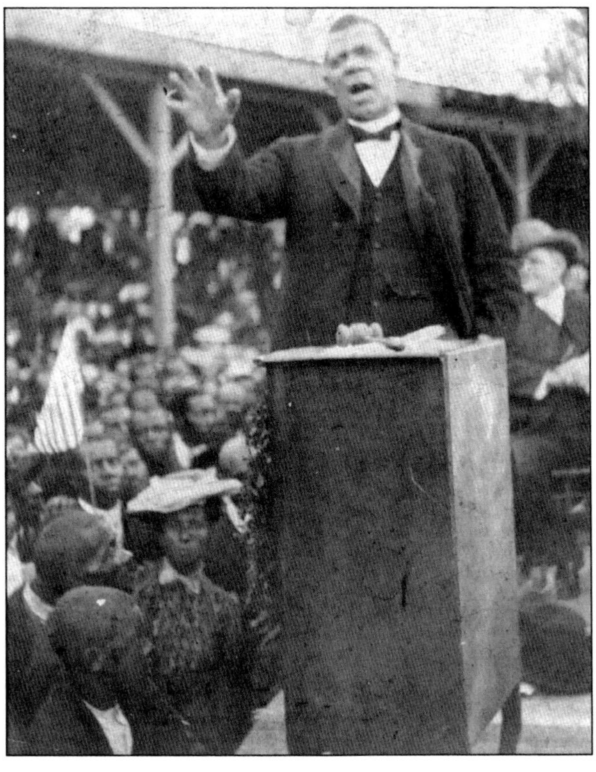

In this image, Booker T. Washington addresses Pine Bluff around 1905. In his book *The Negro In Business*, Washington states, "In the course of my journey through Arkansas and the Territories, I made the acquaintance of no [black] community where it seemed to me to have more real . . . progress than that of Pine Bluff." (Courtesy of Library of Congress.)

George Edmund Haynes, a native of Pine Bluff, was the cofounder of the National Urban League with Ruth Standish Baldwin in 1910. He also became its first executive chief, serving from 1910 to 1917. Haynes was a graduate of Fisk University who also became the first African American to earn a PhD in economics from Columbia University. Pres. Woodrow Wilson appointed Haynes director of Negro economics in 1918. (Courtesy of National Association of Social Workers.)

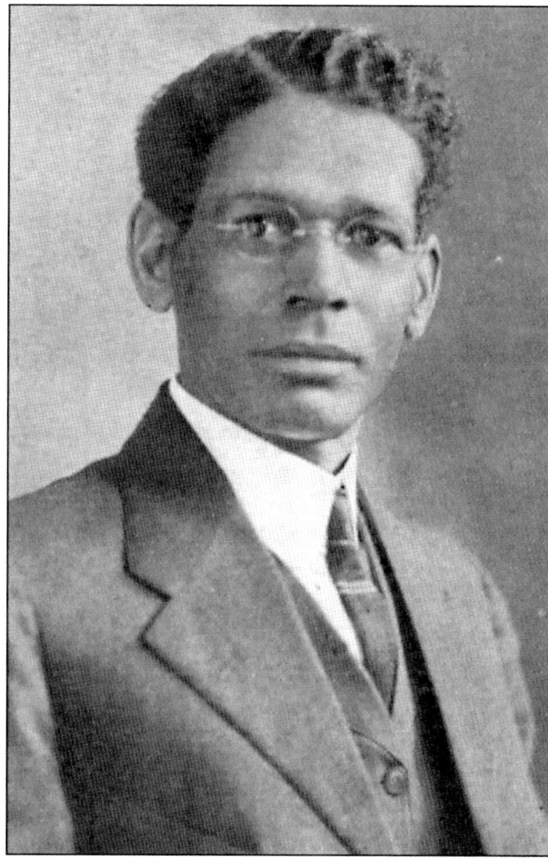

The Ku Klux Klan (KKK) marches down Pine Bluff's Fourth Street in 1922 in front of the African American–owned Masonic Temple. From the period following the Civil War through the 20th century, the Klan maintained varying levels of activity in Jefferson County. (Courtesy of Rick Joslin.)

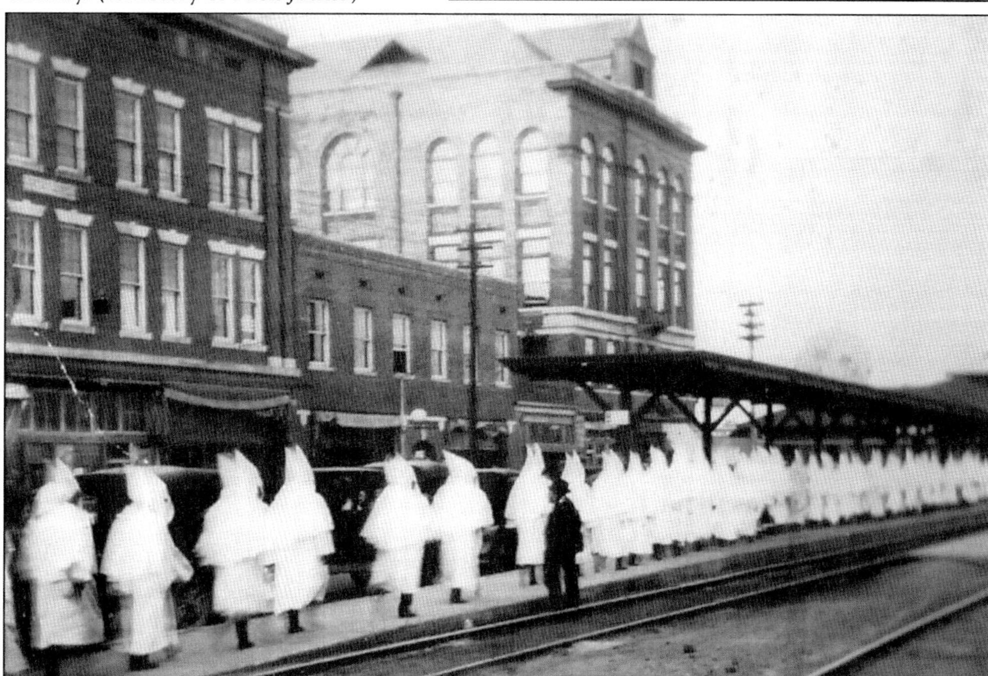

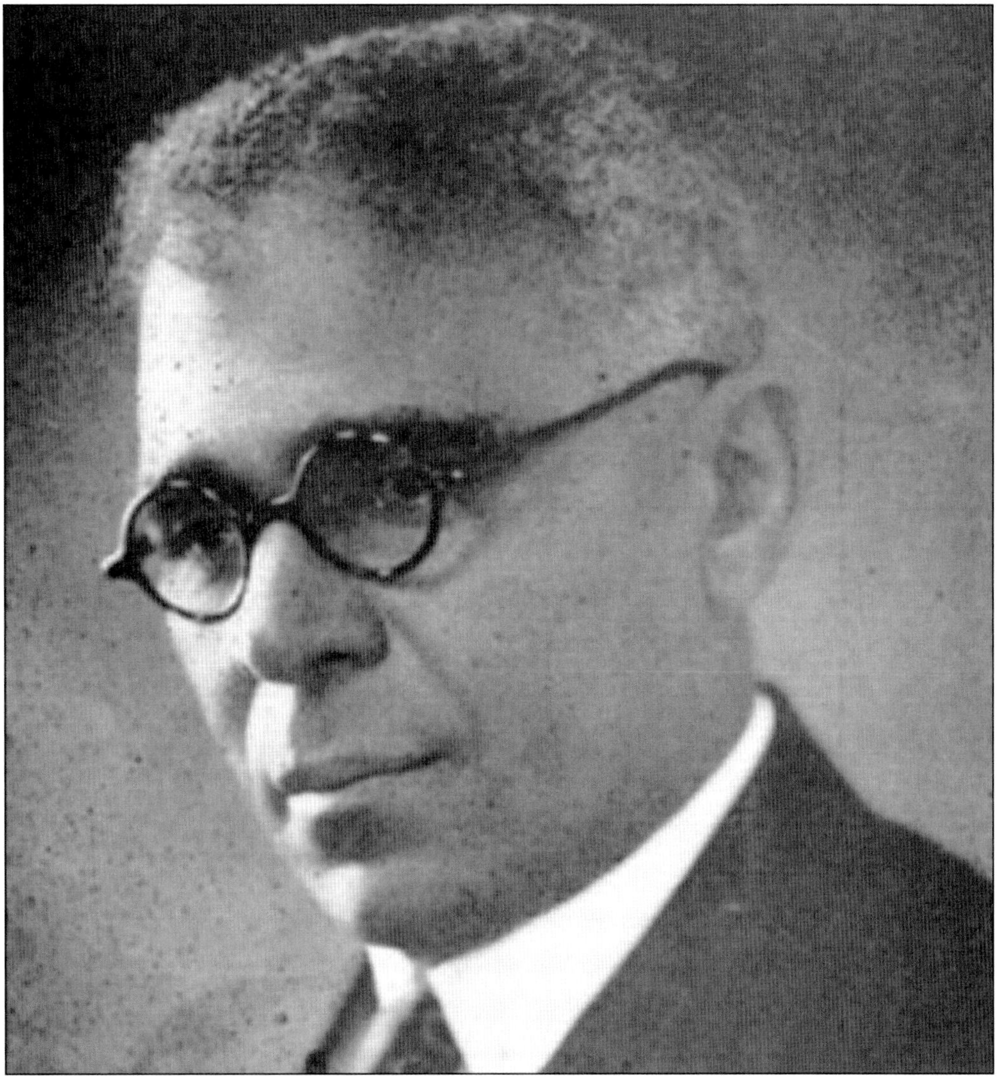

John Brown Watson was the president of Arkansas AM&N College from 1928 to 1940. During his tenure, the school was accredited and built a new campus. However, Watson was also a symbol of resistance and black pride. He is said to have armed his staff with pistols in a confrontation with the KKK, who wanted to shut down the college's water source. When a black youth was charged with assault after defending himself in a confrontation with a white salesman at the Henry Marx store who had called him a racial epithet and punched him, Watson threatened to fire any college employee who patronized the store and expel any student caught doing business there. Black community members in Pine Bluff immediately launched a boycott of the store following his actions. Additionally, Watson would not allow white state officials to visit the campus or call his staff by their first names. On one occasion, he physically ejected one such official from Caldwell Hall. He was often scorned by whites who mistook his boldness for arrogance, as reflected in a 1931 letter sent to him anonymously by "The Committee," which reads in part, "I understand that you and some more Negroes out there have been writing letters to them [white officials at the Pine Bluff telephone company office] to call you 'Mr.' and 'Mrs.' If you don't want a rope around your neck you had better stay in a negroe's place. Do you understand?" (Courtesy of Arkansas History Commission.)

Hattie Rutherford Watson (right), wife of Arkansas AM&N's president John Brown Watson, stands with her friend Mary McLeod Bethune, educator and former director of the Division of Negro Affairs of the National Youth Administration (NYA). In 1936, Hattie Watson became one of only five NYA administrators around the country. Her Pine Bluff camp enrolled 120 young black women and engaged them in academic and vocational training. (Courtesy of Special Collections Department, University of Arkansas Libraries.)

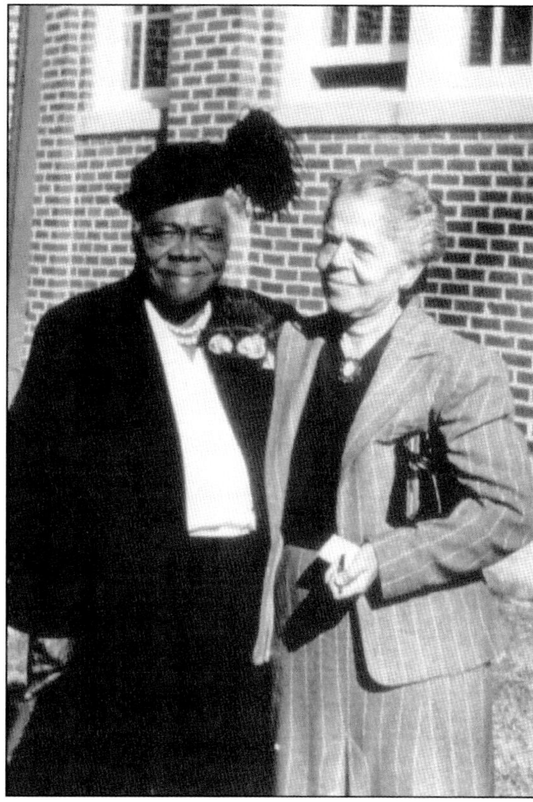

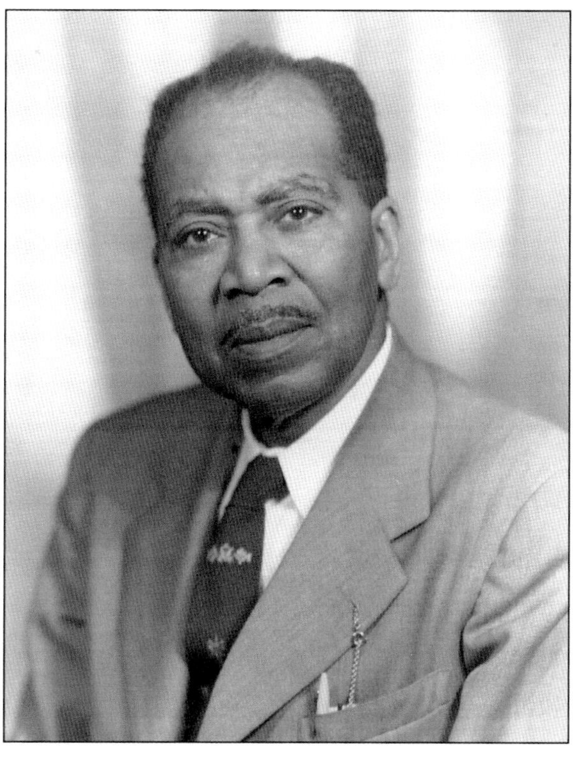

William Sherrill of Altheimer was chosen in 1922 by famed black nationalist leader Marcus Garvey as vice president of the Universal Negro Improvement Association (UNIA). The UNIA was the largest black grassroots organization in US history, with an estimated two million members. Sherill oversaw the administrative functions while Garvey provided the charismatic leadership. Sherrill later became UNIA president. (Courtesy of Universal Negro Improvement Association Records, Manuscript, Archives and Rare Books Library, Emory University.)

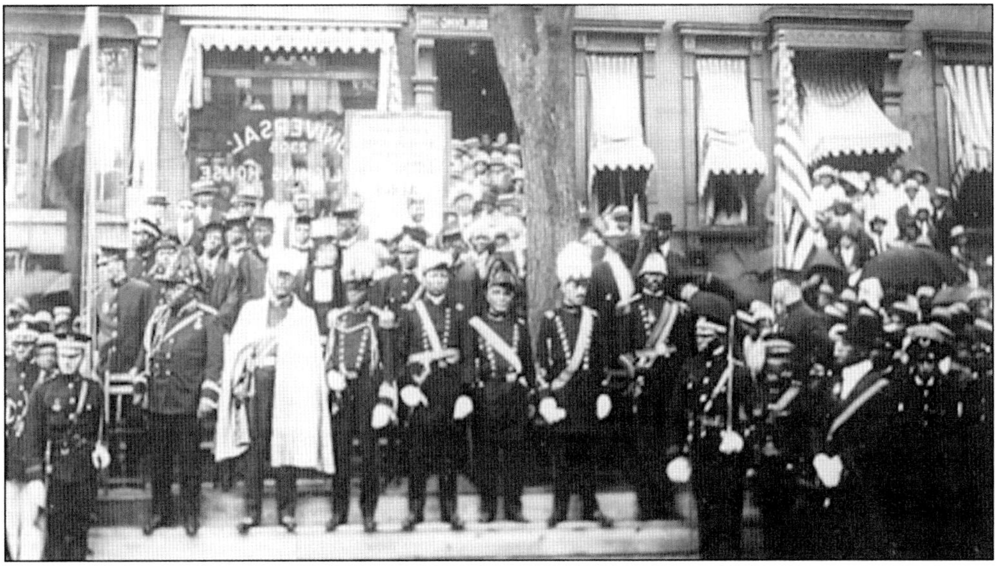

Marcus Garvey (first step, far left) stands in Harlem, New York, with the UNIA leadership in 1922. Altheimer's William Sherrill is assumed to be in this picture as he was elected to the vice presidency at this convention. According to the *Encyclopedia of Arkansas History and Culture*, Jefferson County had three UNIA chapters during the 1920s. (Courtesy of the Marcus Garvey Project and UNIA Papers Project, University of California at Los Angeles.)

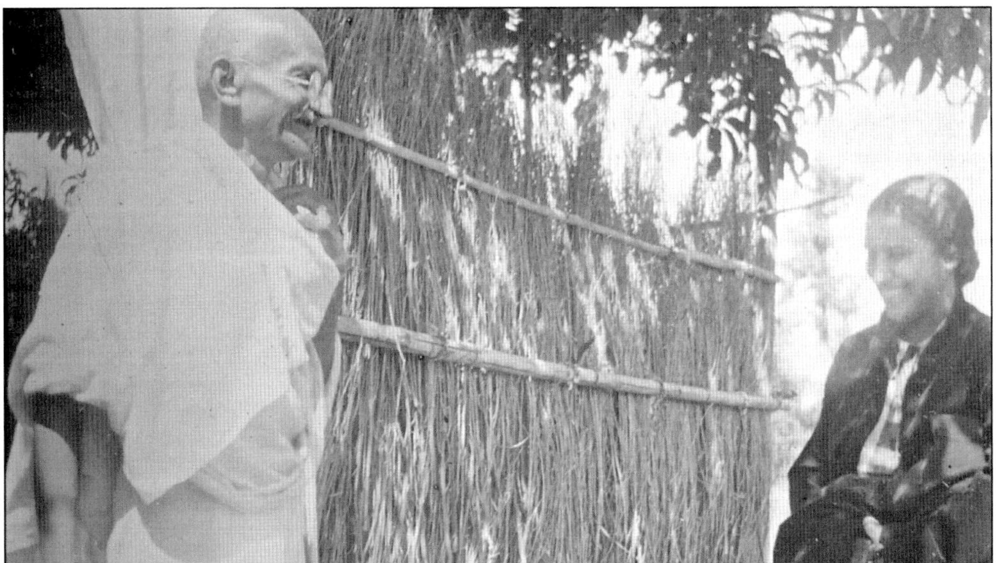

Sue Bailey Thurman (right), a native of Pine Bluff, was a civil rights activist, historian, editor, lecturer, and author. Shown here in 1936, she and her renowned husband, theologian Dr. Howard Thurman, were the first African Americans to meet with Indian leader Mahatma Ghandi (left). She cofounded the nation's first interracial nondenominational church and founded the Museum of Afro American History in Boston. Thurman also worked closely with leader and educator Mary McLeod Bethune as the first editor of the National Council of Negro Women's *Afro American Women's Journal*. (Courtesy of Bailey and Thurman Families Papers, Manuscript, Archives and Rare Books Library, Emory University.)

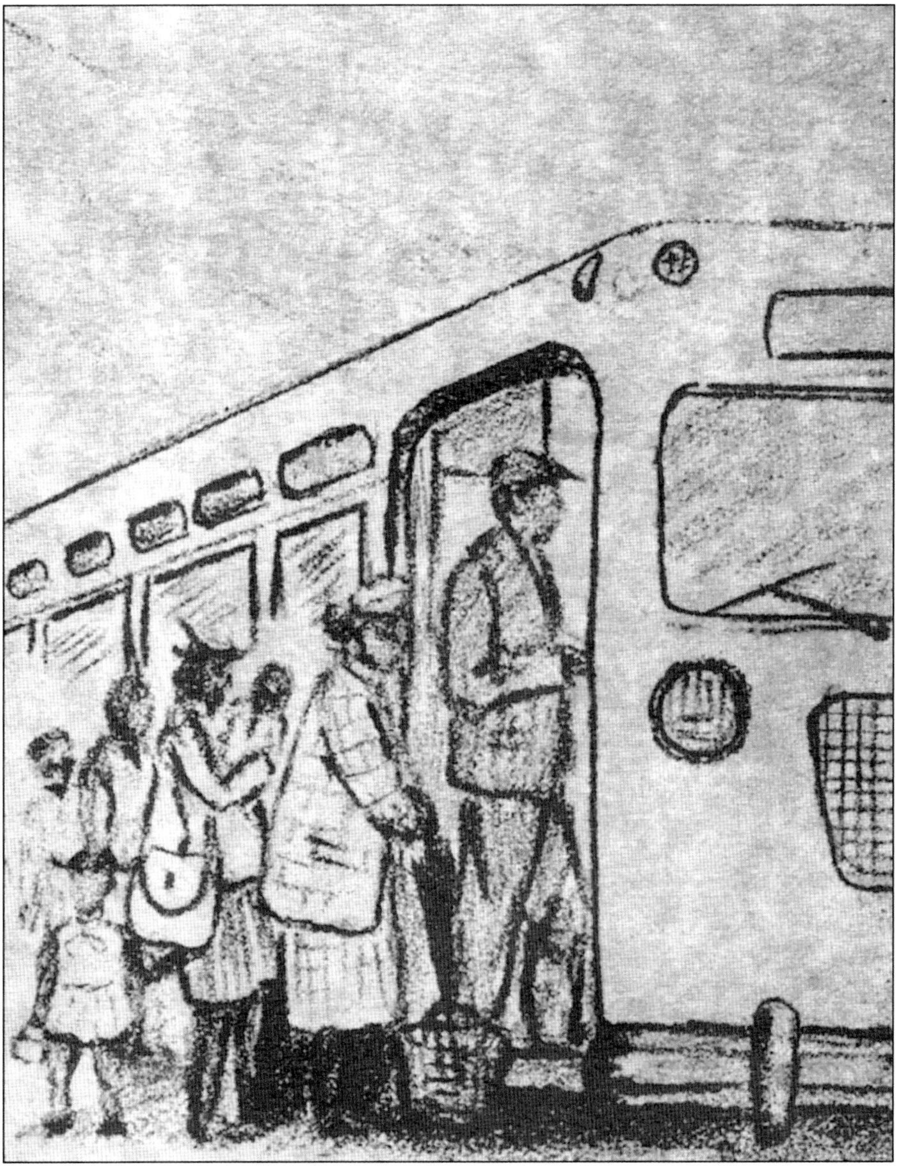

A full decade before Rosa Parks refused to sit in the back of a Montgomery, Alabama bus in 1955, Pine Bluff had already seen at least two similar refusals by defiant African Americans, making the city one of the earliest places in the South to have defied segregation in public transportation. In March 1944, according to the *Arkansas State Press*, a young black World War II soldier who had been handicapped in battle entered a Missouri-Pacific bus headed from Pine Bluff to Little Rock. He took a seat at the front of the bus because the Jim Crow section reserved for blacks was full. The bus driver subsequently stated at the next stop, "Get up n*gger and let that white woman sit down." The young soldier refused, and a white passenger punched him, leading to a fight. Black bus passengers immediately protested his treatment. The incident made news throughout the city. Later in 1946, mail carrier Zack Potts refused to go to the back of a Pine Bluff city bus, instead opting to ride to work in the white section. Consequently, he was badly beaten by police and charged a $25 fine, according to Nan Woodruff in *American Congo: The African American Freedom Struggle in the Delta*. (Courtesy of Poetic Portraits.)

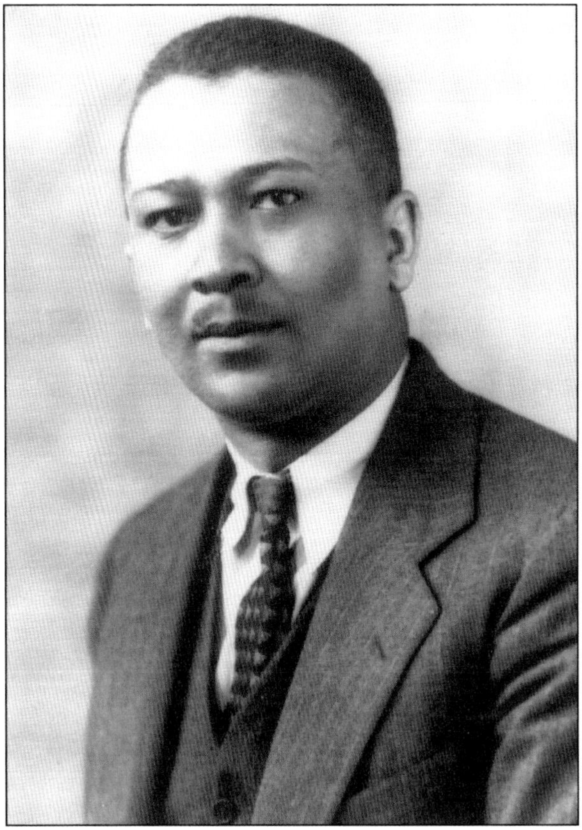

Francis Cecil Sumner, a native of Pine Bluff known as the "Father of Black Psychology," was the first African American in the nation to earn a doctorate in psychology. Sumner conducted extensive research on racial equality issues. He established and chaired Howard University's psychology department, training a cadre of socially conscious psychologists including Drs. Kenneth and Mamie Clark, sister of former UAPB registrar Della Phipps. (Courtesy of Archives of the History of American Psychology, The Center for the History of Psychology, The University of Akron.)

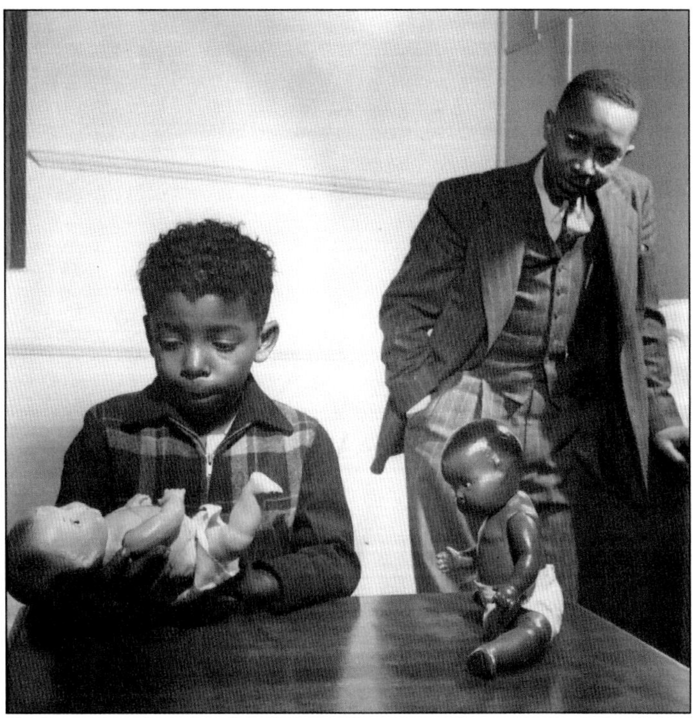

Famed psychologist Dr. Kenneth Clark conducts his famous doll research in 1947 among black children. In one study, he and his wife, Dr. Mamie Clark, administered tests to 134 Pine Bluff children, comparing results with those of 119 Springfield, Massachusetts, youth. This key study, along with others, helped form his thesis about the negative effects of segregation, which he presented in 1954 before the US Supreme Court in *Brown v. Board of Education.* (Courtesy the Gordon Parks Foundation, Photograph by Gordon Parks.)

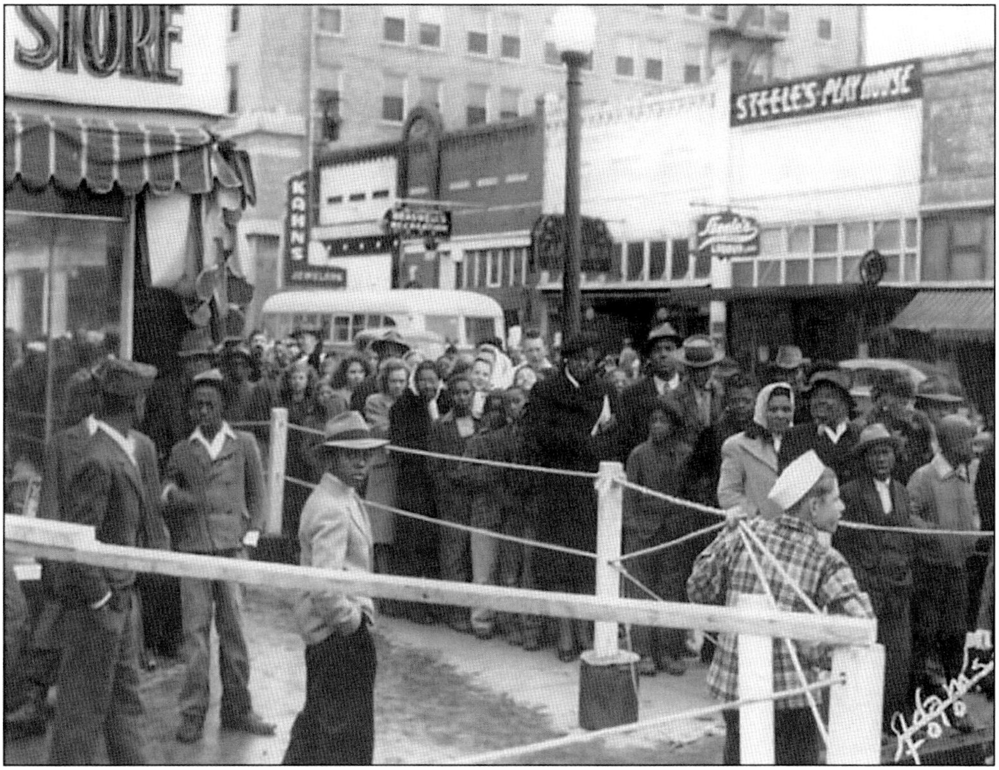

Anxious citizens wait their turn in an integrated Pine Bluff line to view the Freedom Train in 1948. The Freedom Train traveled throughout the United States from 1947 to 1949, showcasing artifacts related to liberty following World War II. The event's sponsoring organization would not allow trips to cities with segregated lines. Hence, in scheduling the train's Pine Bluff stop, public segregation was briefly abandoned, though some whites boycotted the event. (Courtesy of National Archives and Records Administration.)

In 1948, Silas Hunt (seated), a graduate of Arkansas AM&N, enrolled at the University of Arkansas at Fayetteville School of Law, becoming the first African American to do so at a Southern university since Reconstruction. He is shown accompanied by Wiley Branton Sr. (left) and Attorney Harold Flowers. Hunt was part of an elite group called the "Pioneer Six," the first enrolled students of the University of Arkansas School of Law. Of these six, four came from Pine Bluff: George Haley, Chris Mercer, George Howard Jr., and Wiley Branton Sr. They all graduated except Hunt, who died before he could complete his studies. (Courtesy of Special Collections Department, University of Arkansas Libraries.)

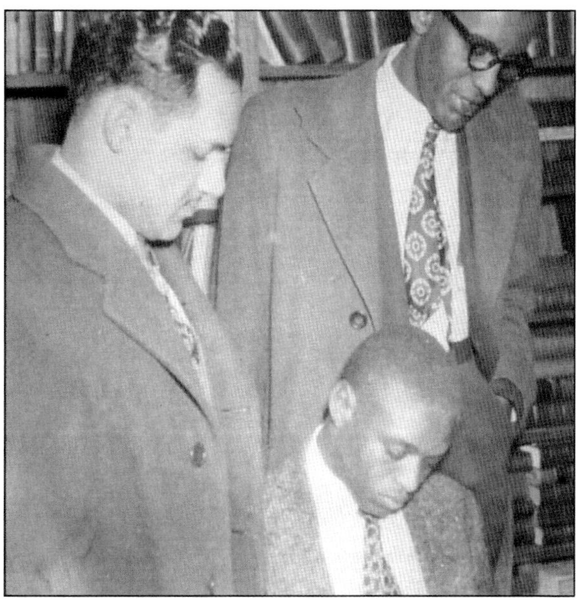

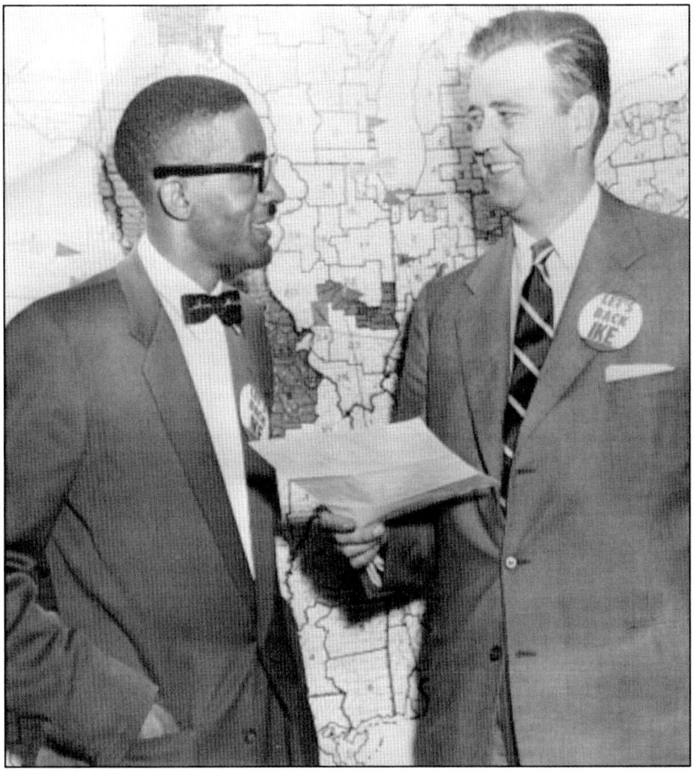

Harold Flowers (left), the longtime Pine Bluff attorney from Stamps, Arkansas, known in the state as the "Dean of Black Lawyers," led the court fight to integrate south Arkansas schools in the 1930s and 1940s and organized dramatic black voter registration drives in the 1940s. Flowers also won a landmark case in 1947, marking the first time a black man had not been sentenced to death for killing a white man in Arkansas. He served as a Gov. Bill Clinton appointee on the Arkansas Court of Appeals in 1980, and championed civil rights causes his entire life. (Courtesy of John Flowers.)

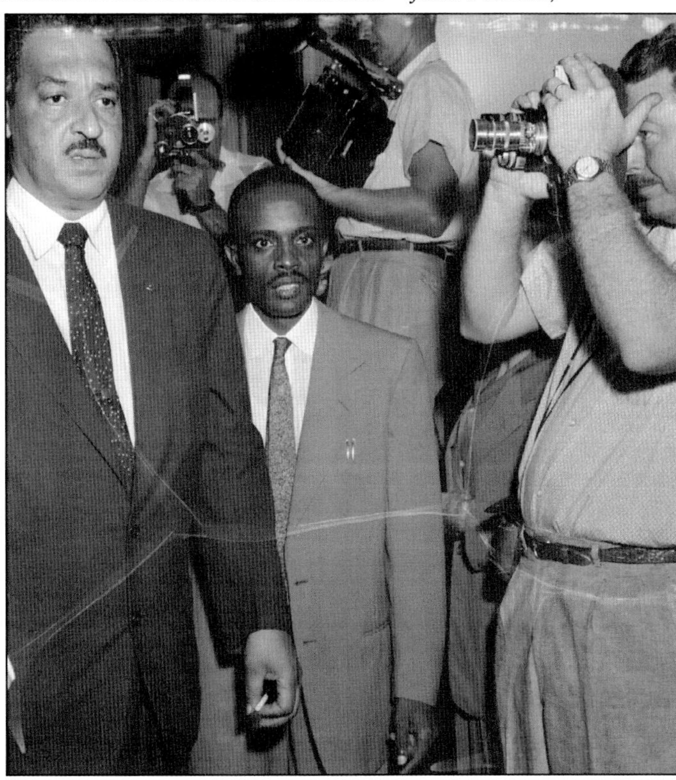

Pine Bluff native and civil rights advocate George Howard Jr. (center) stands next to chief counsel for the NAACP Thurgood Marshall at a Little Rock hearing regarding the integration of Central High School in 1957. Howard served as the president of the Pine Bluff and Arkansas chapters of the NAACP. In 1977, Howard became the first African American to serve on the Arkansas Supreme Court. In 1980, he was appointed by Pres. Jimmy Carter as the first black federal district judge in Arkansas. (Courtesy of Bettman Corbis/AP Images.)

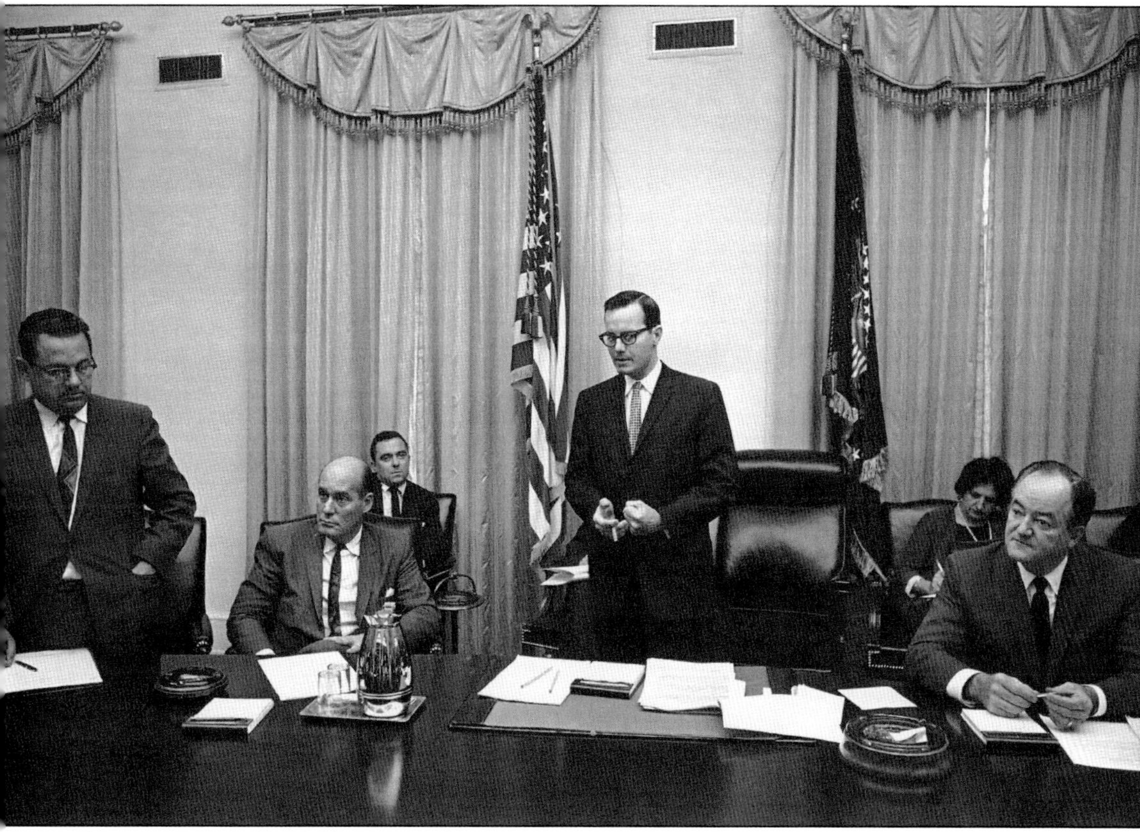

Wiley Branton Sr. (far left), a Pine Bluff native, is introduced to reporters as a member of the Justice Department while Vice Pres. Hubert Humphrey (far right) watches in 1965. Branton was one of the first black law graduates from the University of Arkansas. He served as co-counsel for the Little Rock Nine during the Central High School crisis of 1957 and successfully argued the landmark *Cooper v. Aaron* case before the US Supreme Court. He defended Freedom Riders and civil rights workers in Arkansas and Mississippi, even as he had to engage armed guards for his Pine Bluff home after a cross burning and numerous death threats. He was recommended by Dr. Martin Luther King Jr. and other civil rights leaders to Pres. Lyndon Johnson to head the Voter Education Project in 1962, where he registered 700,000 black voters, transforming the Southern political landscape forever. He served in several other capacities heading civil rights efforts within the federal government before becoming dean of the Howard University School of Law. (Courtesy of AP Images.)

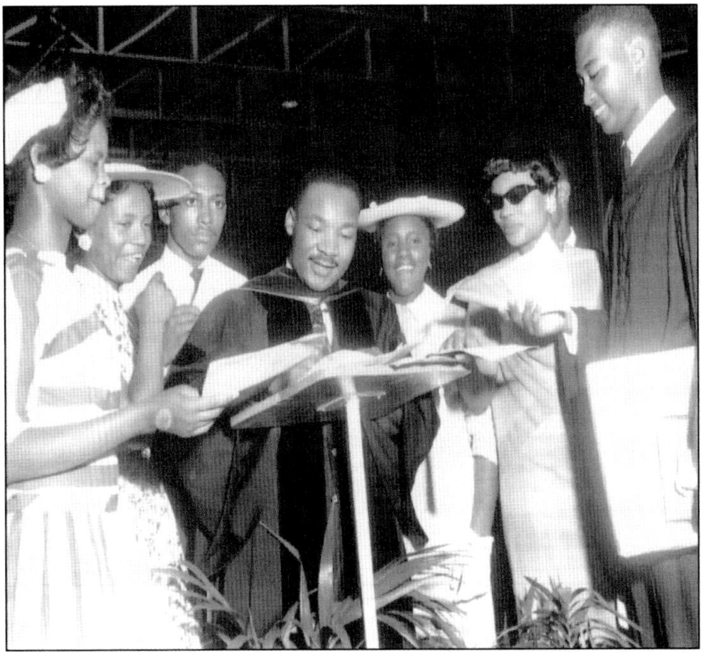

In 1958, Dr. Martin Luther King Jr. delivered the commencement address at Arkansas AM&N College. While his passionate charge to "revolt against segregation" was greeted with enthusiasm by the audience, the president of the college, Dr. Lawrence Davis Sr., was excoriated for inviting King by Arkansas legislators who angrily cut the school's annual appropriation by $50,000 for several years. (Courtesy of Special Collections Department, University of Arkansas Libraries.)

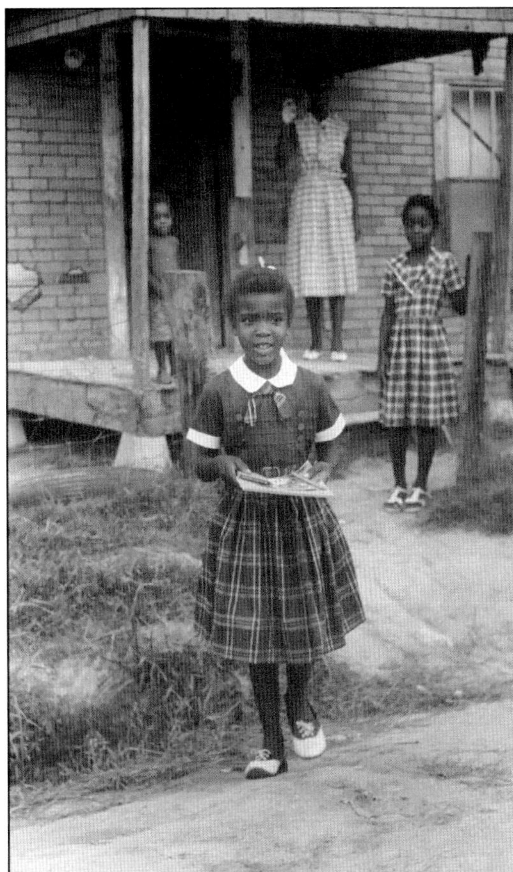

Six-year-old Dolores Jean York is pictured here in 1960 as she prepares to integrate the public schools of Pine Bluff. Both *Ebony* and *Life* magazines covered this because of 1959's massive show of resistance in Pine Bluff to court-ordered integration, which consisted of angry white pro-segregation crowds of over 1,000 at a rally, a hanging effigy of a black child on a tree at school, and attacks against reporters. Nonetheless, by August 1960, York entered Dollarway Elementary School without incident. (Francis Miller photograph, courtesy of Time Life Pictures/ Getty Images.)

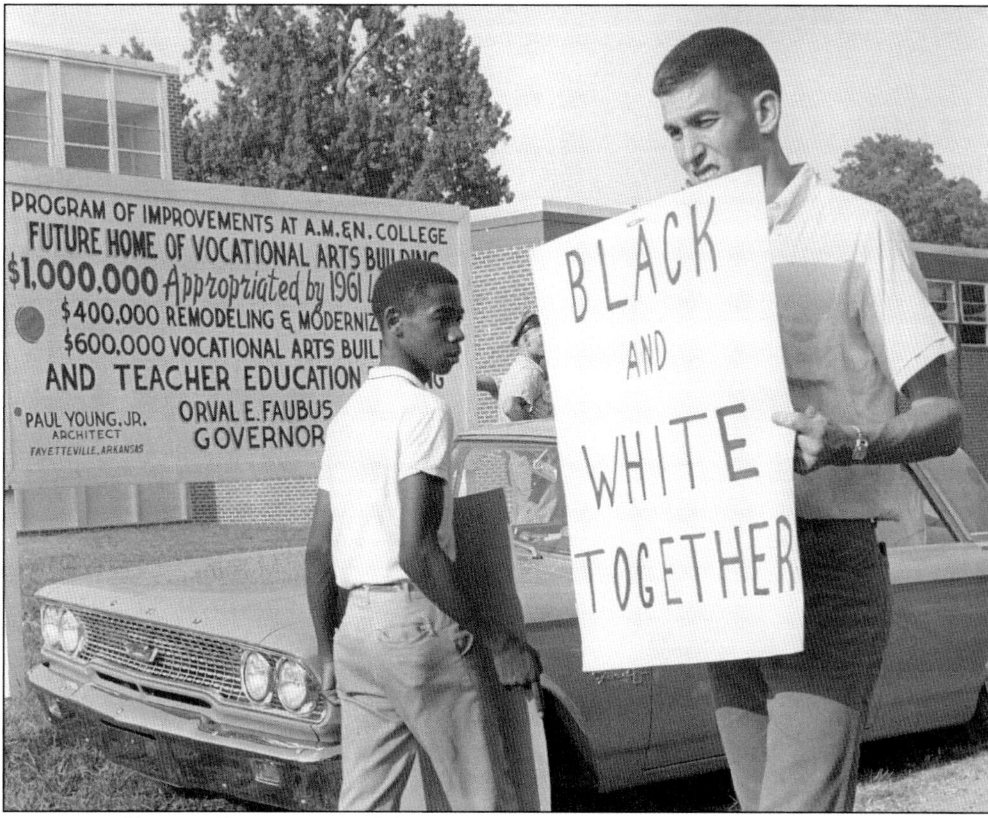

In 1962, William "Bill" Hansen (right), an Ohio native, demonstrates as a field secretary for the Student Nonviolent Coordinating Committee (SNCC) in Pine Bluff. Hansen was one of the first white professionally employed civil rights activists in the nation, as noted in *Black and White in American Culture: An Anthology*. He was jailed several times in Pine Bluff, endured death threats, and was severely beaten at Woolworth's, according to *Arsnick: The Student Nonviolent Coordinating Committee in Arkansas*. (Courtesy of Special Collections Department, University of Arkansas Libraries.)

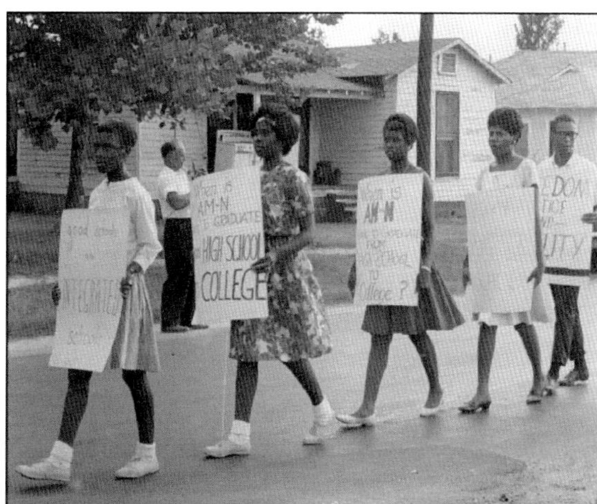

These largely female participants in a 1962 civil rights protest in Pine Bluff march with resolve. Women were critical to the movement, as Arkansas AM&N students like Joanna Edwards and Ruthie Buffington engaged in the first Pine Bluff sit-ins and were eventually expelled with others. Vivian Jones, a high school student, was arrested and jailed in five different protests, expelled from school, and faced vicious police dog attacks with other protesters trying to integrate a McDonald's restaurant. (Courtesy of Special Collections Department, University of Arkansas Libraries.)

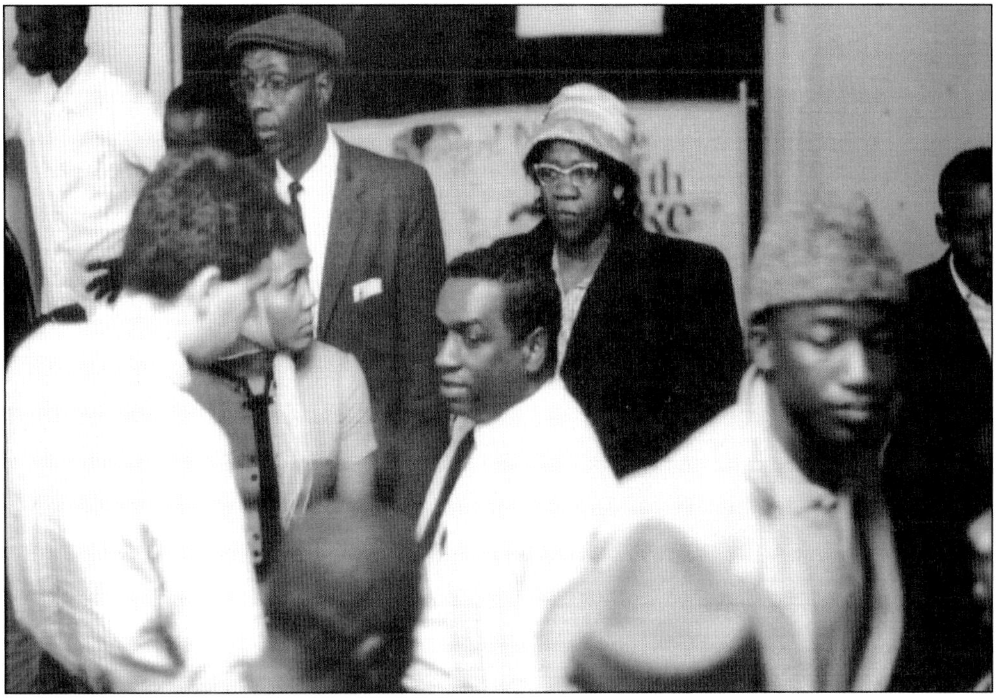

Rev. Ben Grinage (center), Arkansas director of SNCC, talks to Bill Hansen (far left) and Joanna Edwards (between Hansen and Grinage) at a 1960s civil rights–related court proceeding in Pine Bluff. Grinage, along with other demonstrators, was jailed for trying to integrate Pine Bluff businesses such as the Hotel Pines, Saengar Theater, and Woolworth's. During a picket, he was shot at by the white owner of Ray's Barbeque, a restaurant that long resisted integration. (Courtesy of Pine Bluff/Jefferson County Historical Museum.)

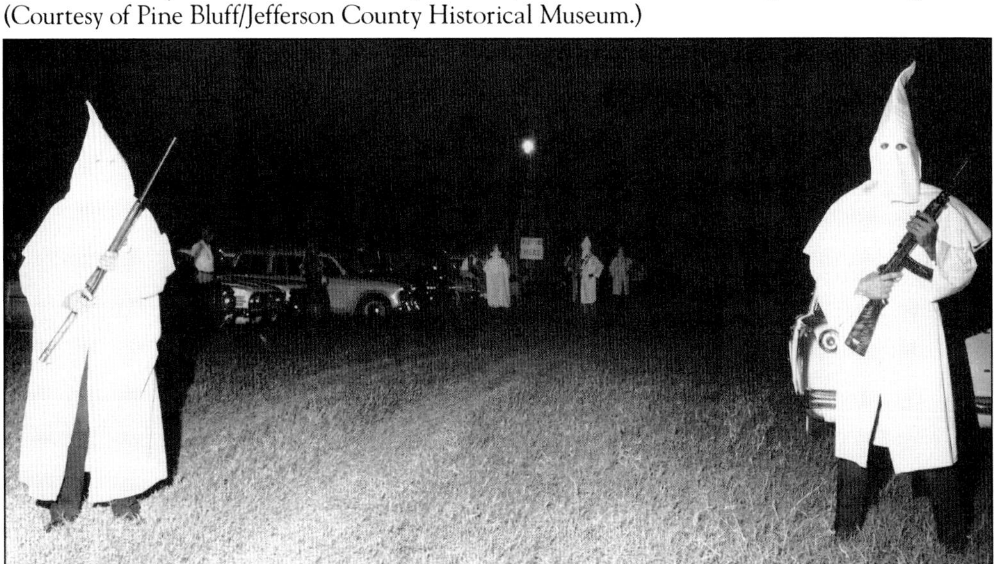

At the height of the civil rights movement in 1965, two armed KKK members guard the entrance of a field as about 250 members and spectators assemble in Jefferson County. Civil rights activists of the area maintained an ever-watchful eye during this period as they were subject to the real possibility of violence by racist elements. (Courtesy of Associated Press.)

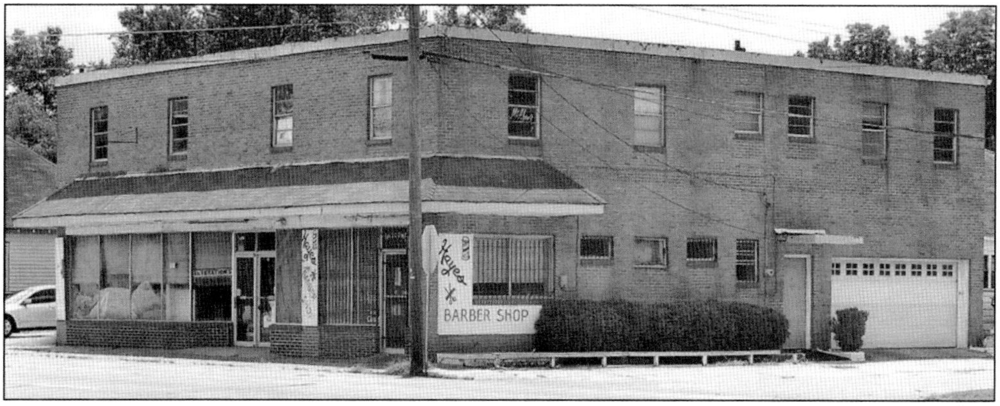

The second floor of the Williams building, built in 1960, served as the Pine Bluff field office for SNCC workers organizing civil rights efforts primarily in Jefferson County, but also in other Arkansas Delta locales. It was frequented by comedian/activist Dick Gregory, SNCC national chairman Stokely Carmichael, and legal pioneer Wiley Branton Sr., among others. Pine Bluff civil rights efforts were supported by many in the black community and some white local businesses and individuals who chose to contribute funds secretly. (Courtesy of Lewis Delavan.)

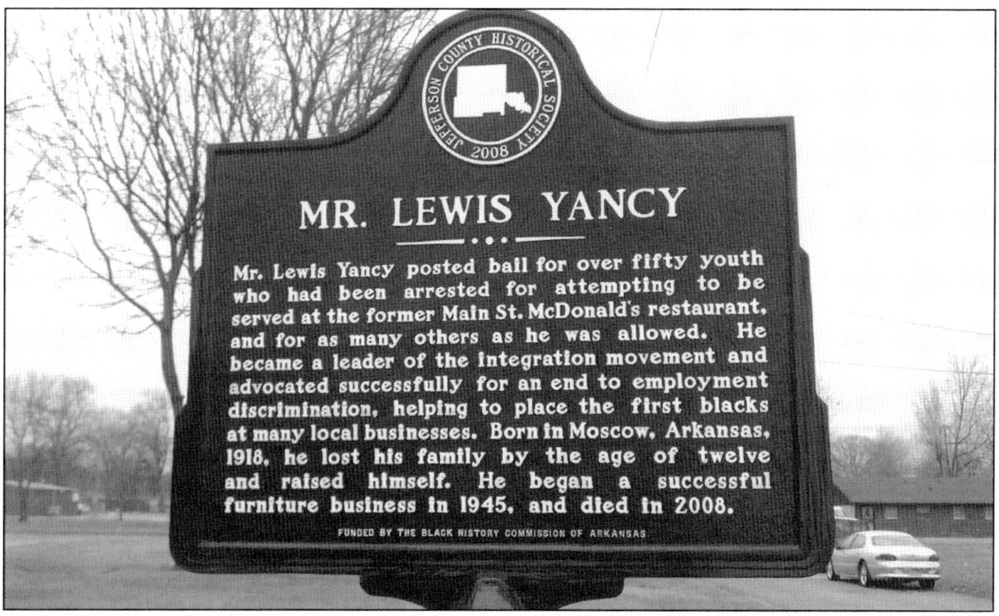

The Lewis Yancy marker is shown in the same vicinity as the Freedom House Marker. It should be noted that Yancy was often accompanied in his trips to visit jailed civil rights protesters by dedicated leaders like H.O. Gray, who not only helped bail them out, but also provided critical emotional support to them and their families. (Courtesy of Jimmy Cunningham Jr.)

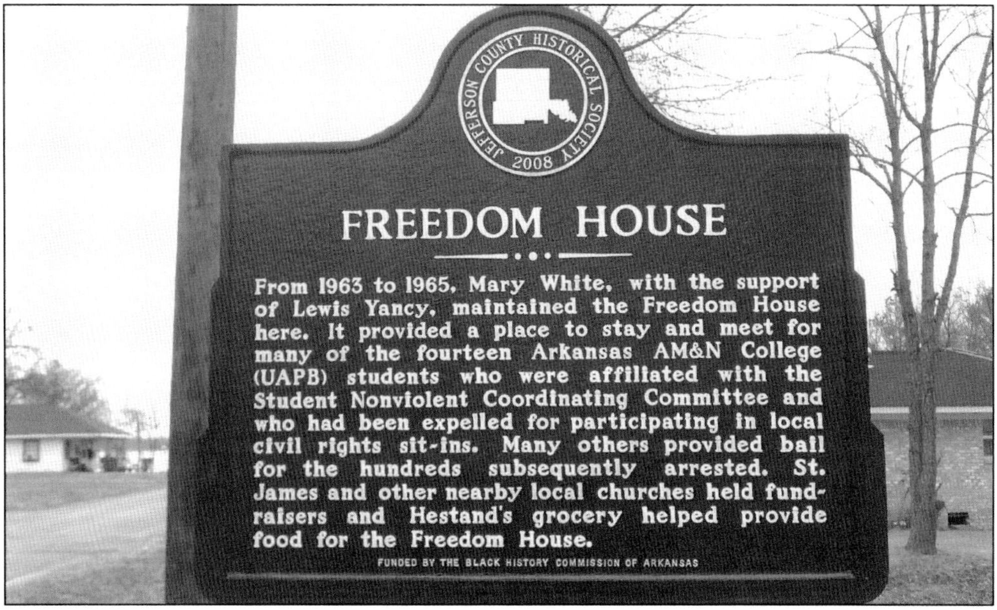

The Freedom House marker stands near Lake Saracen. (Courtesy of Jimmy Cunningham Jr.)

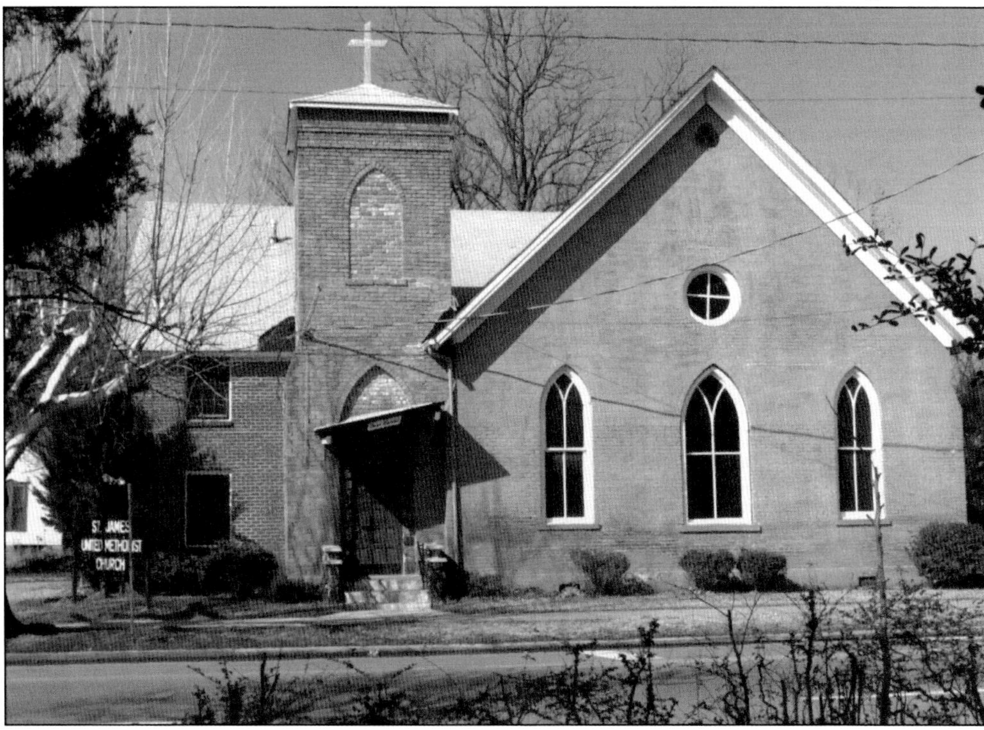

St. James United Methodist Church was one of several churches that held rallies and served as a gathering point for students during the civil rights movement in Pine Bluff. In 1963, racists set off incendiary bombs there, blowing up windows and setting fire to the building, according to Grif Stockley's *Ruled by Race: Relations in Arkansas from Slavery to the Present*. Fortunately, no one was injured, though the danger of participation in the movement was underscored. (Courtesy of Butler Center for Arkansas Studies.)

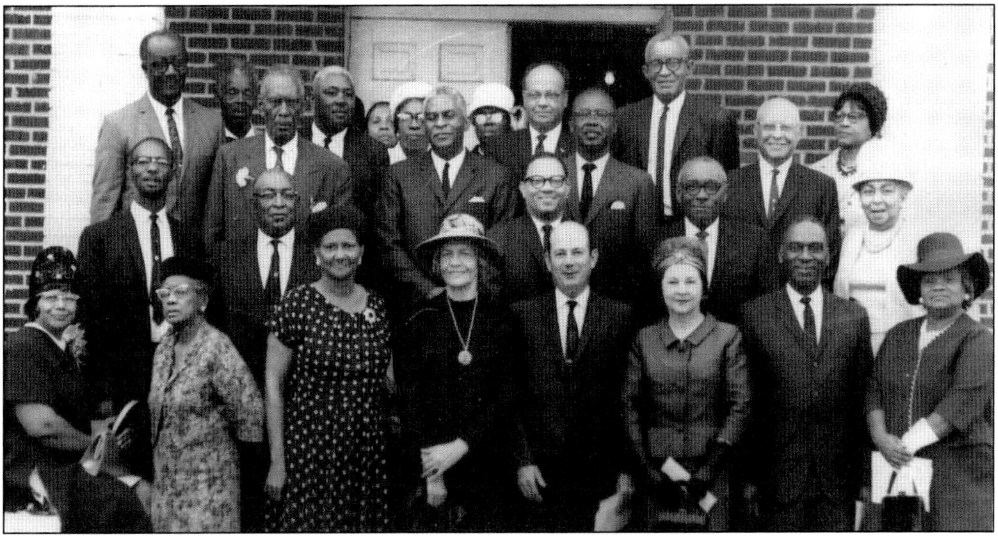

Some of Pine Bluff's most esteemed African American civic leaders meet in the 1960s at a church. With people gathered like William Dove Sr. (second row, second from left), local NAACP chapter president and civil rights champion; U.S. Brown Sr. (second row, left), owner of Brown Funeral Home and successful entrepreneur; Edna Mays (first row, right), tireless youth advocate and community organizer; along with other local luminaries, much was assured to be accomplished here. (Courtesy of Myrtus Henry.)

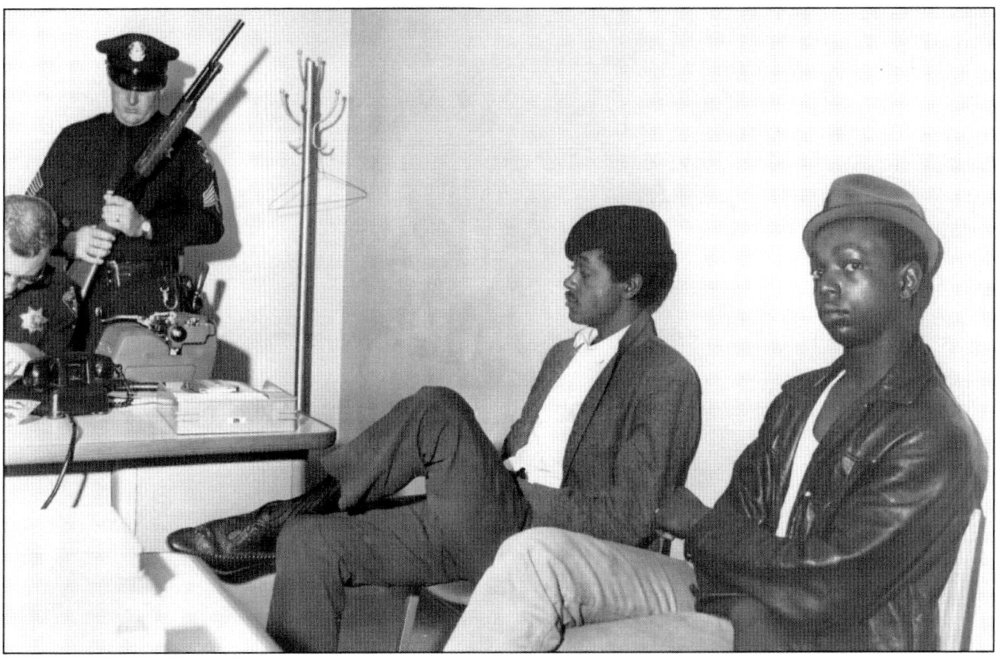

Black Panthers Bobby Hutton (far right, Pine Bluff native), and Bobby Seale (center) are detained by Oakland, California, police in 1967. Hutton lived in an area of Pine Bluff known by locals as "Pot Liquor" until 1953, when his family was visited by racist nightriders. As a result, they decided to move to Oakland. Hutton was the first recruit of the Black Panther Party and the first Panther in the nation to be gunned down in a 1968 police confrontation. His name became a rallying cry against police brutality after his death. (Courtesy of Ron Riesterer.)

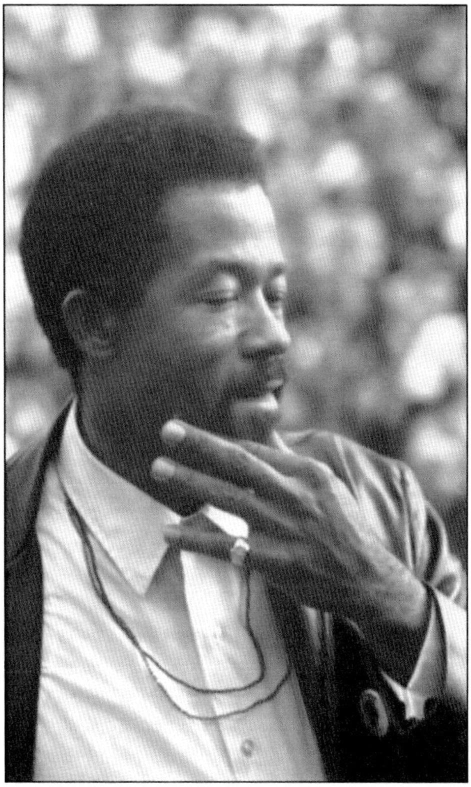

Eldridge Cleaver, a Black Panther Party minister of information and best-selling author of *Soul on Ice,* was born in Wabbaseka. A major figure in the Black Power Movement, Cleaver was a presidential candidate in 1968. He was shot that year along with Bobby Hutton during a police confrontation. Advocating black power, he was one of America's most sought-after speakers during the late 1960s. (Courtesy of Marion S. Triksko.)

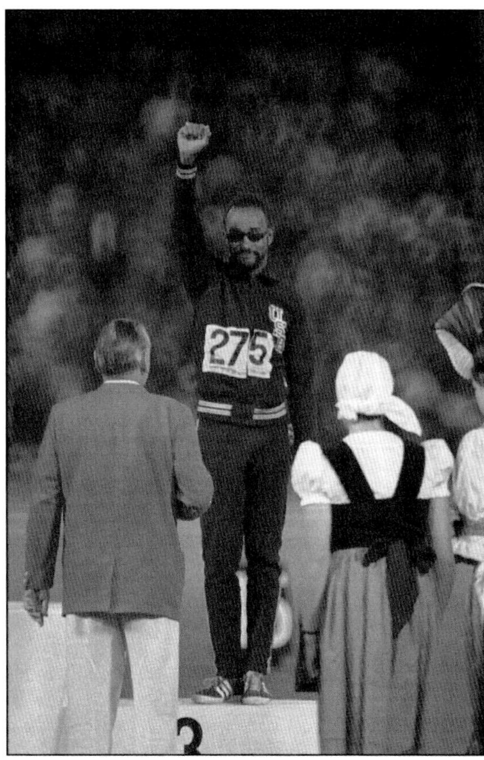

Olympian Charlie Greene, a native of Pine Bluff, raises his fist in a Black Power salute while receiving a medal at the 1968 Olympics. He was a member of the Olympic Project for Human Rights, an organization of black athletes that threatened an Olympic boycott that year. Greene won a gold medal as a member of the 400-meter relay team and a bronze medal in the 100-meter during the 1968 Olympics. He also shared the 100-meter world record in 1968 with renowned sprinter Jim Hines. (Courtesy Magnum Photos/ Raymond Depardon.)

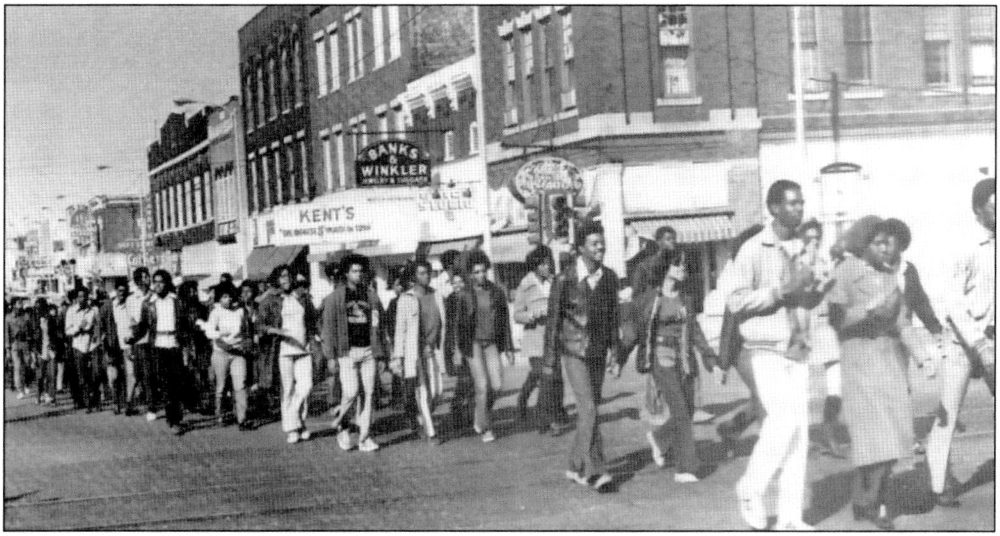

Students of Arkansas AM&N College in 1972 march through downtown Pine Bluff, protesting a proposed merger with the University of Arkansas system. Concerns centered on whether the college would lose its unique identity and mission as a Historically Black College/University because of the merger. (Courtesy of UAPB Archives.)

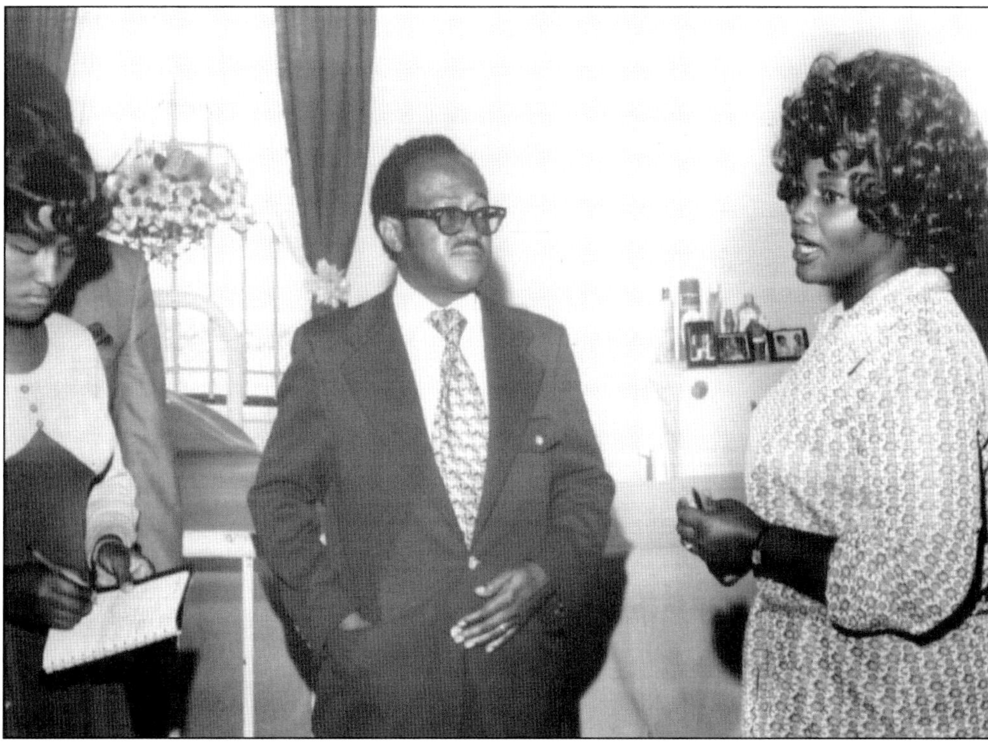

Henry Wilkins III (center) of Pine Bluff became part of an elite group of three legislators in 1972 who were elected as the first African American members of the Arkansas legislature since Reconstruction. Wilkins had many legislative accomplishments, including sponsoring legislation honoring Dr. Martin Luther King Jr.'s birthday as a state holiday. (Courtesy of Special Collections Department, University of Arkansas Libraries.)

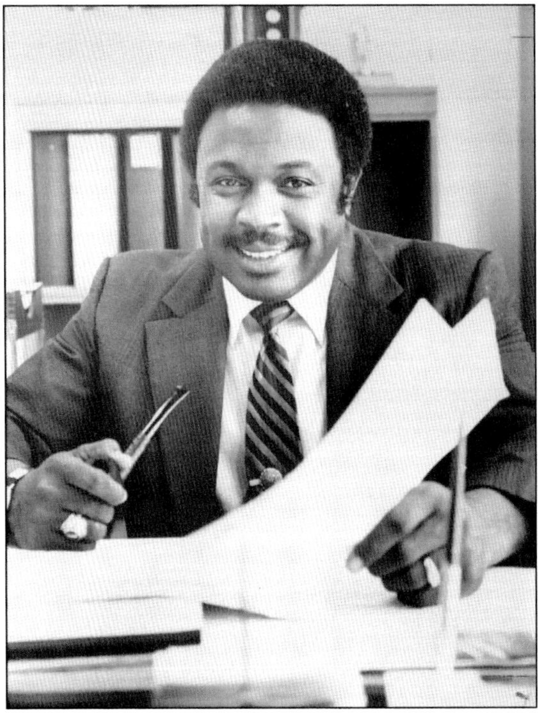

Dr. William "Sonny" Walker, a native of Pine Bluff, was appointed the first African American in the South to hold a cabinet-level position as head of the Arkansas State Economic Opportunity Office in 1969. He also served as the executive director of the Martin Luther King Jr. Center for Nonviolent Social Change in Atlanta. His other numerous civil rights distinctions reflect a lifetime commitment to social justice. (Courtesy of Arkansas History Commission.)

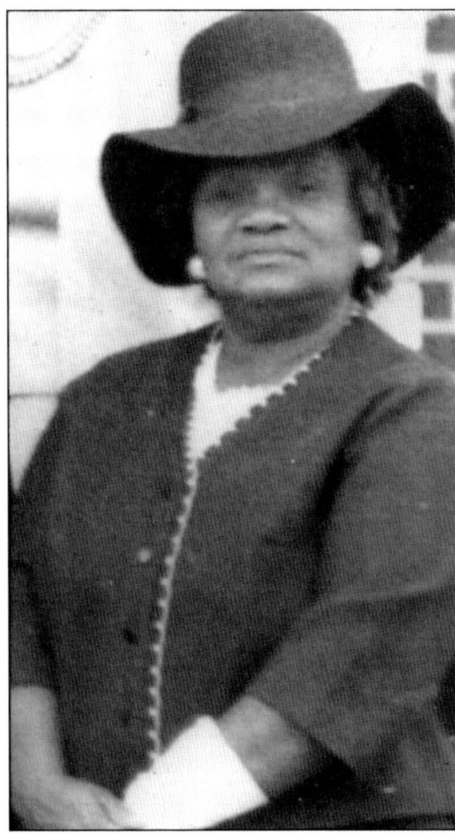

Edna "Mom" Mays of Pine Bluff was one of the city's most dedicated youth advocates. She started organizing in 1928 with the New Town Young People's Club. In 1945, she organized the Better Citizens Boy's Club, which continues today as the Pine Bluff Boys and Girls Club. In 1953, she organized the Negro Youth Organization. Her efforts have touched thousands of young people. Mays received the first citation of an African American by the Arkansas legislature in 1973 for her work. (Courtesy of Myrtus Henry.)

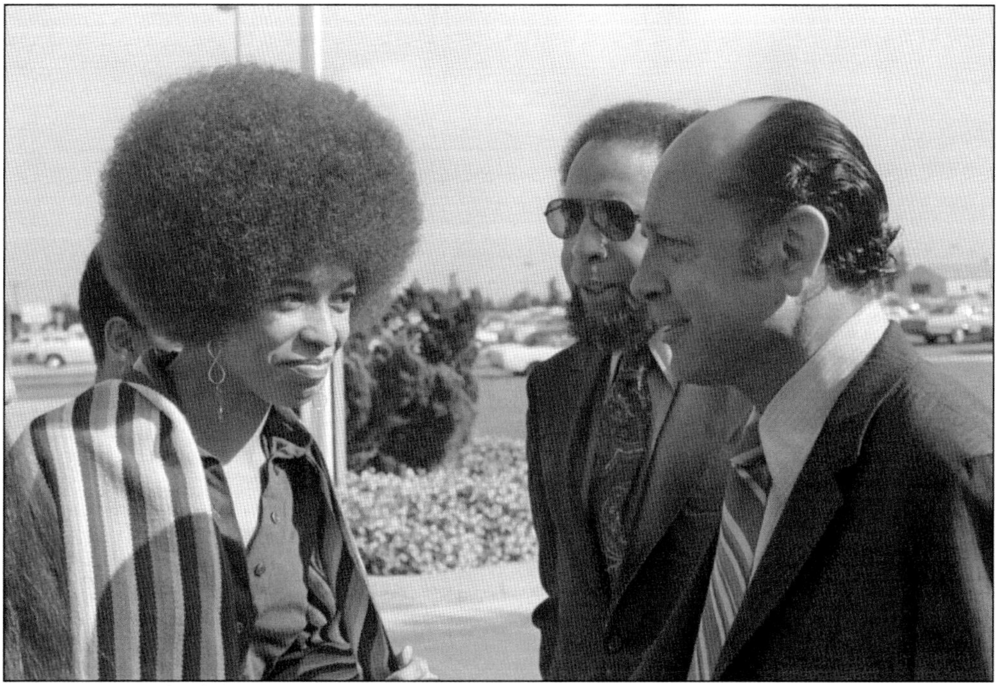

Leo Branton Jr. (right), a native of Pine Bluff, is shown in 1972 with Black Panther activist Angela Davis (left), whom he successfully defended as the lead attorney in the sensationalized case that many called "the trial of the century." A legendary California-based litigator, he also represented the likes of Nat King Cole, Dorothy Dandridge, Jimi Hendrix, Miles Davis, and the Platters. Leo is the brother of deceased legal legend Wiley Branton. (Courtesy of Bettman/Corbis/AP Images)

George Haley (left), diplomat, lawyer, and brother of Alex Haley, famed author of *Roots*, meets with President Nixon during the 1970s. Haley grew up in Pine Bluff, participated in the civil rights movement, and worked as a policy expert in eight US presidential administrations. He served as US ambassador to Gambia under the Clinton administration. His father, Simon, was the head of the agriculture department at Arkansas AM&N College during the 1940s and 1950s. (Courtesy of Pryor Center for Arkansas Oral and Visual History, University of Arkansas–Fayetteville.)

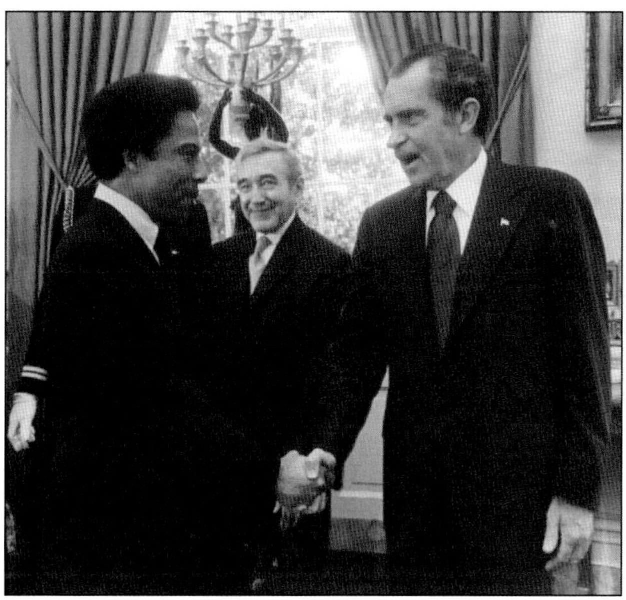

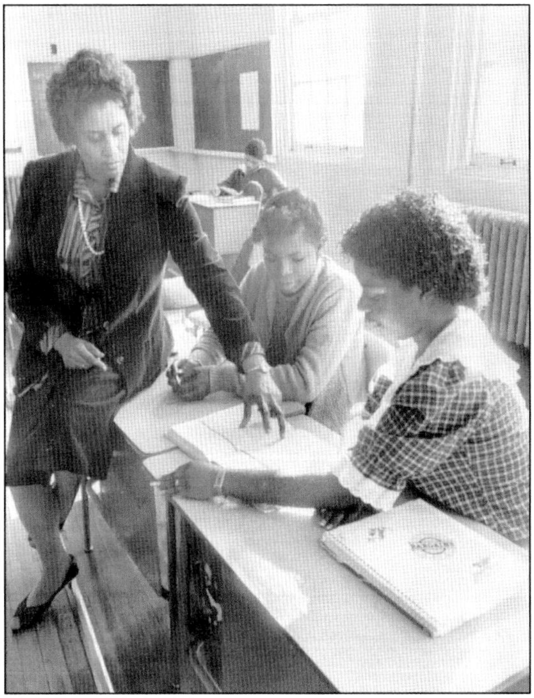

Irene Holcomb, a native of Altheimer, helps students as a longtime teacher during the 1980s. She became the first African American woman to serve on the city council in Pine Bluff. The Holcomb family also owns a local funeral home. (Courtesy of Arkansas History Commission.)

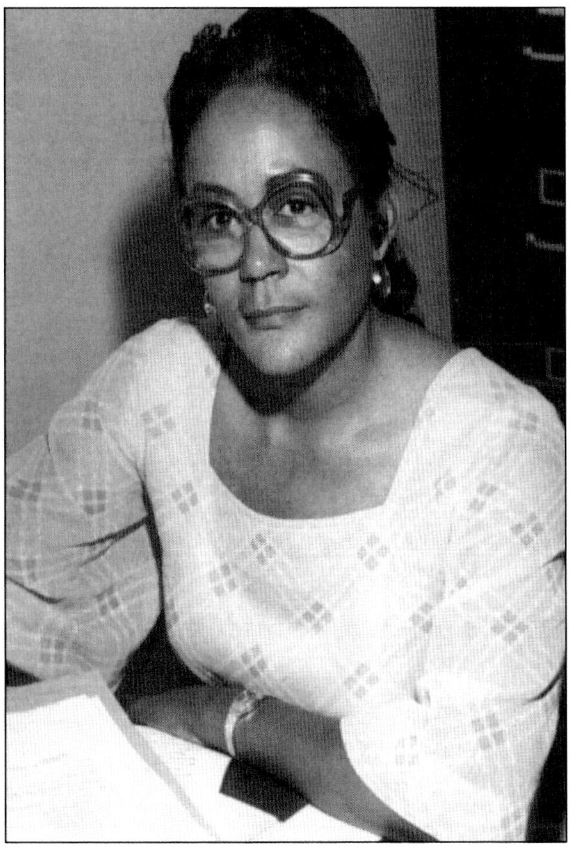

Dr. Josetta Wilkins of Pine Bluff won the vacated seat of her former husband, Henry Wilkins III, in 1991. With her brother Jean Edwards elected the same year to serve in another Jefferson County district, she became part of the first brother/sister team to serve simultaneously in the Arkansas legislature. Wilkins is known for many legislative accomplishments but none more than her advocacy of the Breast Cancer Act of 1997. Her son Henry "Hank" Williams IV later won election to her vacated seat after she served several terms. (Courtesy of Special Collections Department, University of Arkansas Libraries.)

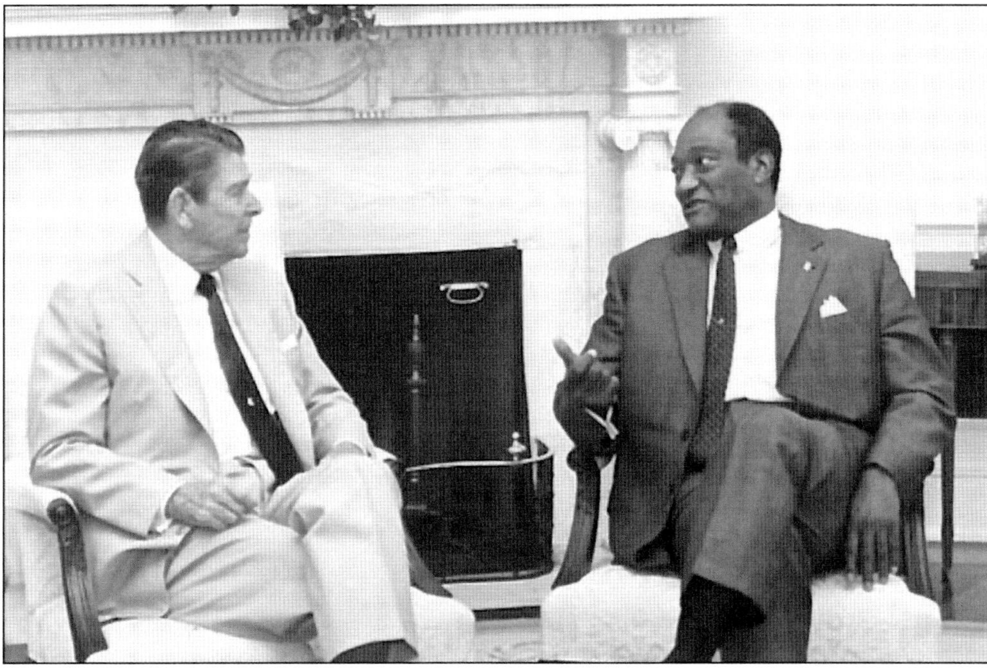

Dr. Edward Perkins, a former resident of Pine Bluff and student of Merrill High School, is pictured discussing diplomatic issues with Pres. Ronald Reagan in the 1980s. In a dramatic appointment in 1985, he was named ambassador to South Africa at the height of that country's apartheid regime. Perkins also served as US representative to the United Nations Security Council, director general of the US Foreign Service, and ambassador to Liberia, Australia, and the United Nations. (Courtesy of University of Oklahoma Press.)

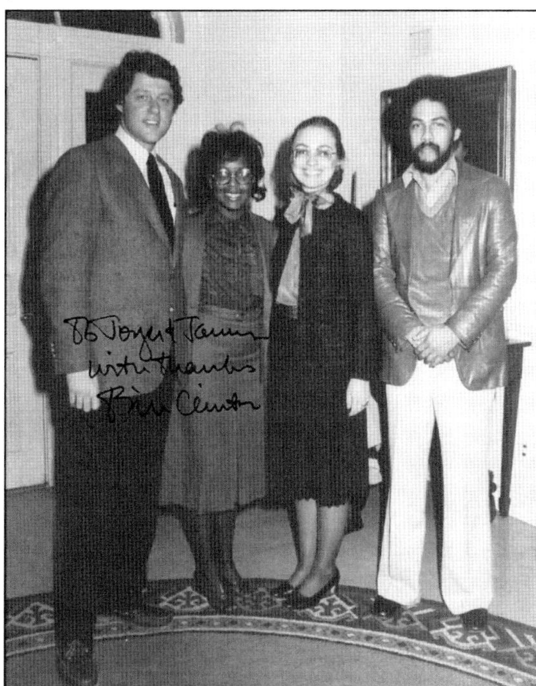

Pine Bluff native Judge Joyce Williams Warren (second from left), the first African American female judge in Arkansas and Pulaski County, stands with then-governor Bill Clinton, first lady Hillary Clinton, and Judge Warren's husband, James M. "Butch" Warren (right). Judge Warren has achieved a multitude of judicial firsts and was voted by the *Arkansas Democrat Gazette* in 2012 as one of the Top 10 Most Influential Black Arkansans in the state's history. (Courtesy of James M. "Butch" Warren.)

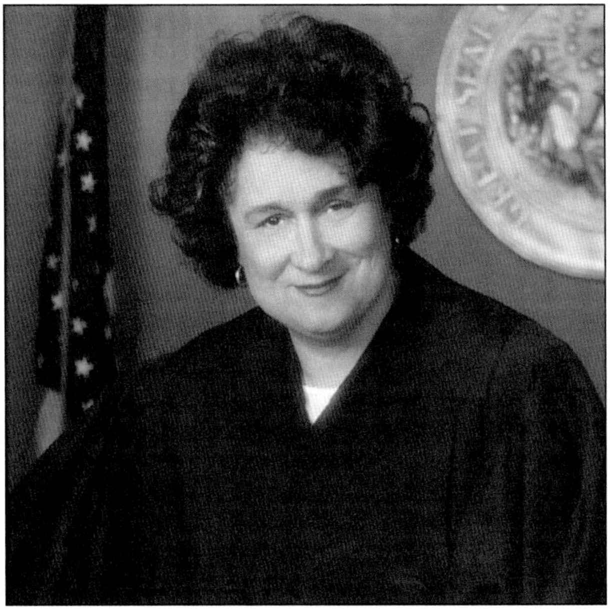

Andree Roaf, a longtime resident of Pine Bluff, was appointed in 1995 as the first African American woman on the Arkansas Supreme Court. She served later in a judgeship as a member of the Arkansas State Court of Appeals. A 1996 inductee in the Arkansas Black Hall of Fame, Roaf was also the mother of Pro Football Hall of Famer Willie Roaf and the former wife of prominent Pine Bluff dentist Dr. Clifton Roaf. (Courtesy of Phoebe Roaf.)

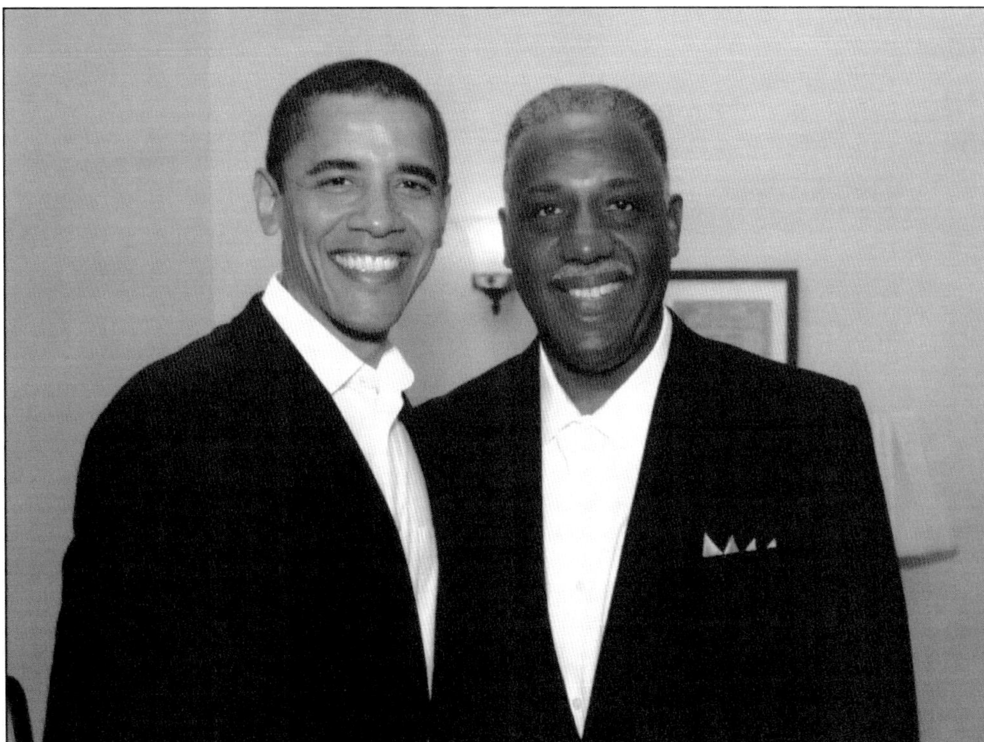

Sen. Barack Obama stands with Pine Bluff mayor Carl Redus. Redus, a Pine Bluff native, became the first African American mayor of the city in 2004, fulfilling a decades-long struggle for more diverse representation in city government. His accomplishments included passing a milestone city tax for improvement of city services, advancing historic preservation efforts, partnering with UAPB to assist small businesses, improving city infrastructure, and a host of others. (Courtesy Richard Redus.)

Seven

EDUCATION AND SCHOOL LIFE

I never saw people learn so fast. It generally took me three months to teach what they [former slaves] *learn in ten or fifteen days.*

—unknown American Missionary Association teacher
Jefferson County Freedmen School (1867)

I can read and write my name. I remember when we thought a newspaper opened out was a bed cover.

—Charlie Hinton, former Pine Bluff slave
WPA Slave Narratives

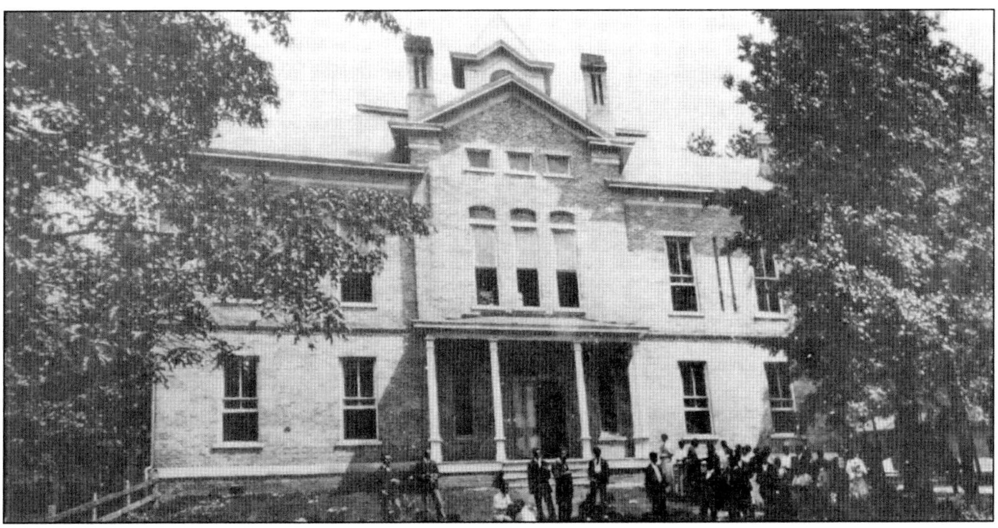

The women's dormitory of Branch Normal College in 1895 had a capacity of 35 residents and a cost of $2 per week paid in advance. Branch Normal College, founded in 1873, later became Arkansas AM&N College in 1927, and then the University of Arkansas at Pine Bluff in 1972. (Courtesy of the Lites-Wallis Collection.)

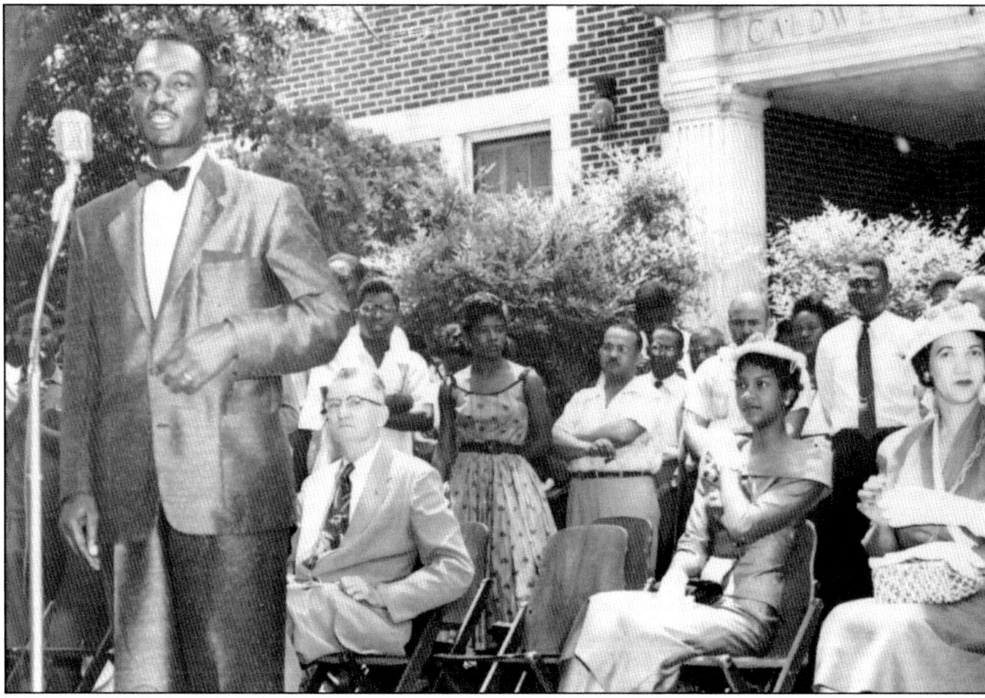

Dr. Lawrence "Prexy" Davis Sr. (at the microphone) was president of Arkansas AM&N College from 1942 to 1972. Under his leadership, the college expanded its physical facilities in an unprecedented fashion while also expanding educational offerings. More importantly, Davis became a beloved leader, finding creative ways to offer students opportunities to enroll in college who had no means otherwise. Thirty years after becoming president of the college, he became the first chancellor in 1972. (Courtesy of Arkansas History Commission.)

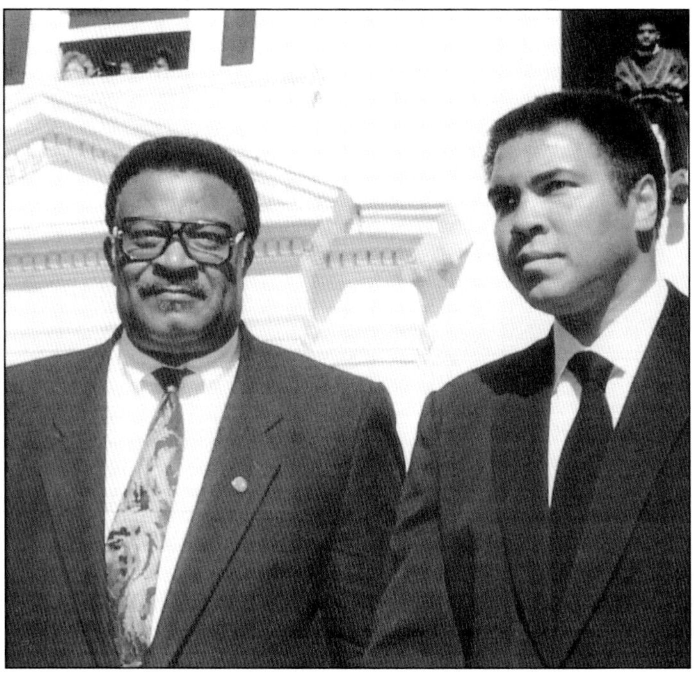

Chancellor Charles Walker (left) and boxing heavyweight Muhammad Ali absorb the sights and sounds of a UAPB homecoming parade around 1990. Walker dramatically increased research grants at UAPB during his tenure (which lasted from 1986 to 1991) ranking the school third in the state for all such money received. The university's first master's degree programs were established during his tenure in elementary and secondary education. (Courtesy of Special Collections Department, University of Arkansas Libraries.)

Dr. Carolyn Blakely, a longtime resident of Pine Bluff, served on the UAPB English department's faculty and later became the first woman to head a major university in the state of Arkansas in her role as interim chancellor of UAPB in 1991. She has also been active in a variety of civic roles, both at the local and state levels. (Courtesy of UAPB Archives.)

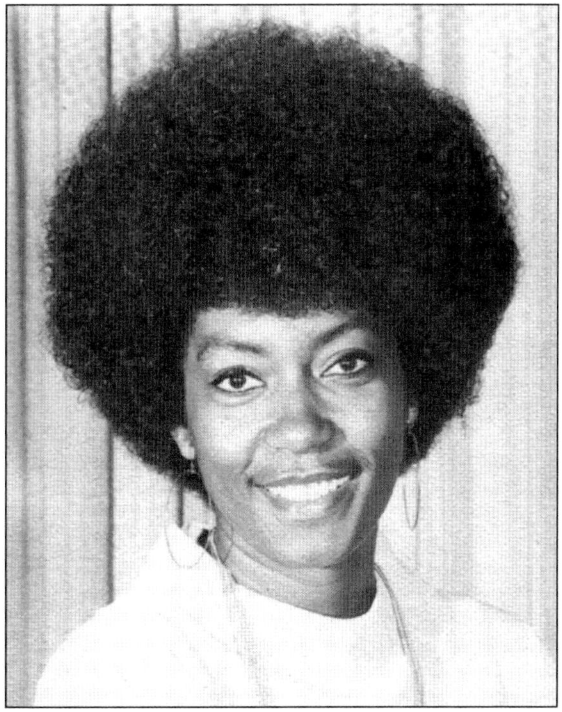

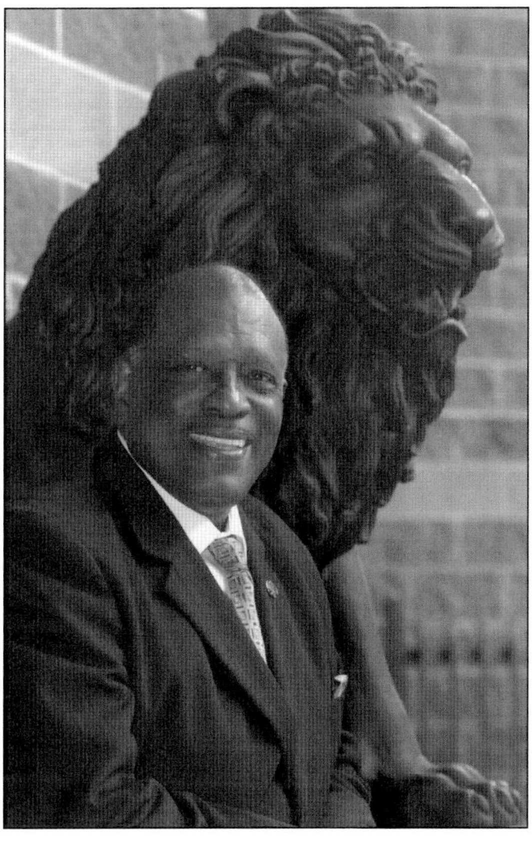

Dr. Lawrence Davis Jr. was the chancellor of UAPB from 1991 to 2012. His exemplary tenure was punctuated by the construction of Dawson-Hicks Hall, Caine-Gilleland Hall, Henderson-Young Hall, the 1890 Extension Complex, Childress Hall, the UAPB Business Support Incubator, Torri Hunter baseball field, Golden Lions football stadium, and the UAPB soccer field. He also fought for the university's first approved doctoral program in aquaculture and expanded numerous academic offerings. (Courtesy of the Pine Bluff Commercial.)

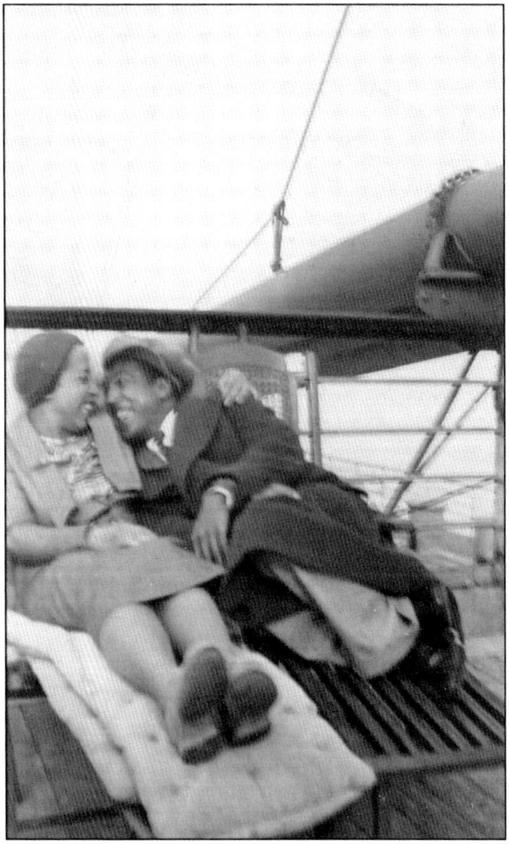

Louise Thompson Patterson, former Branch Normal College professor and Pine Bluff resident, is en route to Russia in 1932 with her friend Langston Hughes to work on a film. Patterson was actively engaged in the Harlem Renaissance, working with both Hughes and folklorist/writer Zora Neal Hurston. She was also a staunch social activist who organized rallies and support for the Scottsboro Boys, Paul Robeson, and Angela Davis over the years. (Courtesy of Louise Thompson Patterson Papers, Manuscript, Archives and Rare Books Library, Emory University.)

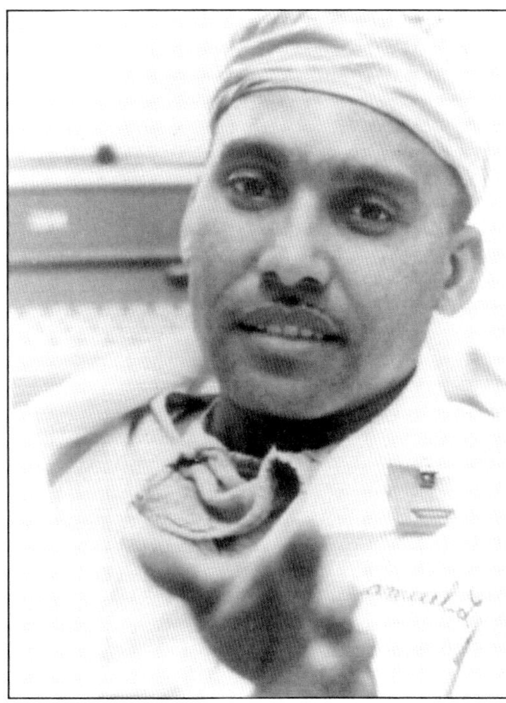

Dr. Samuel Kountz from Lexa, Arkansas, was a 1952 Arkansas AM&N graduate who had failed the college's entrance exam but successfully appealed to the college president for admission. He later became the first person to perform a successful kidney transplant between a recipient and a donor who were not identical twins. He developed the largest kidney transplant and research program in the country at the University of California at San Francisco. (Courtesy of University of California at San Francisco Library, Special Collections.)

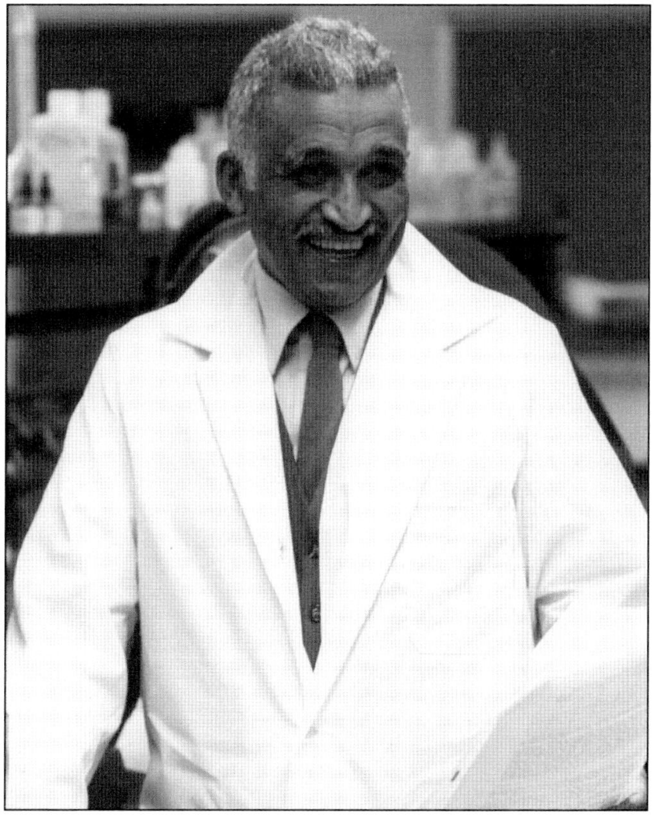

Dr. Samuel Massie, a Little Rock native and an Arkansas AM&N graduate, worked on the Manhattan Project during World War II, focusing on radioactive isotopes for the atom bomb. In 1966, he became the first African American professor at the US Naval Academy. He developed foaming agents that protected soldiers from the effects of poisonous gas and conducted research on drugs to treat infections such as herpes and meningitis. (Courtesy of US Naval Academy, Nimitz Library, Special Collections.)

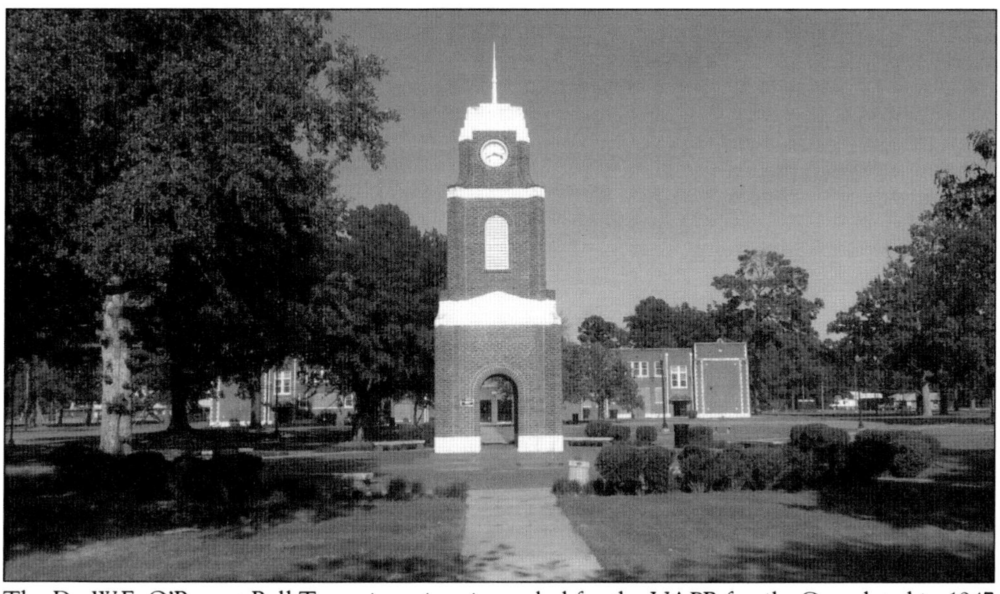

The Dr. W.E. O'Bryant Bell Tower is an iconic symbol for the UAPB family. Completed in 1947 with only private contributions from students, community members, and faculty, the structure was built over a period of four years. Under the supervision of Alexander Mazique, an instructor of bricklaying, students and faculty provided the labor for this undertaking. (Courtesy of Jimmy Cunningham Jr.)

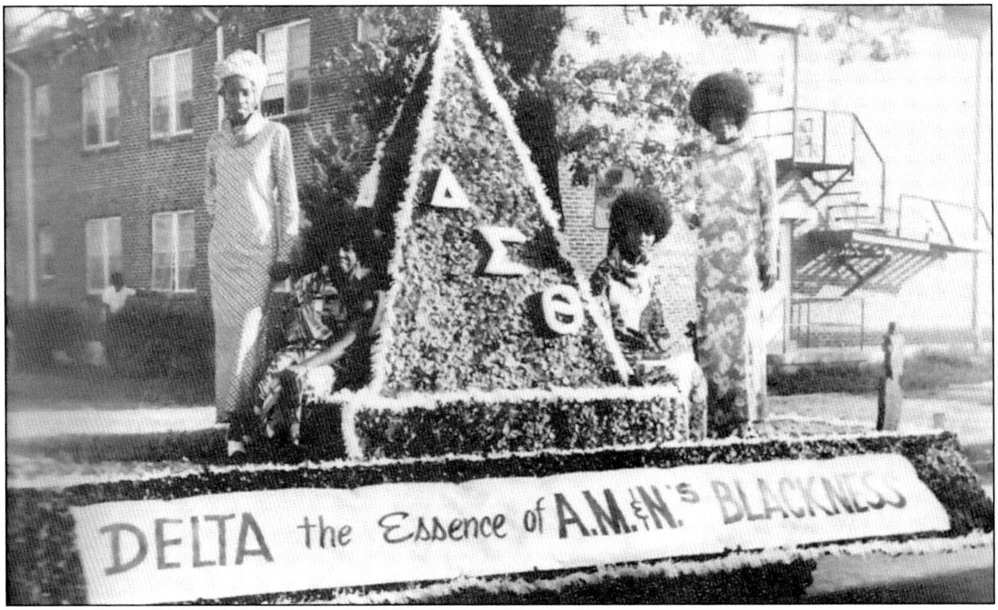

The ladies of Delta Sigma Theta prepare for a homecoming parade in the early 1970s. (Courtesy of UAPB Archives.)

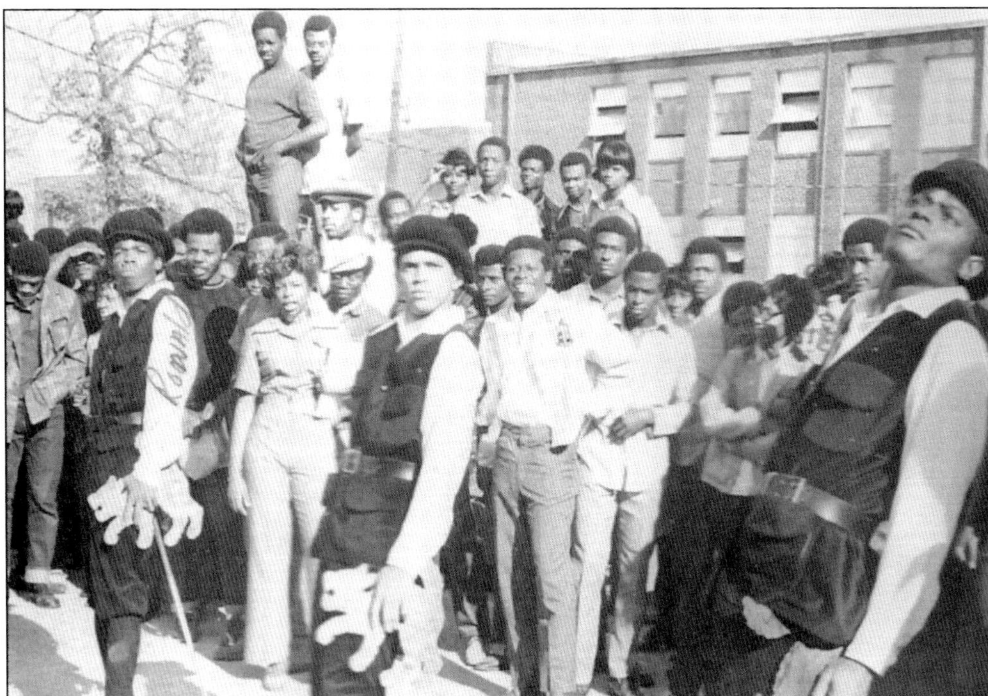

Kappa Alpha Psi pledgees ("scrollers") from 1971 show off their latest coordinated moves on the campus of Arkansas AM&N before an enthusiastic crowd. They hold "fly canes," which were used to complement their unique step routines. (Courtesy of UAPB Archives.)

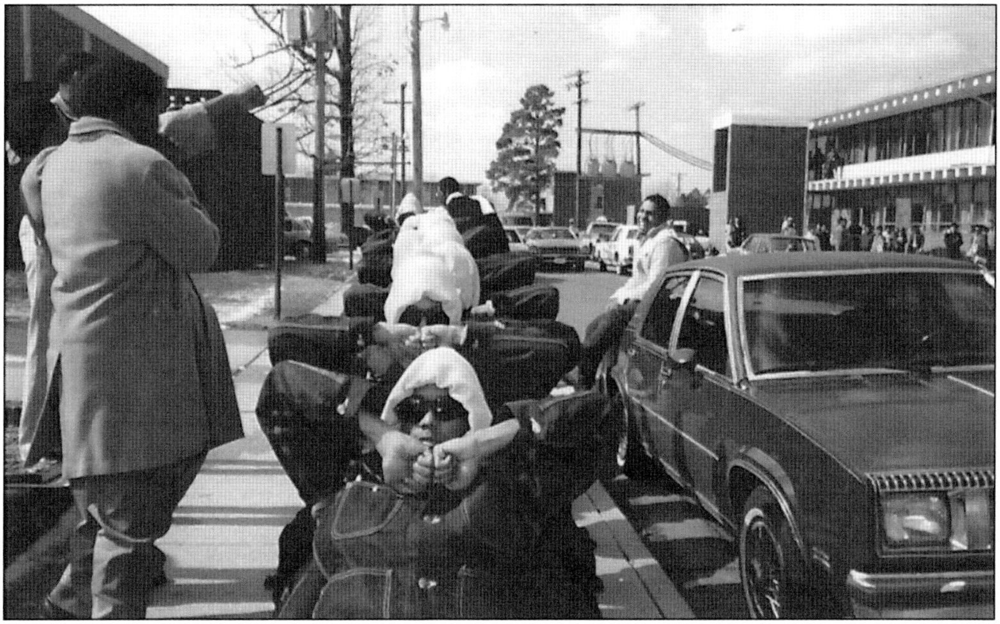

Brothers of Omega Psi Phi carefully inspect pledgees ("lamps") in the mid-1980s. (Courtesy of Renee Peterson.)

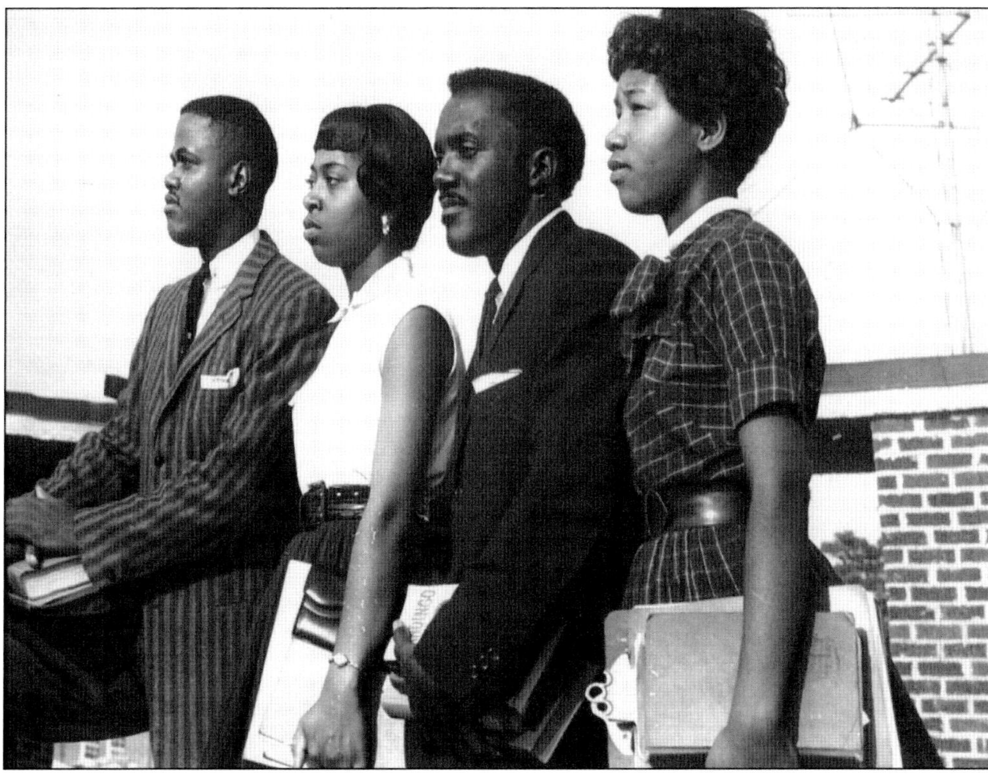

Scholarly Arkansas AM&N College students, including Kwurly Floyd Tate (second from left), who later became the university registrar, look toward the horizon. (Courtesy of Special Collections Department, University of Arkansas Libraries.)

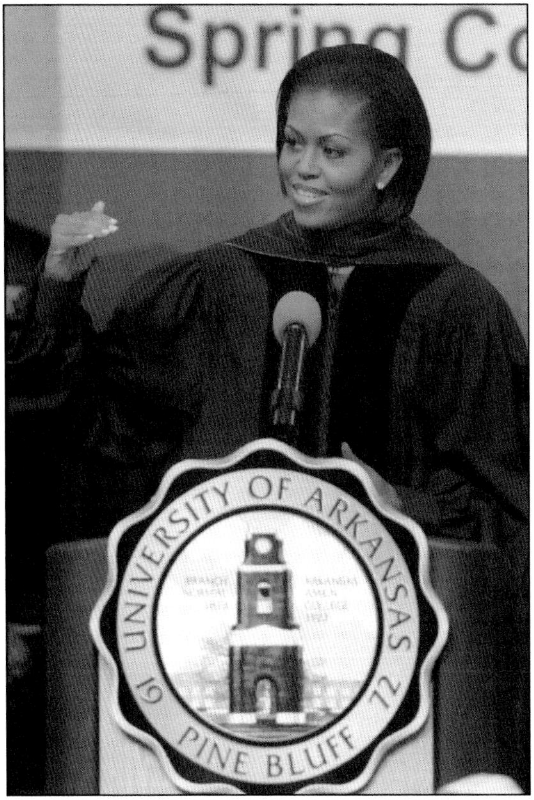

First lady Michelle Obama speaks at the 2010 UAPB commencement. This was Obama's first trip to the Delta since the inauguration of the president and her first trip to Pine Bluff. Her address came a full year after UAPB's 260-piece band was chosen to march in President Obama's inaugural parade. (Courtesy of Associated Press/Danny Johnston.)

A classroom at the Arkansas AM&N Training School in 1949 is filled with elementary students actively engaged in learning. Student teachers from the college's education department received training here under the auspices of experienced teachers. (Courtesy of Donna Cunningham.)

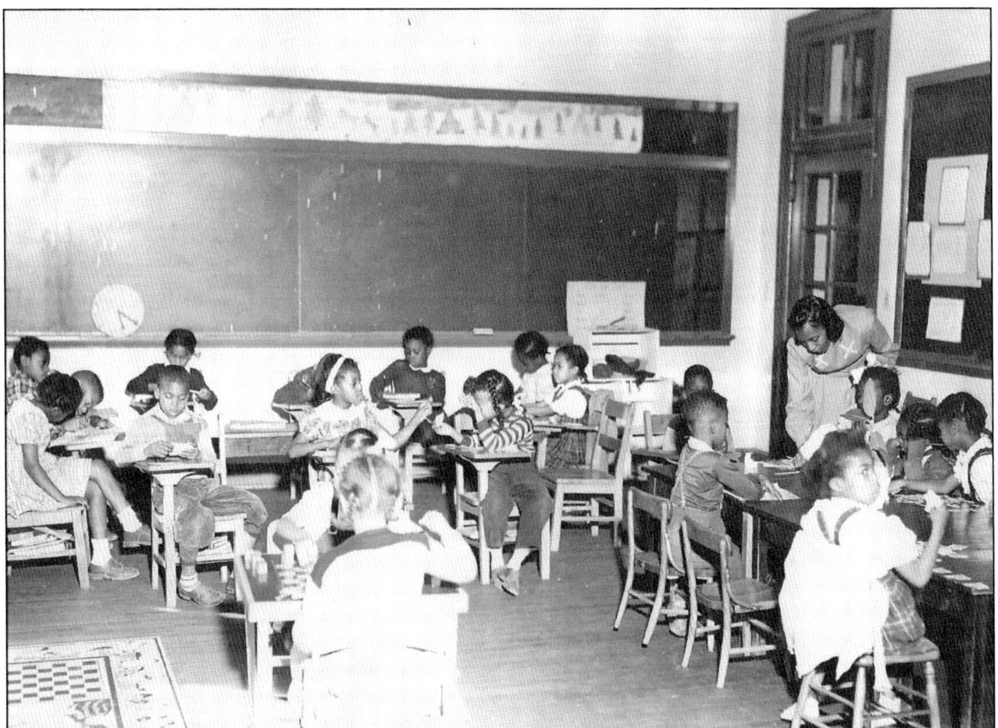

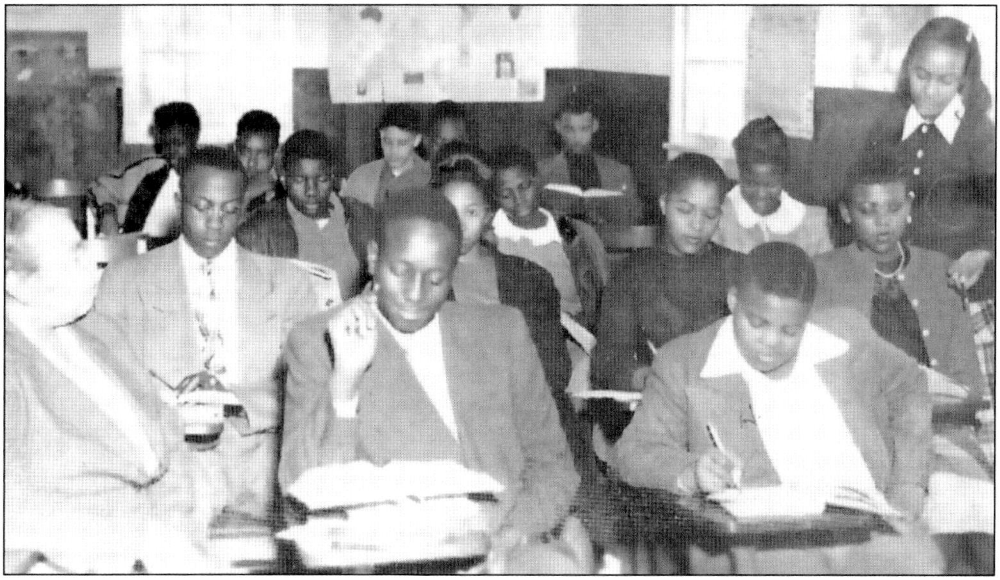

Corbin High School students, pictured here in 1947, were also part of the Arkansas AM&N family as the college coordinated its educational offerings. These students were some of the brightest in the state, including Henry Foster Jr. (first row, right) who later served as dean of the School of Medicine at Meharry College and was nominated by President Clinton for the position of US surgeon general in 1995. (Courtesy of UAPB Archives.)

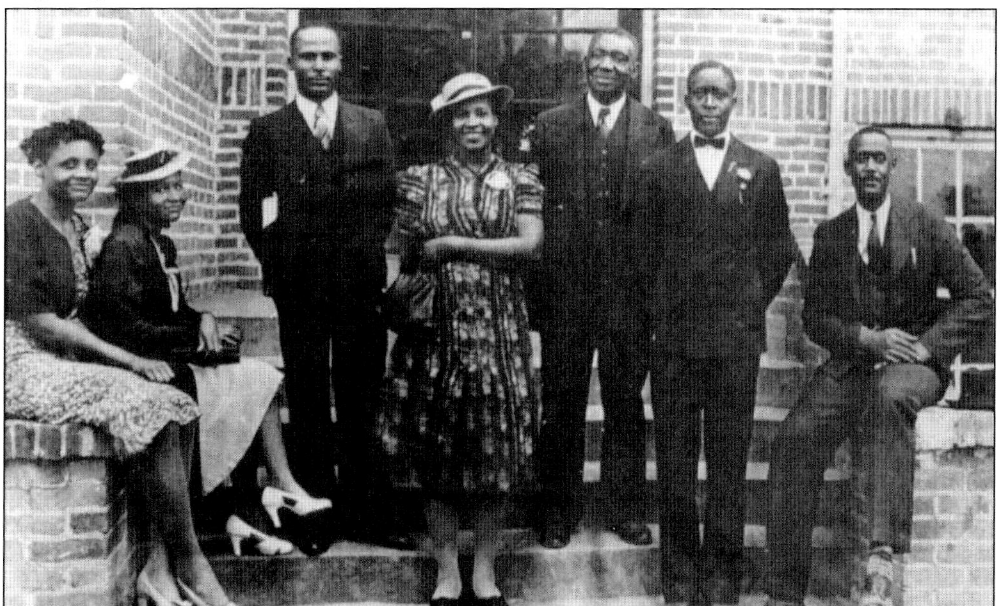

Former students from Arkansas Haygood Industrial College meet with one of their professors at the campus in 1940. The institution was Jefferson County's second historically black college. This Christian Methodist Episcopal–supported school moved just outside of Pine Bluff in 1915 with 300 acres of land and an investment of about $65,000 in buildings. As of 1925, the school had about 400 students enrolled and offered vocational and education courses. It closed by World War II because of financial constraints. (Courtesy of C.C. Neal Jr. Collection.)

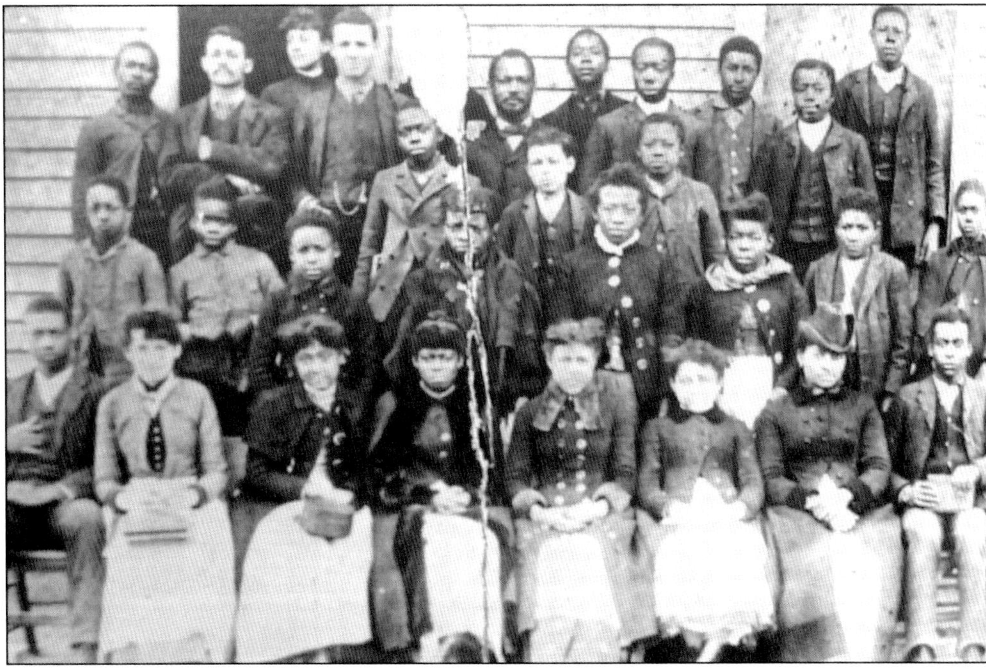

Richard Allen Institute faculty and students stand in front of their school in 1895. Founded in 1886, it was one of the earliest Presbyterian schools for African Americans in the state. The school had as many as 330 students under the supervision of seven teachers and operated until 1932. (Courtesy of Sarah Jones Robinson.)

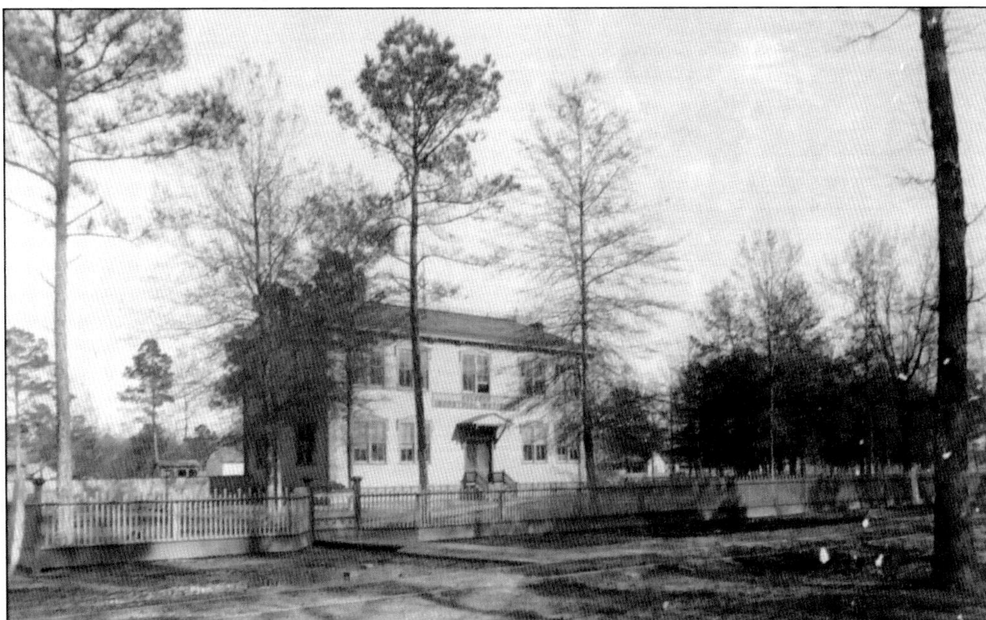

Pine Bluff's Colored Industrial Institute (later renamed St.Peter's Catholic School), pictured here in 1889, was the first Catholic school for African Americans in the state of Arkansas. The idea for the school was conceived by Father John Lucey, the pastor of St. Peter's Catholic Church, and the land was donated by businessman Wiley Jones. (Courtesy of Arkansas History Commission.)

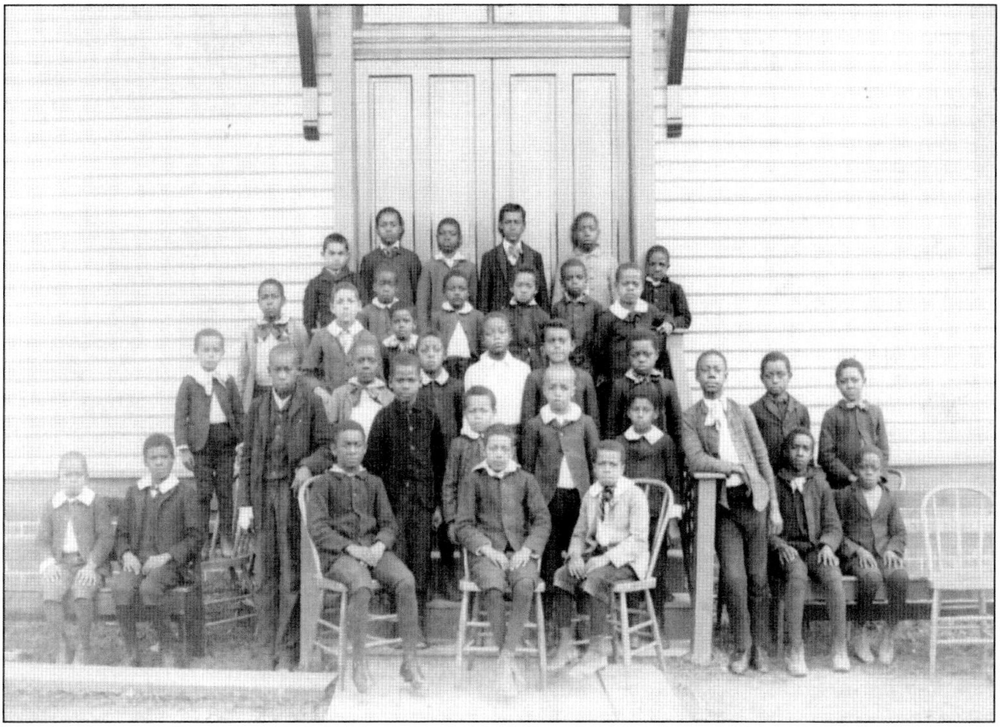

Young boys from the Colored Industrial Institute take a break from classes in 1893. (Courtesy of Arkansas History Commission.)

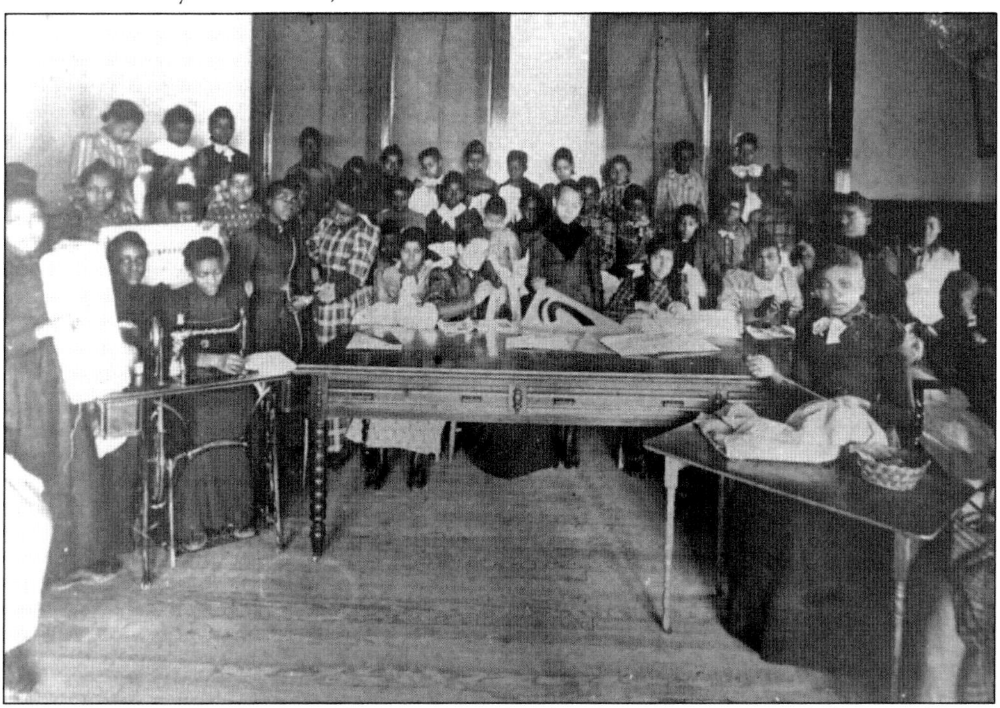

A class at the Colored Industrial Institute teaches female students sewing skills around 1900. (Courtesy of Butler Center for Arkansas Studies.)

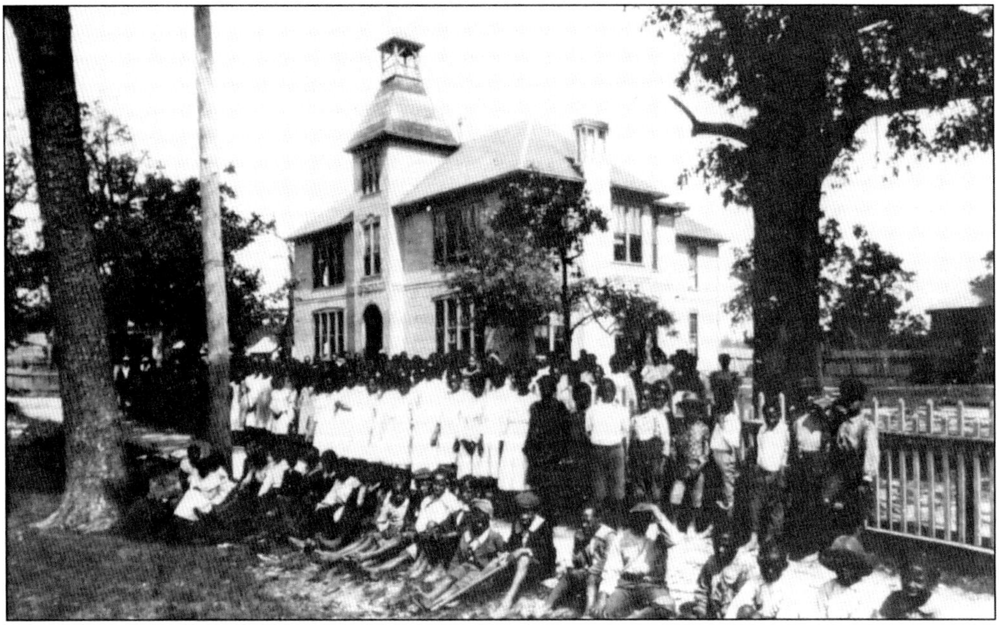

In this 1892 photograph, Merrill Public School students stand in front of their old school, one of the largest frame buildings in the city, boasting 10,000 square feet. Named after white philanthropist Joseph Merrill, who donated money for black education, Merrill School was respected throughout Arkansas because of its outstanding graduates and its educational leadership from principals including Marion Perry Sr., J.C. Corbin, William Townsend, R.N. Chaney, and M.D. Jordan. (Courtesy of Lites-Wallis Collection.)

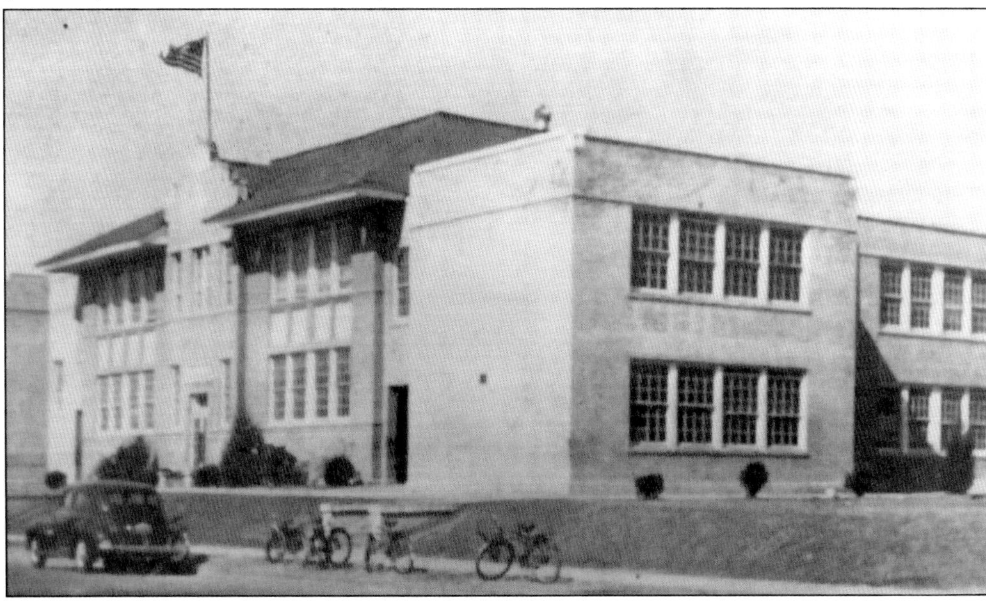

Merrill High School stands proudly in 1948. This building, constructed in the 1930s, also contained an elementary school. According to Merrill graduate Raye Montague, because of Merrill's close relationship with Arkansas AM&N College, students were constantly exposed to African American trailblazers who came to the campus to speak, such as Joe Louis, Mary McCleod Bethune, Jesse Owens, Marian Anderson, and many others. (Courtesy of Connie Elkins Collection.)

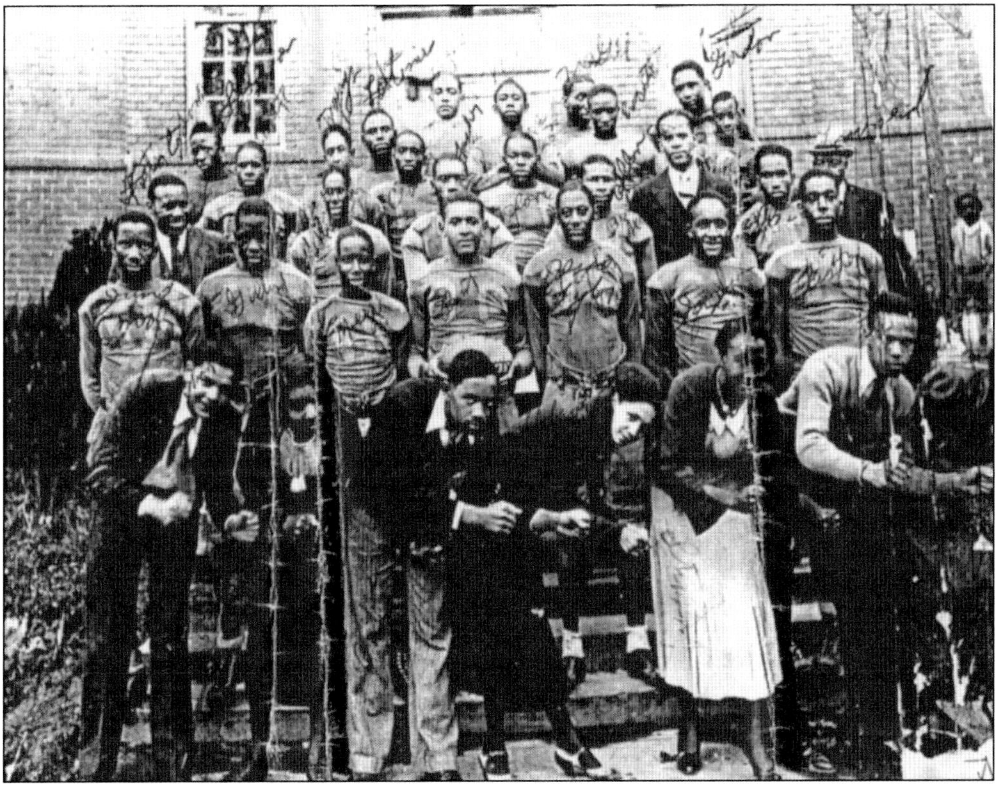

Coach Henry Foster Sr. (third row, left) proudly stands with the 1933 Merrill High School football team and their principal W.M. Townsend (third row, right), as they celebrate winning the black high school national championship. Foster would amazingly go on in 1934 to repeat the championship. A young Japhas Gordon Sr. (last row, right), who would later become a longtime faculty member at UAPB, also stands with teammates. (Courtesy of Juanita Curry.)

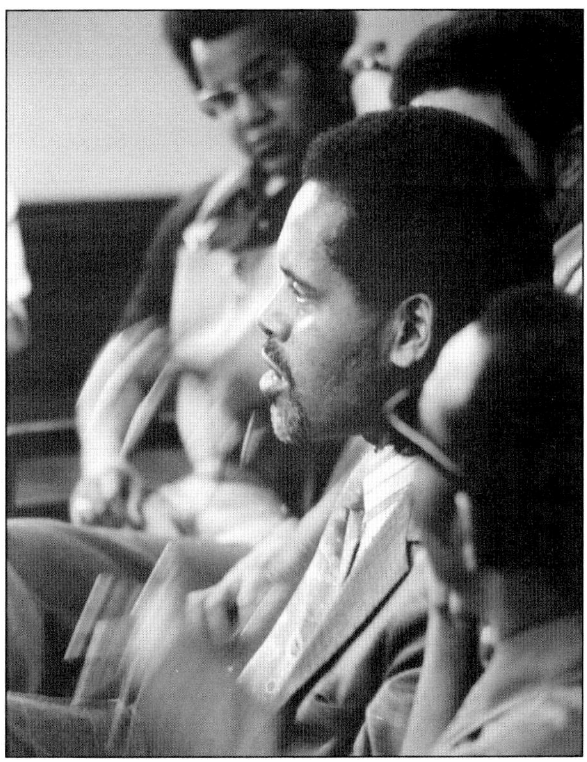

Elijah Coleman, shown here at a meeting in 1971, was a principal of Townsend Park High School in Pine Bluff and a staunch advocate of education and racial equality. He also served as a principal at Tucker-Plum Bayou High School and president of the Arkansas Teachers Association. (Courtesy of Arkansas History Commission.)

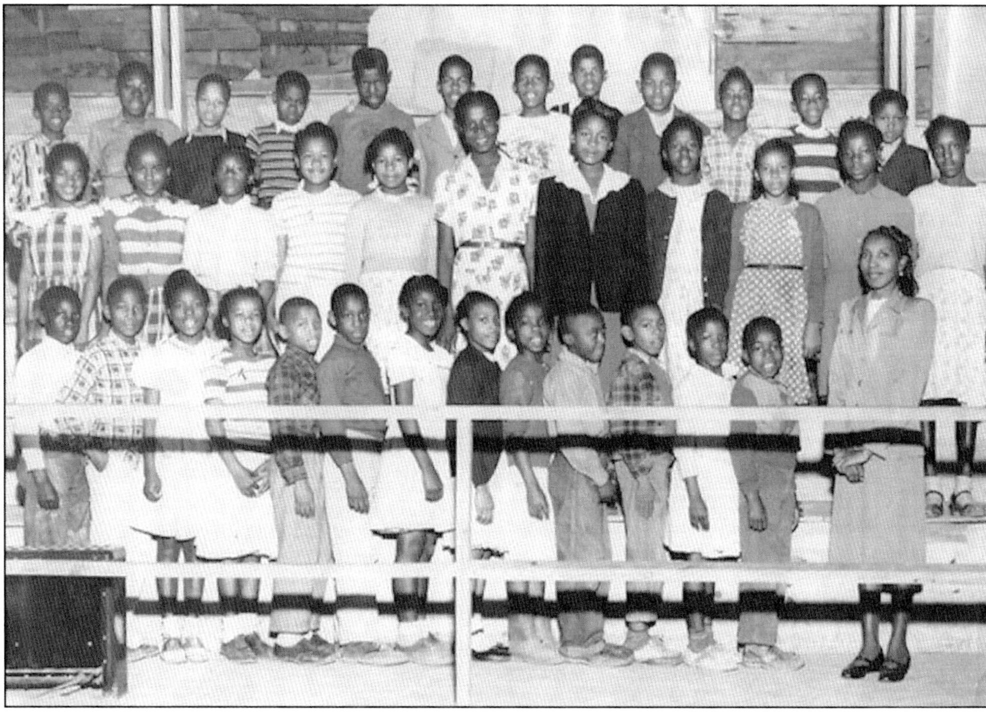

Teacher Bernice Cunningham (first row, right) stands with elementary and secondary students at the Jefferson County Training School in 1949. Renamed C.P. Coleman High School by 1950, it was one of four institutions that provided public high school instruction for blacks in Pine Bluff. The other schools included Townsend Park, Southeast, and Merrill. Missouri Street School was once a high school in Pine Bluff but later became a middle school before closing. (Courtesy of Donna Smith.)

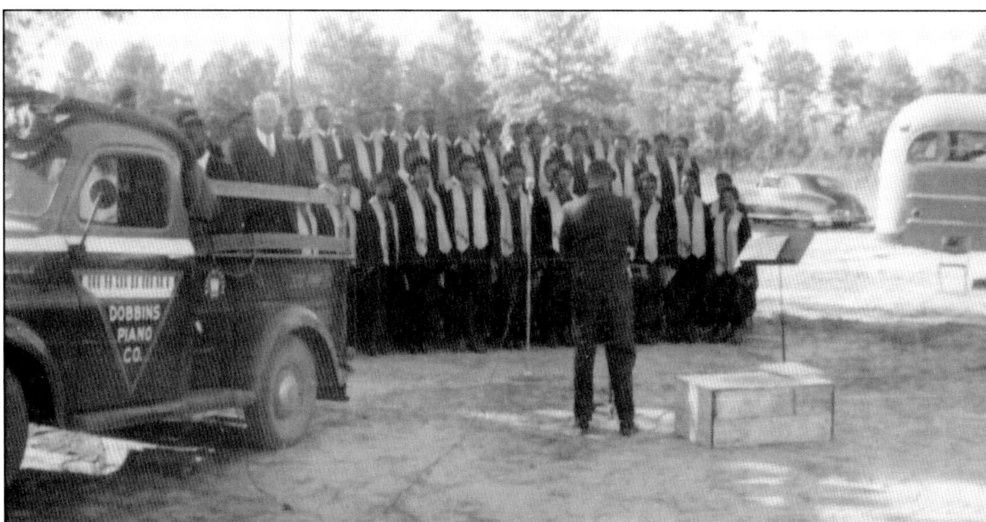

A choir in 1954 assembles during the Marian Year Pilgrimage ceremony at Saint Raphael's Mission, located southeast of Pine Bluff. St. Raphael's Community Center for Colored Education, an industrial school that opened in 1938, was run by the Franciscan brothers from Ohio. In 1955, a fire destroyed the school, and it was not rebuilt. (Courtesy of Arkansas History Commission.)

Eight

RELIGION

I'se a preacher . . . The Lord done left me here for a purpose . . . When we use to pray, we put our heads under a wash pot to keep old master from hearing us.

—Robert Wilson, former Pine Bluff slave
WPA Slave Narratives

Some say the devil loose for a season. I say if he ain't, he tied mighty slack.

—Rachel Harris, former Pine Bluff slave
WPA Slave Narratives

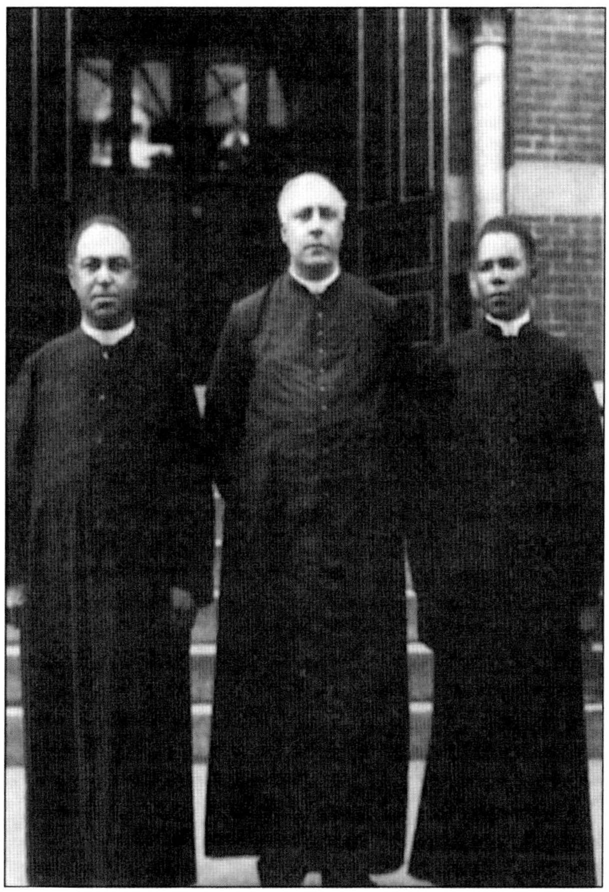

When Father John Dorsey (left) was assigned in 1905 to pastor St. Peter's Catholic Church in Pine Bluff, he became the first African American Catholic pastor in the United States. This was no easy task, as he experienced a series of onerous challenges from within the church and the community. Nonetheless, Dorsey advocated expanded opportunities among black priests in the Catholic Church throughout his career. (Courtesy of Church of St. Cecilia.)

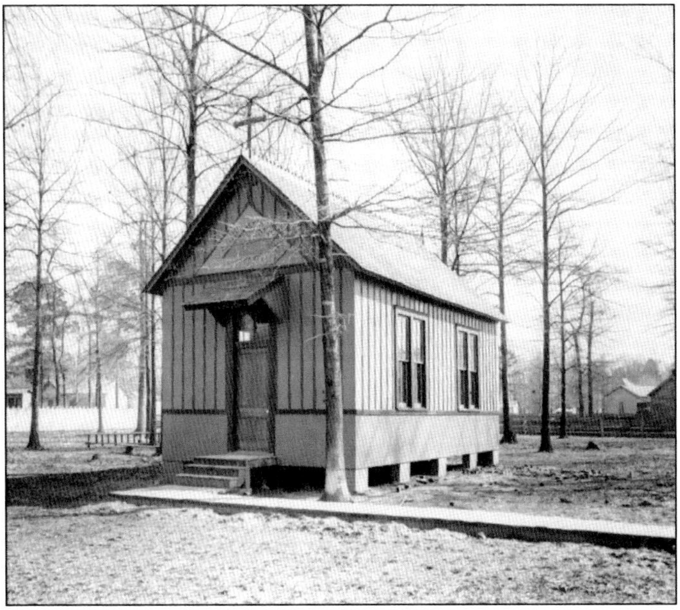

St. Peter's Catholic Church, pictured here in the 1890s, was originally located in this quaint building. The church was built for African American Catholics by Monsignor John M. Lucey in 1894. The money for construction came largely from the efforts of the editors and readers of the *Pilot*, a Boston, Massachusetts, newspaper. With the establishment of St. Peter's Catholic School, the church has been able to fuse religion and education in profoundly meaningful ways for youth. (Courtesy of Arkansas History Commission.)

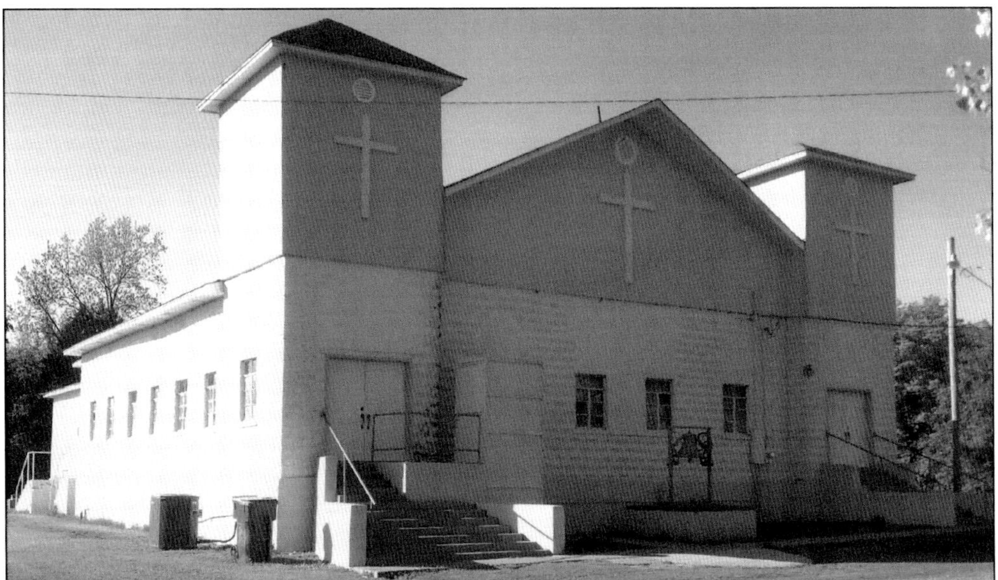

Antioch Missionary Baptist Church in Sherrill was founded by former slaves in 1868. Both the church and the adjacent cemetery represent the oldest resources related to the Good Hope Plantation slaves who were moved from their South Carolina plantation to the Sherill/Pastoria area. The church became the center of a thriving black community with members and descendants who homesteaded the land. Relatives of these same descendants continue in modern times to serve the Sherrill community spreading the gospel with equal passion and vigor. (Courtesy of Jimmy Cunningham Jr.)

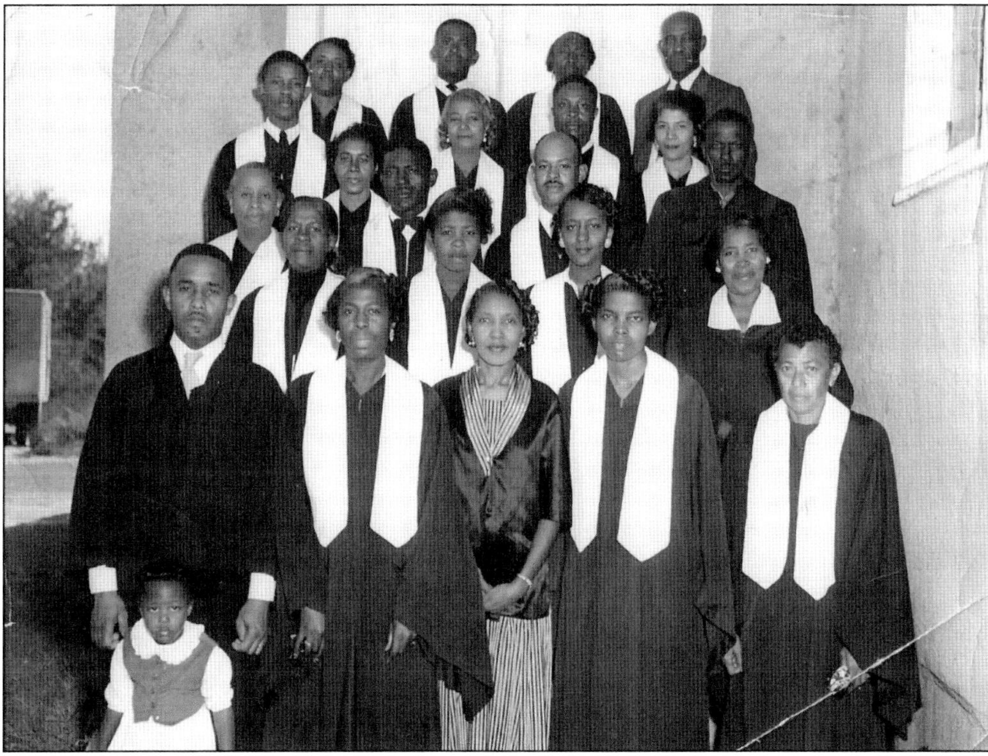

Members of Barraque Street Missionary Baptist Church's choir pose in this 1953 photograph. The church, founded in 1885, became a strong force in Pine Bluff under Rev. J.C. Battles's leadership. Booker T. Washington mentioned Rev. Battles's committed efforts to secure housing for blacks throughout Pine Bluff in *The Negro in Business*. Like many other black churches in Pine Bluff, Barraque Street met only twice per month for many years. It continues today with an array of unique ministries utilizing both a social and spiritual gospel. (Courtesy of Donna Cunningham.)

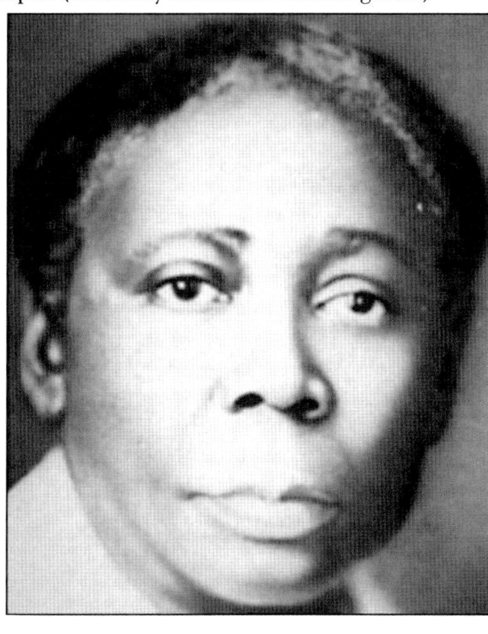

"Mother" Lizzie Woods Robinson, a 20-year Pine Bluff resident, became the first national church mother for the Church of God in Christ (COGIC) in 1911. She organized women in auxiliaries nationwide and introduced international ministry to the church. She was interrogated by the FBI for preaching pacifism during World War I, jailed for her beliefs, taunted by the KKK, and egged by crowds as a female church leader. Robinson and her auxiliaries of women raised over half the funds used to construct the COGIC national headquarters in Memphis, Tennessee. Her later Nebraska home is listed in the National Register of Historic Places. (Courtesy of COGIC Museum.)

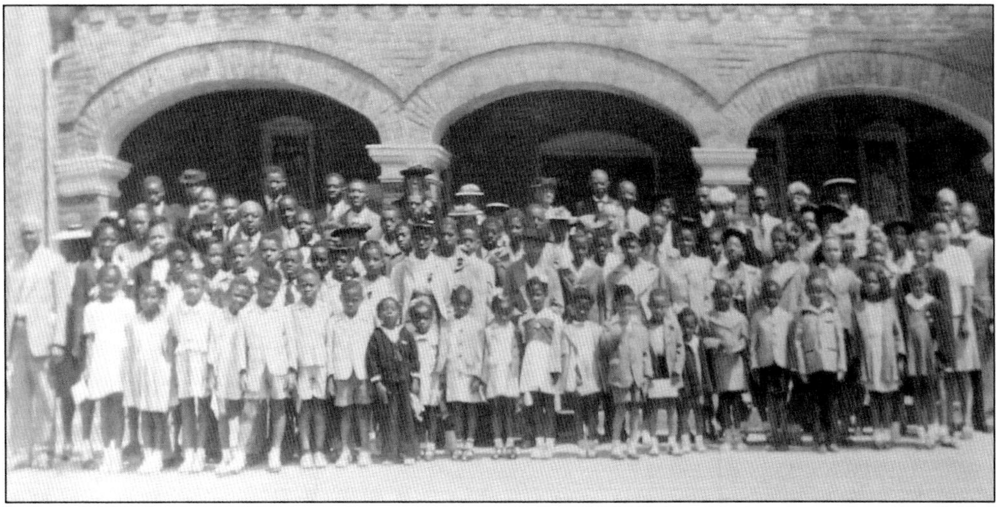

Rev. H.M. Green stands with youth and other members in front of St. John AME Church in 1941. The building pictured had been in use since 1897 and was replaced in 1966. With a critical emphasis on facilitating affordable housing opportunities along with important work in civil rights, social activism, and spiritual instruction, St. John has made biblical teachings tangible and relevant for all, including "the least of these." (Courtesy of Connie Elkins Collection.)

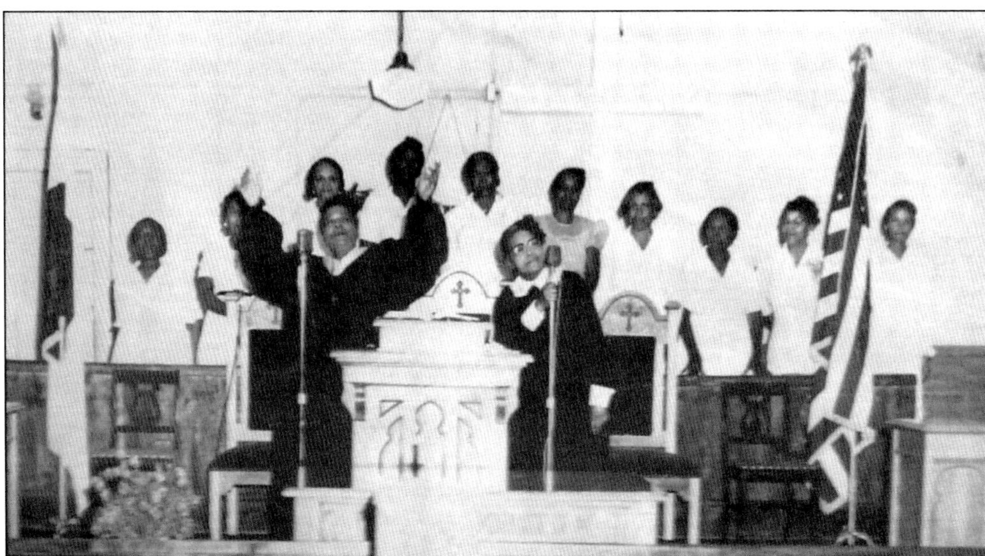

The First Community Church was a rarity in 1956, as it had two female ministers. Pictured in black robes are Rev. L.R. Tolar (left), a former pastor, and its current pastor at the time, Rev. K.R. Player. Female ministers anywhere were few in number during this time, but female pastors in Pine Bluff were almost unheard of. This church served the community and residents of the Tolar Convalescent Home. (Courtesy of Juanita Currie.)

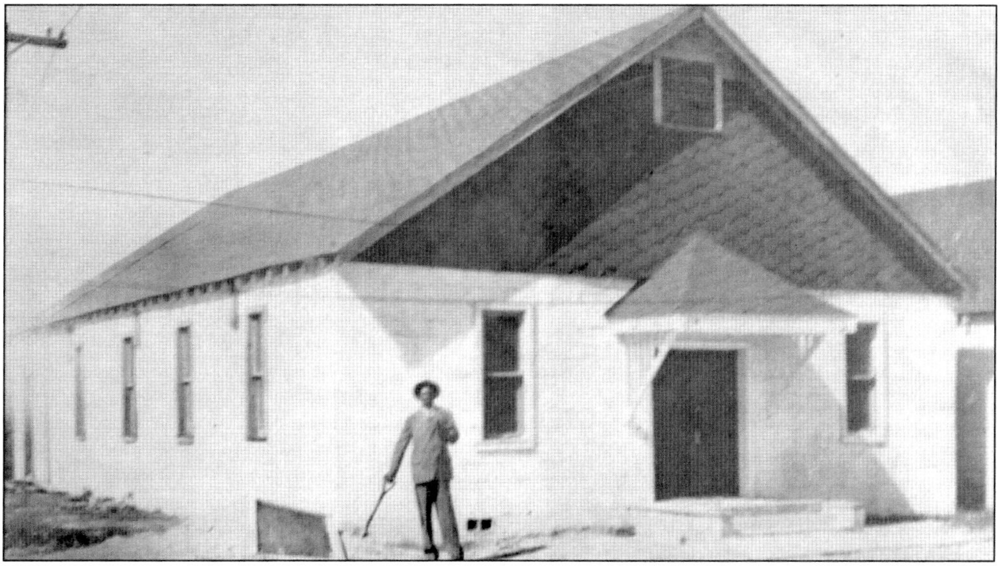

A First Community Church program booklet from 1956 gives some context for this image, stating, "After two years of hard work by himself, Haywood Carter, a cripple, with the use of only one hand and one foot, finished our church in 1951. Layed every stone without help. Haywood is seen standing with the shovel in hand and is now one of the stewards of the church." (Courtesy of Juanita Currie.)

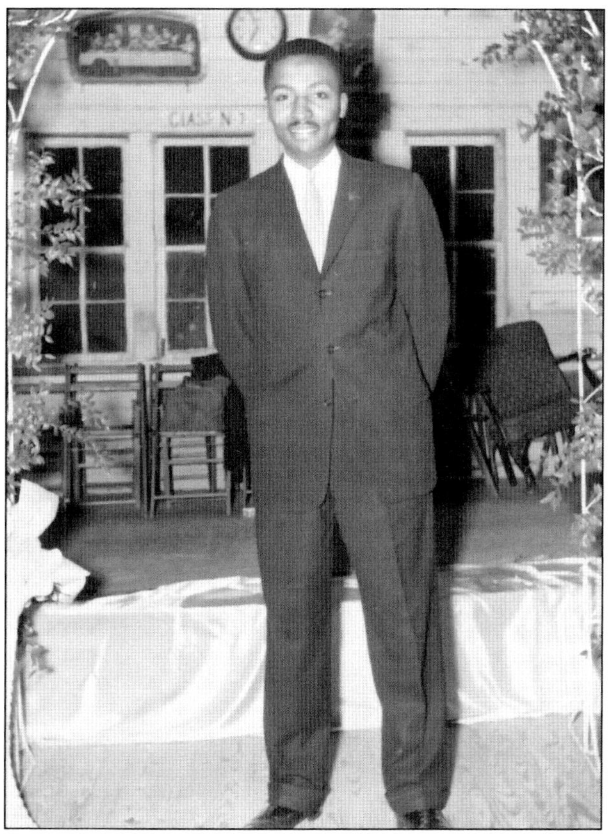

A debonair Rev. Clifton O'Neal visits Kings Highway Missionary Baptist Church for an early 1960s wedding. Kings Highway was formed in 1921 with 15 families. The first baby born to a charter member was local icon Dr. Carl E. Hyman, the first residency-trained African American obstetrician/gynecologist in the state of Arkansas. With successive buildings constructed in 1943 and 1965, Kings Highway now maintains a beautiful worship facility that was dedicated in 2002, serving more souls than ever in its history. (Courtesy of Ethel O'Neal.)

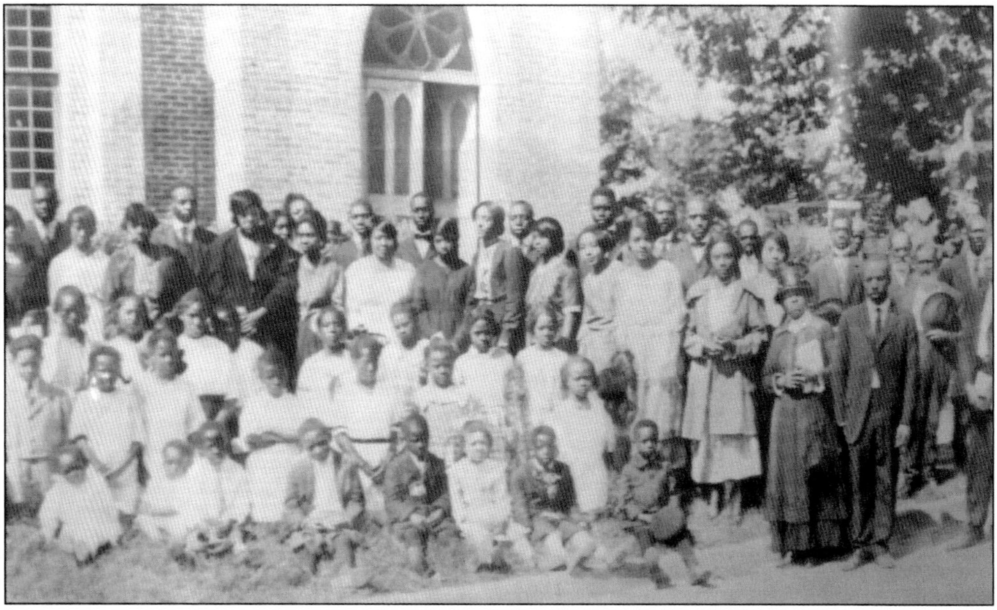

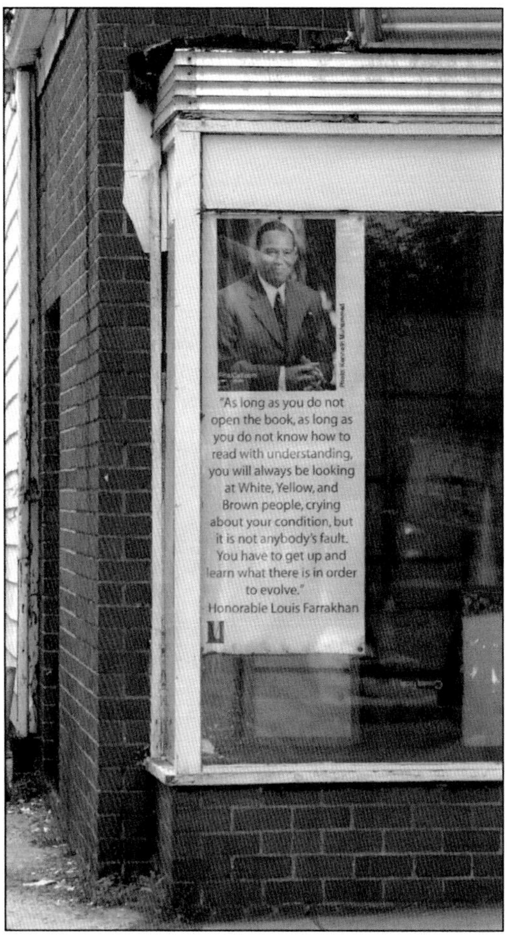

A partial photograph of St. Paul Missionary Baptist Church's congregation shows members in front of their edifice, which was built in 1894. St. Paul ran a school for black youth around 1877 and boasted a brief pastorate by Rev. E.C. Morris, the first president of the National Baptist Convention. St. Paul's members have served proudly in the community as university chancellors, principals, doctors, lawyers, teachers, and in a host of other professions. They have taken the gospel to the masses through highly dedicated and respected community leadership. (Courtesy of St. Paul Missionary Baptist Church.)

The words of Minister Louis Farrakhan, leader of the Nation of Islam (NOI), resound for admirers on a poster. Farrakhan spoke at UAPB in 2012. The NOI has maintained a Pine Bluff presence at least since the 1970s. In 1928, Pine Bluff was home to one of Noble Drew Ali's earliest Moorish Science Temples (forerunner to the NOI), according to Moorheritage.com and the *Encyclopedia of African and African American Religions*. Ali visited the Pine Bluff temple several days in 1928. (Courtesy of Takoma Bibelot.)

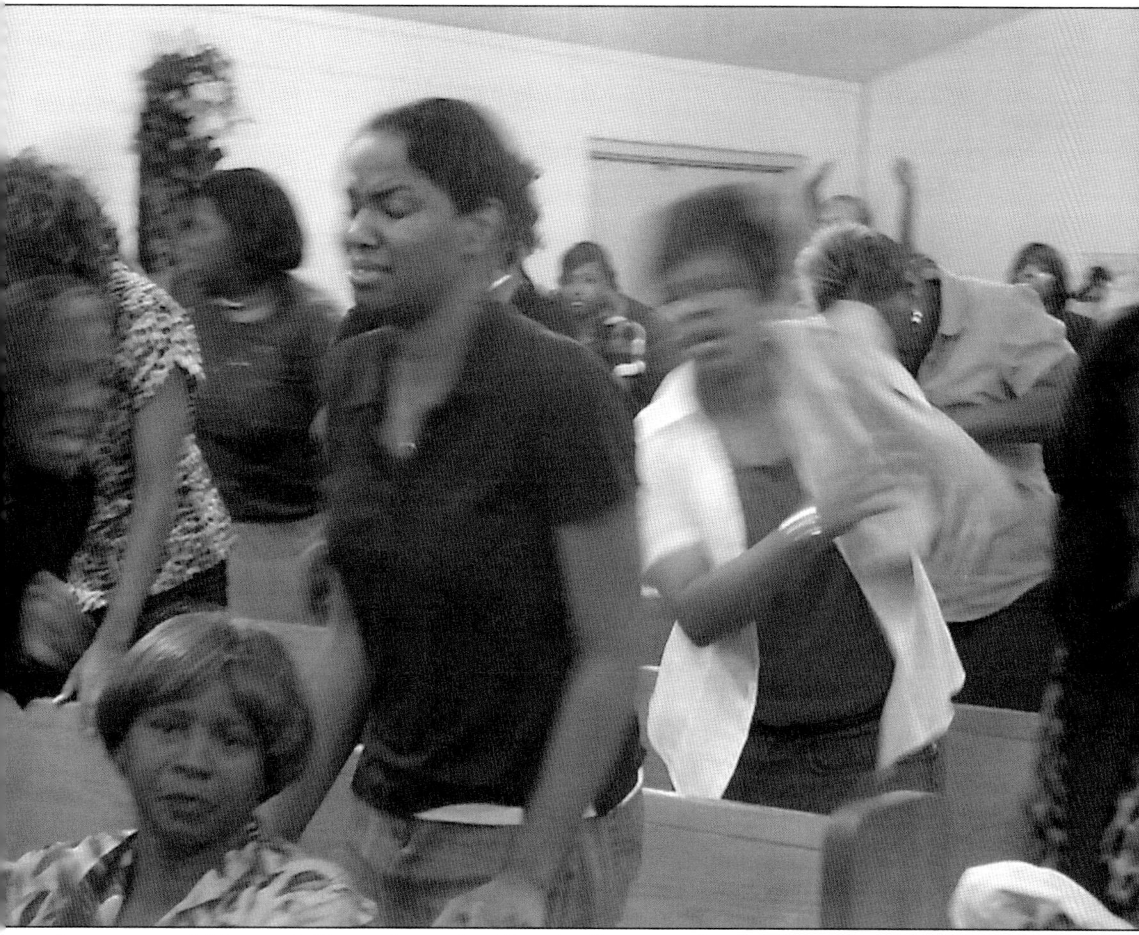

A service at Altheimer's Unity Apostolic Church illustrates the passion and praise of African American religion. Congregants focus their attention on seeking an ever-increasing spiritual connection. At the end of the day, most blacks in Pine Bluff/Jefferson County acknowledge what their ancestors knew centuries before: that their faith in God is the key to the bright future they seek for themselves, their families, and their community. (Courtesy of Dr. Loyd Lasker Jr.)

Consistent with our mission to preserve history on a local level, this book was printed in South Carolina on American-made paper and manufactured entirely in the United States. Products carrying the accredited Forest Stewardship Council (FSC) label are printed on 100 percent FSC-certified paper.

MADE IN THE USA